ALICE MUNRO'S NARRATIVE ART

ALICE MUNRO'S NARRATIVE ART

Isla Duncan

palgrave
macmillan

First published in hardcover in 2011by PALGRAVE MACMILLAN® in the
United States—a division of St. Martin's Press LLC, 175 Fifth Avenue, New York,
NY 10010.

Where this book is distributed in the UK, Europe and the rest of the world, this is by
Palgrave Macmillan, a division of Macmillan Publishers Limited, registered in England,
company number 785998, of Houndmills, Basingstoke, Hampshire RG21 6XS.

Palgrave Macmillan is the global academic imprint of the above companies and has
companies and representatives throughout the world.

Palgrave® and Macmillan® are registered trademarks in the United States, the United
Kingdom, Europe and other countries.

ISBN: 978-1-137-45122-4

The Library of Congress has cataloged the hardcover edition as follows:

Duncan, Isla.
    Alice Munro's narrative art / Isla Duncan.
        p.   cm.
    Includes bibliographical references.
    ISBN 978-0-230-33857-9
    1. Munro, Alice—Criticism and interpretation.   2. Women and literature—
Canada—History—20th century. I. Title.

    PR9199.3.M8Z595 2011
    813'.54—dc23   2011018681

A catalogue record of the book is available from the British Library.

Design by Scribe Inc.

First PALGRAVE MACMILLAN paperback edition: September 2014

10 9 8 7 6 5 4 3 2 1

This book is dedicated to my partner, Gill.

CONTENTS

ACKNOWLEDGMENTS

I would like to acknowledge my gratitude to librarians at the University of Chichester, West Sussex, England, who have always been extremely helpful to me.

Parts of this work have been published before, in slightly different form. They are: "'It seems so much the truth it is the truth': Persuasive Testimony in Alice Munro's 'A Wilderness Station,'" *Studies in Canadian Literature* 28, no. 2 (2003): 98–111; "Disparity and Deception in Alice Munro's 'Lichen,'" *British Journal of Canadian Studies* 19, no. 1 (2006): 61–77; "Social Class in Alice Munro's 'Sunday Afternoon' and 'Hired Girl,'" *British Journal of Canadian Studies* 22, no. 1 (2009): 15–31. I am grateful to *Studies in Canadian Literature*, New Brunswick, Canada, and to Liverpool University Press, England (publishers of the *British Journal of Canadian Studies*) for their kind permission to reprint those materials here.

INTRODUCTION

IN HER ESSAY, "ROSE AND JANET: ALICE Munro's Metafiction,"[1] Canadian academic Helen Hoy documents the extraordinarily tortuous publication history of Alice Munro's fourth book, the collection entitled *Who Do You Think You Are?*, published in Canada in 1978, and as *The Beggar Maid* in the United States in 1979 and Britain in 1980. She explains that Munro had submitted the original manuscript with stories by two different first-person narrators, Rose and Janet, but by the time the stories reached the stage of galley proofs, she had decided that their narrative voices were indistinguishable from each other. At considerable financial cost to herself, she succeeded in arresting the publication, extracting from her publisher (Macmillan) a fresh deadline, before which she had transformed the collection into ten third-person stories about Rose. The Janet narratives were revised, to be included in the subsequent collection, *The Moons of Jupiter* (1982).

In her examination of the archival correspondence between Munro and her editors, both Canadian and American, Hoy illustrates the writer's overriding concern for the consistency and coherence of her narrative viewpoint, pointing out that the faith in her own insight proved to be rewarding, for the book won the prestigious Governor-General's Award for Fiction in 1978.

Munro's biographer, Robert Thacker, provides further evidence of his subject's meticulous attention to the integrity of narrative voice. Discussing the "long gestation" of Munro's "most successful stories,"[2] he reveals how the writer vacillates over the eventual perspective for the title story of *The Progress of Love* (1986), presenting it originally in the first person, before sending "a new, *finally final*, third-person version" of her story to the *New Yorker*, where, after 1976, her narratives often appear first before they are anthologized.[3] When "The Progress of Love" is published in the book, however, it has been revised yet again, changed back into the first person. When she was asked in an interview, if she "often change[d] perspective or tone" in her revisions, Munro replied, "Oh yes, sometimes I'm uncertain, and I will do first person to third over and over again."[4]

It is not only with regard to voice and point of view that Munro's particular narrative concerns are documented. Her respect for structure is articulated in several publications, with the passage from the essay "What Is Real?" being frequently cited: "Everybody knows what a house does, how it encloses space and makes connections between one enclosed space and another . . . This is the nearest I can come to explaining what a story does for me, and what I want my stories to do for other people."[5] Catherine Sheldrick Ross, in the biography *Alice Munro: A Double Life* (1992), quotes a passage from the writer's 1986 interview with Connolly, Freake, and Sherman, where Munro explains her desire for narrative density, asserting: "What I want . . . is a lot of overlap. I want things to come in as many layers as possible."[6] Appositeness and coherence of voice, intricacy of structure, networks of connections, density of layering—these are among the essential components of Munro's narrative art. It is an art that she affirms is best developed in the genre of short fiction, and evidence of her resistance to the novel is well documented. In 2004 she told *New York Times* journalist Daphne Merkin: "I've tried to write novels . . . They turn into strange, hybrid stories"—defiantly adding, "I haven't read a novel that I didn't think couldn't have been a better story."[7]

Those who read, review, study, and publish her work can have no grounds to question Munro's desire to concentrate on the short story, for her success and critical acclaim are assured. Her books have been translated in at least twenty languages, and each collection of short stories has outsold the previous one. Several Canadian universities have offered to bestow honorary doctorates on her. She has won numerous literary prizes and accolades, notably, the National Book Critics Circle Award in the United States and the Trillium, the Jubilee, the Giller Prize (twice), and the Governor-General's Award for Fiction (thrice) in her native land (Canada). In 2009 she was awarded the Man Booker International Prize, being chosen over authors such as Joyce Carol Oates, Peter Carey, V. S. Naipaul, James Kelman, and Mario Vargas Llosa. As she approaches her eightieth year, she has indicated that she may write less. In a profile on the writer in the *Guardian Review* of April 2003, Aida Edemariam explains that Munro "feel[s] some diminishment of power," although she is not entirely sure of the cause, concluding: "I've decided that there isn't going to be a next book. I think there will be posthumous stuff but I'm not sure that I will publish again."[8] Her agent and publisher wore her down, however, as Edemariam predicted, for Munro has published *The View from Castle Rock* (2006) and *Too Much Happiness* (2009).[9]

Since her first collection of short stories, *Dance of the Happy Shades* (1968), for which she won her first Governor-General's Award, she has produced 11 short story collections as well as her only novel, *Lives of Girls and Women* (1971). Her stories have become longer and more complex with each publication, a fact that the writer herself acknowledges. When the writer and interviewer Eleanor Wachtel asked Munro why her stories have become so elaborate, suggesting the image of "a three-dimensional chess game [with] so many layers of things going on and crosscutting in time and memory," Munro explains that she needs this complexity: "It's that I see things now, in this way, and there is absolutely no other way I can deal with the material of fiction."[10] In their length, profundity, and structural elaborateness, her later stories could more accurately be termed novellas; the title story of *The Love of a Good Woman* (1998), for example, runs to an astonishing 76 pages and contains so many mysteries, ambiguities, and evasions that it might usefully serve as an "apprenticeship in reading Munro," where "the reader is challenged to make sense of a text that contains so much and that refuses to subordinate the plurality of its detail within a single frame."[11]

The word "complexity," and terms akin to it, recur in studies and reviews of Munro's later fiction. Dennis Duffy raises the ways in which her stories "condense a wealth of implication and detail within a minute space," comparing her motifs to "small stones thrown with great force, spread out to lap the whole pond."[12] Coral Ann Howells observes, "Her stories have become increasingly complex and elusive, with their shifting narrative perspectives, their apparent digressions, their spatial and temporal gaps."[13] The essay from which the preceding quotation was taken is included in a double edition of *Open Letter* (2003–4) devoted to Alice Munro. All the essays in the journal were delivered at the Alice Munro Conference entitled "*L'écriture du secret*/Writing Secrets," held in May 2003 at the University of Orléans. The conference papers and resulting scholarly essays examine Munro's "writing of secrets," her "aesthetic of indirection."[14] Some of the essays, in their focus on secrecy, indeterminacy, ambivalence, obliqueness, and what Caterina Ricciardi calls the "relentlessly uncapturable" in Munro's fiction, are among the most dauntingly theoretical in Munro scholarship.[15]

The writer's work has been and continues to be studied by academics and theorists from many different schools of thought. Ajay Heble observes that "Over the years, Alice Munro's art has been stretched to accommodate various trends in literary studies."[16] The MLA Bibliography lists four hundred entries under the writer's name. Most of the critical work consists of essays devoted to individual stories, in which phenomena such as particular stylistic traits, recurrent themes, or remarkable structural arrangements are identified and examined. Several books on Munro's work have been published, among them the often-cited *Controlling the Uncontrollable: The Fiction of Alice Munro* (1989), by Ildikó de Papp Carrington, and *Critical Essays on Alice Munro* (1999), edited by Robert Thacker. These books are, respectively, American and Canadian publications. To date, there have been, to my certain knowledge, only two monographs published in Britain on the writer: both are entitled *Alice Munro*—the first, in 1998, by the prolific Coral Ann Howells; the second, in 2004, by Ailsa Cox. This dearth is surprising, considering that the writer should now be more familiar to the British reading public than she was more than a decade ago: for example, she was interviewed, long-distance, at the 2009 Edinburgh Book Festival, by Margaret Atwood, and reviews of her work appear in all the British broadsheets. According to research conducted by the British Association for Canadian Studies, Munro's novel *Lives of Girls and Women* frequently appears as a core text on Canadian literature syllabi in British universities.[17]

In "The Lamp in the Mausoleum," a summary of recent books by and about Alice Munro, Alison Lurie declares that "there is a clamoring clutter of scholarly articles treating her work from various fashionable and unfashionable perspectives: religious, anthropological, sociological, historical, biographical, psychological, structuralist, deconstructionist, symbolist, etc."[18] There is one perspective—narratological—that I would add to Lurie's list, and it is one, whether fashionable or not, I have found invaluable in my own research on Munro.

My introduction to Alice Munro's work took place nearly thirty years ago, via the volume *Something I've Been Meaning to Tell You* (1974), which became available in Scotland much later than the date it was first published in Canada.[19] It was "Memorial" that most fascinated me, but it also puzzled me: although it was third-person narration, the events seemed to be filtered through the main character, Eileen. She was not telling the story, but I could clearly discern her voice. I noted all the questions she asked herself, and the reader, and I became aware of her distinctive qualities—her fallibility, and her accommodating politeness. I wanted to discuss how these traits were manifest, and I was also intrigued by when and how the narrator could comment so smugly on Eileen's faults. My wonderings led me into the exciting world of narratology, where I met concepts such as free indirect discourse (FID), focalization, analepsis, ellipses, heterodiegesis, terms with which I could, with greater precision and authority, examine and clarify the puzzles that "Memorial" posed.

Since that heady period of discovery, I have fully exploited the rich resources of the discipline, for narratology, and literary linguistics, provide the researcher and teacher with a panoply of explicative and explorative tools. The epistolary narrative "A Wilderness Station," for example, as I will argue later in this work, offers a variety of competing testimonies, the claims of which are more fairly evaluated with an understanding of polyphony and the differences between public and private narration. My reading of the later story "Save the Reaper" is enriched when I mentally reorder the anachronous sections and see how the textual dislocations reflect the protagonist's disordered memories. Dislocations and disarrangements in her fiction are meticulously and deliberately configured by a writer whose narrative aesthetic is concerned with patterns and connections that may not be immediately discernible, and may be muffled under layers of narrative or time. Stephen Regan, writing in *Narrative Strategies in Canadian Literature* (1991), lists as Munro's most impressive ploys, "the subtle modulation of tense, the interplay of active and retrospective voices, the collusion of memory and history, the unsettling shifts in perspective, and the sustained effects of overlapping and multi-layered narratives."[20] Narratology enables me to identify and explain such ploys, to discuss their workings, and celebrate their effects.

Narratology is, of course, the study of narrative. Gerald Prince defines the term thus: "Narratology is a theory of narrative. It examines what all narratives, and only narratives, have in common as well as what enables them to differ from one another qua narratives, and it aims to describe the narrative-specific system of rules presiding over narrative production and processing."[21] The word is translated from the French *narratologie*, first used by Tzvetan Todorov in *Grammaire du Décameron* (1928, published in English 1969). Narratology is regarded as following in the traditions of Russian formalism and structuralism, for like these disciplines, it is also concerned with the rule-governed ways in which humans organize their worlds. Structuralism sees language as a structured system, with each linguistic element perceived and defined in relation to other linguistic elements, in combination or contrast with them. The term "structuralism" was coined in 1929 by Roman Jakobson, a founding member of the school of Russian formalism, a movement of literary criticism and interpretation that emerged in the 1920s. Formalism emphasizes the autonomous, discrete nature of literature, regarding it "as neither a reflection of the life of its author nor as a by-product of the historical or cultural milieu in which it was created."[22] In the discipline of formalism, as the name suggests, the *formal* properties of a text are identified; in particular, the poetic and aesthetic qualities are examined for what and how they contribute to the *literariness* of the piece.

Besides Todorov, prominent theorists in the discipline of narratology include Roland Barthes and Vladimir Propp, whose respective works

"Introduction to the Structural Analysis of Narrative" (1966) and *Morphology of the Folktale* (1928, published in English 1968) are acknowledged as germinal influences in the study of *what* is narrated, the set of events or the story presented. The focus at this stage in the history of narratology seemed to be on functions and agents in narrated events: for example, scholars considered matters such as the typology of roles; the relations between the participants in the story; and the fundamental schema of narrative, and what might constitute but later disrupt that schema. The discipline gradually moved, in the latter part of the twentieth century, toward a focus on *discourses*, the *texts* that transmit the stories, and in this direction the book *Narrative Discourse: An Essay in Method* (1980), by Gerard Génette, played a vital role. Génette considers narrative as a primarily verbal presentation, arguing that the same set of events can be recounted in many different ways, that is, discourses. His book has become a rich source for researchers in narrative literature, providing as it does a necessary methodology in the discipline, in addition to "the systematization of [a] formalist terminology."[23]

The impact of postmodernism and poststructuralism in the late 1990s saw a broadening of the scope of narrative studies, as directions in the discipline sought to explore general narrativity in genres as heterogeneous as medical interviews, hypertext, and avant-garde poetry. Narrative theorists now speak and write of *narratologies*, the title of an important, relatively recent collection of essays confirming the ways in which "narrative theorists have drawn on [other] fields . . . to broaden and diversify our conception of stories and to provide new ways of analyzing their structures and effects."[24]

However, it is with literary narrative that my book is concerned, and it is to this genre that narratology has made, and continues to make, a substantially enriching contribution. From the discipline there emerges a more precise metalanguage for the description of such aspects as point of view, voice, structure, layering, connections—those very constituents of narrative to which Munro accords her careful attention. It is in contemporary narrative theory that one finds "the best possible descriptive and explanatory models" for analyzing Munro's strange, hybrid, thickly imbricated stories.[25]

What, then, constitutes the *metalanguage* of narratology? How are its expository models formed? One theorist who has clarified for me the most recondite recesses of narrative is Shlomith Rimmon-Kenan, whose germinal book *Narrative Fiction* (1983) is regularly cited by fellow narrative theorists, and in whose revised edition, published in 2003, the "renaissance of narratology" is proclaimed.[26] Drawing on, primarily, "Anglo-American New Criticism, Russian Formalism, French Structuralism

[and] the Tel-Aviv School of Poetics and the Phenomenology of Reading," Rimmon-Kenan asserts that her work is not indebted to any particular school or theoretician, but is a synthesis of "existing theories" and the "presentation of [her] personal view."[27] In this study of Alice Munro's narrative art, I acknowledge my indebtedness to Rimmon-Kenan and to other theorists of narrative for their exposition of "the *differentia specifica* of narrative fiction." How these are illustrated in Munro's fiction, however, and how they distinguish her work are the presentation of my personal view and argument.[28]

Narrative fiction is a succession of fictional events, a sequence that has three fundamental components: the story, that is, the events themselves; the text, namely, the discourse in which these events are written (or told); and the narration, the act or process of production and transmission. How events are chained to make a story depends on two factors, two "principles of combination" of time and causality, familiarly perceived as answers to the questions of *when* and *why* something happens in fiction.[29] Not all events are of a uniform nature in terms of narrative dynamic: some, called kernels, drive or accelerate the action, while others, sometimes called catalysts, serve to shed new light on, or expand upon, or even retard the kernel events.

In Munro's "Lichen" from *The Progress of Love*, for example, David's gleeful display of the nude photograph of his new lover, Dina, is exploited for more than one purpose by Munro: on its first appearance, when David shows the photograph to Stella's neighbors, he tantalizingly ensures that Stella, his former wife, does not see it. At this point the action is a kernel event, for it generates narrative suspense, since the nature of the image is withheld from the reader. The action assumes later significance in the story when David offers to show the photograph to Stella, who declines to view it, and her reticence tells the reader that she suspects its hurtful import. Further on, David finally succeeds in confronting Stella with his trophy, and his determination to provoke can be inferred from the following: "He reaches quickly into his inside pocket, and before Stella can turn her head away, he is holding a Polaroid snapshot in front of her eyes."[30] The action of *displaying* the photograph is crucial to "Lichen," a story that is the focus of my discussion in a later chapter. At this point in the introduction, I draw attention to the event to illustrate Munro's skillful use of it. The event can be seen as a kernel, for it drives the narrative, but it is also a catalyst, in its functions as a retardatory device and as a character index.

Events in Munro's fiction usually stretch over generations, creating what Howells describes as "the sense of individual lives scrolling out over many decades."[31] While some of the events in her earlier stories, for example, "The Office" and "Boys and Girls," follow a primarily linear sequence, the same does not apply to most of her later work, where the elaborate manipulation of time is a hallmark. Text time is linear, of course, for language prescribes a sequential figuration of signs. Although the text "scrolls out," to use Howells's arresting image, the events depicted may not correspond to this one-directional chronology; indeed, in modern fiction, they tend not to. The principal types of anachrony in text time are flashback and "flashforward," which in narratology are referred to as analepsis and prolepsis. The latter is less common than the former. There are countless examples of analepsis in Munro's fiction, and in the following chapter I examine the phenomenon in two of her earlier stories, "The Peace of Utrecht" and "Material." Both first-person narrators return to significant episodes in the past in an attempt to justify, and perhaps exorcise, feelings that trouble them in their present lives.

An example of the rarer phenomenon, prolepsis, can be found at the conclusion of "Mischief" in *The Beggar Maid*. The third-person narrator has recounted Rose's continually frustrated efforts to launch into a full-blown extramarital affair with Clifford, the husband of her friend Jocelyn. Although they meet surreptitiously, several times, their sexual union is always being postponed, until the occasion of another of the couple's infamous parties, where Rose drinks too much. She has her wish, but she shares Clifford with Jocelyn, in a threesome. The experience shames and angers her afterwards, and she resolves to write to them both, expressing her outrage; however, the letter is not sent, and Rose eventually calms down. In the conclusion, the narrator wryly observes that "Sometime later she decided to go on being friends with Clifford and Jocelyn, because she needed such friends occasionally, at that stage in her life."[32] The discrepancy between contemporaneous and future time is evidenced by the adverbial "sometime later" and the distal deictic determiner "that," referring to a period in the protagonist's future life.

Another aspect of time in fiction, duration, is less easy to discern and measure. With regard to the order of time, the norm is the possibility of an "exact coincidence between story-time and text-time," but it would be impossible to postulate some kind of symmetry between an event and the textual expression of it.[33] In response to the need to posit a relationship between story time and textual space, Génette uses constancy of pace, proposing two forms of modification: acceleration and deceleration. The former is often effected by synopsis, or summary, when a long piece of narrative is expressed in a short textual segment, with the maximum speed being ellipsis (zero textual space). Since the term also denotes, in syntax, an omitted structure in a sentence, it is useful at this point to clarify its specific meaning in narrative theory. Normally signaled by a blank space in the text, one that is sometimes marked by asterisks in a line, it corresponds to and represents "narratively pertinent situations and events that took time."[34] The minimum speed is a descriptive pause, where a sizable piece of text is devoted to hardly any action. The term *scene* is reserved in narratology for a situation where the story duration and the text duration are roughly alike—in dialogue, for example, which on the page has the appearance of a scene in a drama script. Anything other than an approximate synchronic correspondence between story duration and text space is impossible, and unreadable, as Mieke Bal asserts, noting that "the dead moments in a conversation, the nonsensical or unfinished remarks, are usually omitted."[35] The scene is, in good literary fiction, a highly significant moment in the narrative, marking a kernel event. Moreover, the dialogue in the scene will yield character indices. The various means by which Munro adjusts narrative pace are amply illustrated in the later story "Nettles," from *Hateship, Friendship, Courtship, Loveship, Marriage* (2001), a story I examine in a subsequent chapter.

These adjustments of narrative pace are one of the reasons why reading a Munro story is so necessarily a careful, unhurried experience. When the reader encounters an ellipsis, she or he asks why it is placed there and considers what has happened in that blank space. In a descriptive pause of substance, lucid images, particular details of setting, may adumbrate pivotal events, or shed light on inscrutable characters, or draw attention to important themes. In "Five Points," from *Friend of My Youth* (1990), Brenda and Neil carry out their clandestine sexual relationship in a side road off the highway near Logan. As Brenda drives, excitedly, to their meeting place, the narrator describes the profusion of "goldenrod and milkweed, with the pods burst open, and dangling branches of bright, poisonous fruit, and wild grapevine flung over everything."[36] The luxuriance of growth suggests the extravagance of her sexual desire; in some of the detail are hints of dangerous excess. The third-person narrator observes that Brenda and Neil "have a history of passion, the way families have a history [and] have come through complicated adventures together" (*Friend of My Youth*, p. 37). This authoritative statement lets the reader know that the risky, passionate liaison has gone on for some time.

It is, of course, easier to directly define and describe characters from the perspective of omniscience. Definition and categorization were more readily acceptable in the early days of literary fiction, when human personality was understood as a combination of traits shared by many others; in this relativistic era, "generalization and classification are less readily tolerated, and the economy of definition is grasped as reductive."[37] Modern writers tend to develop characters obliquely, allowing their traits to be revealed by their actions and speech, as well as by the responses they provoke in others. Other factors that contribute to characterization include details of setting, external appearance, and what Rimmon-Kenan calls "reinforcement by analogy," where, for example, a character is recurrently associated with certain images, or where a character's name seems to indicate an abiding personal quality.[38] In the title story of Munro's *Friend of My Youth*, the initial description of the nurse Audrey Atkinson illustrates this kind of reinforcement. She is described as "a stout woman with corsets as stiff as barrel hoops, marcelled hair the color of brass candlesticks, a mouth shaped by lipstick beyond its own stingy outline" (*Friend of My Youth*, p. 13), and it becomes clear that her external appearance yields clues as to her personality, for she is presented as greedy, vain, and self-indulgent, stern in her judgments of others.

In this vignette there is evidence of narrative tendentiousness. The narrator is reporting her mother's account of events when she was a young teacher in the Ottawa Valley. She had lodged at a farm owned by two sisters, the younger of whom, Ellie, required nursing care, as she was terminally ill. She was married to Robert, who also lived on the farm, and who had previously been engaged to the older sister, Flora, but had married the younger woman after impregnating her. "Friend of My Youth" consists, in the main, of the story of Flora's unfortunate life, a life that, according to the narrator's mother, was spent in saintly devotion to her sister, to the farm, and to a strict Presbyterian religion. The narrator is consistently at pains to depict characters and events from the perspective of the mother, whose attitude toward the nurse is conveyed in the firm assertion: "She disliked the nurse far more than Flora did" (*Friend of My Youth*, p. 13). Her dislike is discerned in the unflattering descriptive detail and in the evaluative informality of the adjective "stingy."

Narratology has given literary studies a precise term, focalization, for the viewpoint, in narrative, from which things are "seen, felt, understood, and assessed . . . where 'seen' is interpreted in a broad sense."[39] The term, introduced by Génette, is considered more exact than, for example, angle, viewpoint, perspective, or filter, although its visual sense should be broadened to include cognitive, emotive, and ideological orientation. Thirty years and more of narrative theory have produced a typology in focalization: the holder of the point of view in a narrative is the focalizer, or the subject of the focalization, while the character, scene, or event presented in terms of the focalizer's perspective is the focalized, or the object of the focalization. Thus to return to "Friend of My Youth," the narrator's mother is the focalizer in her description of the nurse, Audrey Atkinson, who in the passage quoted previously, is the focalized.

The narrator, who tells the story, and the focalizer, through whom (or which) the narration is mediated, are not necessarily the same, although they often are, especially in first-person narratives. All the stories in Munro's third collection, *The Beggar Maid*, are narrated in the third person, by a narrator who takes no part in events, while the subject of the focalization is almost invariably Rose, around whom most of the action revolves. In the passage that follows, the narrator explains Rose's reaction to the painting of the beggar maid, whom Patrick, her cultured, imperious fiancé, thinks Rose resembles. The "cognitive, emotional and ideological orientation" of the focalizer is evident in the narrator's reporting of Rose's impressionable incredulity: "She had a look at the painting. She looked it up in an art book in the library. She studied the Beggar Maid, meek and voluptuous, with shy white feet. The milky surrender of her, the helplessness and gratitude. Was that how Patrick saw Rose? Was that how she could be?" (*The Beggar Maid*, p. 80).

There is an important difference between external and internal focalization. The former is close to the narrating agent and is traditionally associated with objective narration, such as that exemplified in the canon by Henry Fielding's *Tom Jones* (1749). External focalization creates the impression that "an anonymous agent [is] situated outside [events] functioning as a focalizor."[40] An outstanding instance of Munro's use of external focalization can be found at the beginning of "Lichen," where the narrator presents the setting where most of the action will take place— Stella's "summer house, on the clay bluffs overlooking Lake Huron." The narrator explains, "It was and is a high, bare wooden house, painted grey—a copy of the old farmhouses nearby, though perhaps less substantial" (*The Progress of Love*, p. 32). The juxtaposed simple present tenses of the verb furnish incontrovertible proof of this type of focalization, which, interestingly, gives way to that of a perceptual focalizer, the character of David. He and Stella are the principal protagonists in this fascinating narrative of *shared focalization*. In the passages where Stella and David are featured as the focalizers, the narrative "Lichen" exemplifies internal focalization, a type of narration "whereby information is conveyed in terms of a character's conceptual or perceptual point of view."[41]

In her reporting of her mother's perception of events, and of characters in her story, the narrator in "Friend of My Youth" tries to faithfully reproduce her mother's words, to replicate her idiolect. The mother's account is reported speech, but it is colored by her idiosyncratic choice of vocabulary and idiom. What is exemplified in the brief excerpts given previously from "Friend of My Youth" and "The Beggar Maid" is a type of discourse representation that Munro richly exploits in her fiction, a type labeled FID. A term first used by the French stylistician Charles Bally in 1912, who calls it *le style indirect libre*, it "refers to a kind of indirect speech or reported speech in which the speech of a character and the words of the narrator are blended, but with no reporting clause indicated (hence 'free')."[42] FID is one of several varieties of discourse representation in fiction, which are listed as follows. The subsequent definitions are paraphrased from Leech and Short's lucid explanations in *Style and Fiction*:

- NRDA (narrative reports of discourse acts)
- ID (indirect discourse)
- FID (free indirect discourse)
- DD (direct discourse)
- FDD (free direct discourse)[43]

The noun "discourse" may be used to refer to both speech and thought, but if a distinction has to be clarified, then the convention is to substitute speech (S) or thought (T) for the discourse (D) in the previously listed varieties (i.e., "indirect speech" or "indirect thought," as opposed to "indirect discourse"). The norm for the representation of speech is direct, while the norm for the rendering of thought is indirect.

Possibly the least familiar in the aforementioned list is the phenomenon known collectively as NRDA, which are "useful for summarizing relatively unimportant stretches of conversation."[44] Examples of such discourse are few in Munro's fiction, where dialogue is so copious, so richly meaningful and revelatory. One instance can be found at the beginning of "Chance," from *Runaway* (2004).[45] The narrator informs the reader that the protagonist, Juliet, a young classics teacher, is about to embark on a detour in her journey home to visit a "friend who lives up the coast" (*Runaway*, p. 48). The reader learns that shortly before this time Juliet had gone to a movie with a teaching colleague, who "confessed that she herself, like the woman in the picture, was in love with a married man" (p. 48). Since the woman makes this confession verbally, we can classify it as a report of a speech or discourse act, the content of which in this case is not especially important, for Juanita does not figure in the ensuing narrative. The disclosure serves only to induce the narrator to report that Juliet has similarly found herself attracted to a married man, after which the account of her involvement begins.

The presentation of the varieties that are considered the norms, that is, direct speech and indirect thought, need no exemplification. It is useful at this point to discuss FDD and FID, since both are less common, although Munro frequently exploits them in her stories. FID is a form of discourse representation that is a combination of indirect and direct. It enables the writer to align the values and perspective of a narrator with a character in the narrative. Indicators of FID are the omission of a reporting clause; the retention of the tense and pronoun usage of the narrative; markers of deixis, or references to the situation of utterance; vestiges of a character's idiolect; and evidence of modality, for example, modal verbs and certain sentence adverbials.

There are several passages of such discourse in the story "Chance," in which Juliet takes a bold risk, visiting, unannounced, the married man she met on a train journey six months before. Encouraged by a letter he had sent to her at her school in which he declares "I often think of you" (*Runaway*, p. 51), Juliet sets off on her detour to find this man, Eric, who lives "on Whale Bay, somewhere north of Vancouver" (p. 69). After several journeys in buses and ferries, through unfamiliar landscapes, she begins to doubt the wisdom of her undertaking, but then she remembers the urgency of the message. The narrator explains:

> But there will have to be a hotel, or tourist cabins at least, at Whale Bay. She will go there. She has left her big suitcase at the school, to be picked up later. She has only her travelling bag slung over her shoulder, she won't be conspicuous.
> She will stay one night. Maybe phone him.
> And say what? (p. 51)

In this passage some indicators of FID are in evidence. First, there is modality, in the form of the repeated modal auxiliary "will," the determined optimism of which is diluted somewhat by the more speculative "Maybe phone him." The elliptical informality of this sentence fragment can be considered idiolectal, like the interrogative that succeeds it, and Munro accentuates the question's uncertain, even plaintive quality by isolating it in a paragraph. FID (in this instance, thought) blends the narrative and the reflections of the subject of the focalization, the character Juliet. One can ascertain that the focalization is internal when one attempts to render the previously given passage in the first person. The experiment works reasonably well, although the resulting piece would lack the knowingness of the third-person narrator's referential statements.

The free indirect variety of speech and thought presentation thus blends narratorial and characterological traits; in Munro's fiction it is used with such subtlety, and so often, that the reader is not always conscious of its workings. FDD does not occur as frequently in her work. It is a variety that is easier to identify, for all that distinguishes it from direct speech or thought is the absence of the reporting clause or the quotation marks that conventionally surround dialogue and thought in narrative fiction. A fascinating example of the phenomenon of FDD, in this case, speech, can be found in "Fits" from *The Progress of Love*. I discuss the story in Chapter 2 of this book, when I consider the shifts of focalization in Munro's fiction.

The central event in "Fits" is the murder-suicide of an elderly couple, the Weebles; the husband murdered his wife with a shotgun then killed himself. The bodies are discovered by Peg, their next door neighbor, who is a protagonist in the third-person narrative. This tragedy happens in the small Ontario town of Gilmore, whose residents are understandably shocked by it, and Munro conveys the various reactions of the townspeople—shock, disbelief, curiosity, prurience—in a series of questions and answers that individuals would have uttered.

> Talk ran backward from the events of the morning. Where were the Weebles seen, and in what harmlessness and innocence, and how close to the moment when everything changed?
>
> She had stood in line at the Bank of Montreal on Friday afternoon.
>
> He had got a haircut, on Saturday morning.
>
> They were together, buying groceries, in the IGA on Friday evening at about eight o'clock.
>
> What did they buy? A good supply? Specials, advertised bargains, more than enough to last for a couple of days?
>
> More than enough. A bag of potatoes, for one thing. (*The Progress of Love*, p. 119)

The Gilmore people ask each other mundane, fact-finding questions, exchanging evidence, trying to piece together the circumstances of this terrible event in their search for rational explanations. All their questions and responses are rendered without quotation marks and without reporting clauses. In the presentation of sustained dialogue, the reader might expect to identify interlocutors, unambiguously, by the presence of clauses such as *she asked, he replied, it was suggested*. The reader would then begin to recognize characters from their idiolects, and from the manner in which their speech or thought is delivered. That is how characterization is developed. In this particular passage, however, the individuality of each interlocutor is not pertinent to Munro's design, which is to create a plurality of speakers, a "genuine polyphony of fully valid voices"[46] that constitutes the fictive community of Gilmore, working *en masse* for a solution to the mystery.

The narrative "Fits" is remarkable not only for the inclusion of polyphony, but principally, as I argue later, for the singular narration of the kernel event, the discovery of the murder-suicide. Instead of being narrated directly, from the point of view of Peg, who is first to see the bodies, the event is related vicariously by Peg's husband, Robert, who reconstructs the experience from several sources, although not from his wife herself, the witness. The reader is thus presented with an account that is not first hand, but subject to a kind of double distancing, and this adds to the "many layers of mystery concerning the true nature of the Weebles."[47]

Howells observes that "the 1980s fashion for paradox as the key to interpreting Munro's fiction seems to have been displaced in the 1990s by the concept of "layering."[48] The layering may be multiply caused, but it is often the result of factors such as the blurring, doubling, diffuseness, or transfer of focalization. Another kind of layering can be traced to the actual *level* of narration. It is a truism to assert that there is always a teller in the tale, what Rimmon-Kenan calls "a higher narratorial authority responsible for 'quoting' the dialogue or 'transcribing' the written records."[49] In the hierarchy of narrative levels, the highest is the one concerned with narration—in narratology it is called the extradiegetic; the noun diegesis and its adjective diegetic are used for the story, as defined earlier in this chapter. When the narrator is also a participant character, then she or he is intradiegetic, like most of the narrators in *Dance of the Happy Shades*.

One other type of narrative level must be mentioned, and that is the hypodiegetic, which refers to a story told by a fictional character. A well-known example of such a narrator is the governess in Henry James's novel *The Turn of the Screw* (1898); instances of hypodiegesis occur in Munro's story "The Progress of Love," when the narrator relates her mother's memory of a pivotal incident in her childhood and then later reports her aunt Beryl's version of the same incident, an account that casts doubt on the accuracy of the former. Both accounts are hypodiegetic narratives, competing for their claim to veracity. Munro's use of hypodiegesis is yet another narrative strategy that amplifies the "layering" in her fiction. Indeed, in the densely structured, cryptic novella "Love of a Good Woman," the subject of a later chapter, I discuss how it intensifies the irresoluteness.

The terms explained in this chapter illustrate what is regarded by some as the "forbidding terminology and mania for taxonomies" characterizing the discipline of narratology.[50] I would defend the use of its metalanguage, providing it is not intended to complicate or obfuscate. As I observed earlier, narratology, in combination with literary linguistics, offers, to me, the best possible descriptive and explanatory models for analyzing and discussing Munro's work.

In the ensuing chapters I examine the many facets of Munro's narrative art, as they are best illustrated in particular stories. I begin with a discussion of her first-person, confiding narrative, concentrating on two familiar stories, "The Peace of Utrecht" from *Dance of the Happy Shades* and "Material" from *Something I've Been Meaning to Tell You*. The first-person narrator of Munro's early fiction returns to past events that provoke feelings of predominantly guilt, anger, or shame, but in spite of her resolve to understand and expunge these negative emotions, perhaps even to atone for what has caused them, she remains dissatisfied and troubled. In these narratives, the temporal leaps are not as frequent, nor do they span the great sweeps of time that are found in Munro's later fiction. But they are significantly marked, by ellipses, by nuances of tense, modality, and aspect that are elaborate and become more intricately patterned with each volume.

Munro's experiments with linear narrative and point of view are clearly evident in her third work of fiction. The title story of *Something I've Been Meaning to Tell You*, for example, a story that features a third-person narrator, covers an ambitious time span of nearly four decades and is arranged in 15 sections that are not sequenced chronologically. This story breaks new ground for Munro in the degree of its extensive fragmentation and anachrony. In addition, "Tell Me Yes or No" is delivered by an unreliable first-person narrator, "an artificer and a manipulator . . . an illusionist,"[51] whose entire account can be read as a letter to an absent lover or as an exercise in catharsis, "a journey inwards, a journey in words."[52] In her next three volumes of short fiction—*Who Do You Think You Are?* (*The Beggar Maid* in the United States and Britain), *The Moons of Jupiter*, and *The Progress of Love*—Munro continues to experiment, notably with regard to focalization and narrative authority. Two stories from *The Progress of Love*, "Fits" and "Lichen," provide rich material for studies in focalization, and they are the focus of Chapter 2. By examining phenomena such as polyphony, FID, adjustments in narrative speed, and recurrent tropes, I argue that the shifts in focalization in these two stories achieve particular effects: in "Fits" they serve to expose the emotional distance and the latent violence repressed by the two protagonists, while in "Lichen" the changes in perspective reflect the nuances of sexual tensions evident in the character relations.

The limits of narrative authority are explored and tested by various means in *Friend of My Youth* and *Open Secrets* (1994). The title story in the former collection, and "A Wilderness Station" from the latter, constitute the core of my discussion in Chapter 4. I am interested in "Friend of My Youth" because it illustrates Munro's sustained use of hypodiegetic or metadiegetic narrative, one that is embedded within the primary narrative. The narrator delivers a version of her mother's oral account, but she wishes to discredit parts of it, believing she could see "through [her] mother's story and put in what she left out" (*Friend of My Youth*, p. 20). The mother's status as a credible narrator is undermined mainly because she has *told* her story to an often skeptical listener and has incorporated material gleaned from less reliable sources such as local gossip and hearsay. The daughter's claim to greater textual truth, however, is weakened by her tendentious speculation and by her emulous nature. What emerges is aptly described by Deborah Heller as "a site of contestation between the narrator and her mother," a struggle that neither wins.[53] Claims to narrative reliability and truth are ubiquitously challenged in "A Wilderness Station," an epistolary narrative composed of 12 letters and reports, all of which are gathered by an historian in an attempt to shed light on events in Ontario's pioneering past. I examine how the various textual sources are woven into a narrative that purports to have the authority of biography, of historiography, while at the same time it teems, as "Friend of My Youth" teems, with uncertainties, omissions, and instabilities. My analysis of these two stories I entitle "Competing Testimonies."

The title of Chapter 4 is "The Queer Bright Moment," the phrase Munro uses for the sudden illumination she likes her stories to contain.[54] Writing in the *New Republic*, Wendy Lesser notes that, with *Open Secrets*, Munro moves into a "new terrain of the fantastical, the psychologically introverted, the purely suppositional."[55] What makes this "new terrain" secretive and mysterious are the ways in which the "queer bright moment" is prepared for, and then revealed. I examine "Open Secrets," as well as "Save the Reaper" and "Cortes Island" from *The Love of a Good Woman*, discussing the various ways Munro throws doubt on the reliability of witness and memory in the construction of narrative, all the time expecting her reader to retain clues that might clarify the "cryptically expressed reality" her characters inhabit.[56] These clues are carefully inserted into "The Love of a Good Woman," which is the focus of my analysis in Chapter 5. In its length and complexity, this story of some 27,000 words is more accurately termed a novella. It has attracted the attention of several Munro scholars, notably Catherine Sheldrick Ross, who sagely observes that it sometimes feels that there are "too many things to be held together in the same frame."[57] Among the qualities that distinguish the piece, and which interest me in particular, are the diffuse center of consciousness, the withdrawal of any closure, and the steady accumulation of retardatory and digressive devices that deflect the cautious reader.

In Chapter 6 I consider how Munro, in her fiction of the last decade, concentrates more and more on "what is remembered" and what is forgotten—the foibles, tricks, and defensive mechanisms of memory. For my purposes I consider stories from both *Hateship, Friendship, Courtship, Loveship, Marriage* and *Runaway*, concentrating on "Nettles" and "Tricks." In Chapter 7 I discuss how Munro, in *The View From Castle Rock*, revisits and reworks in singular transformations certain key themes and strategies manifest in preceding publications. I explore what her redrafts reveal not only about her narrative aesthetic, but also about the role of social commentary in her work. For example, concentrating on "Hired Girl," I argue that Munro's treatment of social class is more incisive, more combative than in earlier pieces such as "Half a Grapefruit" or "The Turkey Season"

In her most recent book the writer returns to the territory of childhood and late adolescence, but imbues it with greater menace. For example, in "Child's Play," she explores the consequences of a sinister childhood secret, creating a narrator whose callous cruelty has rarely been encountered before in her *oeuvre*; and "Wenlock Edge," far from evoking an idyllic rural setting, deals with sexual perversion and ritual humiliation in seedy urban rooms. As Peter Kemp observes in his review, the title *Too Much Happiness* "could hardly be more savagely ironic."[58] With particular focus on "Child's Play," I discuss what particular methods of "disarrangement" Munro is exploiting in stories that seem "darker than anything [she] has previously published."[59] As always, I rely on the solid tools of narratology and literary linguistics in my search for clues in the cryptically expressed reality that is Munro's fictive world.

CHAPTER 1

THE CONFIDING FIRST-PERSON NARRATOR

THE FIRST STORIES PUBLISHED BY ALICE MUNRO (as Alice Laidlaw) appeared in *Folio*, the magazine of the University of Western Ontario, in 1950 and 1951. They are written from an omniscient narrative perspective and their subject matter is not entirely within the writer's experience.[1] The story "At The Other Place," published in the *Canadian Forum* in September 1955, marks a significant change, for in it Munro draws upon her family's circumstances, employing the first-person narration that, according to Robert Thacker "became characteristic" of her fiction.[2] Of the 15 stories in Munro's prize-winning collection, *Dance of the Happy Shades*, twelve are written from a first-person narrative perspective. Most of these are what the writer, in the often-cited interview with J. R. (Tim) Struthers, describes as her "real material" stories, for example, "Walker Brothers Cowboy," "Boys and Girls," and "The Peace of Utrecht."[3]

"The Peace of Utrecht" is recognized as one of her "breakthrough stories" and it represents a watershed in her writing.[4] It is the first of several stories recurring regularly in Munro's *oeuvre*, which explore the female narrator's filial guilt after the prolonged illness and death of her mother. In addition, "The Peace of Utrecht" illustrates several traits that characterize the writer's first-person narrative, which are developed and more fully exploited in her later work. Among these traits are temporal and spatial shifts; the systematic, purposeful arrangement of narrative sections; and the use of tense and aspect to convey nuances in the narrator's retrospection. The adult narrator is not the same as the young girl who is sometimes the subject of the focalization; this "dialectic between present and past, between experience and understanding" creates a kind of dual voice akin to the narration in Harper Lee's *To Kill A Mockingbird* (1960), and Margaret Laurence's *A Bird in the House* (1970).[5]

Both the aforementioned texts exemplify the genre of the *Bildungsroman*, whose narrator/protagonist develops greater wisdom and understanding in the course of the narrative by dint of several educative experiences and often painful lessons. In the final pages of Lee's novel, Scout Finch surely affirms the author's moral message when she acknowledges, "you never really know a man until you stand in his shoes and walk around in them."[6] And Laurence's narrator Vanessa MacLeod has learned, through processes of mourning, to value her indebtedness to her ancestors, especially her grandfather, who "proclaims himself in my veins."[7] Munro's narrator neither finds comfort in nor derives any benefit from the new knowledge she gleans: what she does learn serves only to confirm the gulf between her and her sister, Maddy, and to augment the burden of her filial guilt. In this story, the darkest recesses of the narrator's "secret, guilty estrangement" are thrown open for scrutiny.[8]

"The Peace of Utrecht" is the longest story in the collection, and it is more formally arranged than its companions, for not only does it contain several ellipses, it is also divided into two numbered sections. The use of numerals is unusual in Munro's fiction, and in this instance I believe the numbers draw attention to how similar the opening sentences of both segments are. Each section begins with an announcement of the return of Helen, the narrator, to her former home, now her sister's house, and each return has brought unwelcome truths. In the first section she realizes that the two sisters have grown irrevocably apart from each other, Helen having left her hometown, Jubilee, many years before, while her younger sister stayed in "that discouraging house" to look after their stricken mother in "her ten-year's vigil" (p. 195). Helen's visit to her former home takes place a few months after their mother's funeral. In the second section, the narrator learns of the harrowing nature of her mother's last few weeks, discovering, from her aunts, that her sister might have been more of a comfort during that time.

The opening sentence of the first section reads, "I have been at home now for three weeks and it has not been a success" (p. 190). The perfective aspect of the present tense conveys anterior time, during which certain events have occurred that substantiate the narrator's assertion that her visit home has not gone well. Successive statements document the extent of the sisters' disharmony. Most of these contain simple present tense verbs, and in the contiguous clauses, "Silences disturb us. We laugh immoderately" (p. 190), the tense could more precisely be labeled the state present, a category used to express timelessness and stasis. Another category of the present tense, the habitual present, is used when the narrator describes how the sisters spend their evenings: "At night we often *sit out* on the steps of the verandah, and *drink* gin and *smoke* diligently to defeat the mosquitoes" (p. 190, italics added). These verb phrases, as the adjective "habitual" denotes, imply both an unrestricted time span and the frequency of an event's repetition.[9]

The perfective aspect in the first sentence indicates a state of affairs that has pertained before the present moment, and indeed may continue into the future, while the simple present tenses that cluster in the rest of the paragraph confirm the narrator's current unease. All these tensual and aspectual nuances in the opening paragraphs are a foretaste of the subsequent temporal shifts that distinguish this narrative. The episode of retrospection, when the narrator recounts events of the night when her sister "took [her] to a party at the lake" (p. 191), allows Munro to elaborate on the distance that has grown between the two sisters. The narrator has become disdainful about her hometown: twice she makes captious reference to how her sister speaks, "with the harsh twang of the local accent"; she tends to categorize her friends, observing that they "had copper rinses on their hair, and blue eyelids, and a robust capacity for drink" (p. 192). The reader can sense the narrator's regret when she concedes that Maddy is aligning herself with "these people" from Jubilee, that she wants to feel part of the community. The regret stems from the realization that her younger sister is, unlike her, now "repudiating the monstrous snobbery" they had both been keen to cultivate when they were young and wished for "much bigger things than Jubilee" (p. 192).

The narrator feels alienated from her hometown, from her sister, and from childhood memories they share. This sense of alienation, of keeping a distance, is often made salient by Munro's carefully placed ellipses. For example, the first ellipsis occurs after Helen has revealed that she has to share her sister's company most evenings with someone who may or may not be Maddy's lover. Fred Powell is depicted as "this strange man" to whom the sisters make "a present of [a] childhood which is safely preserved in anecdote" (p. 193), and it is clear that the narrator is troubled by her reactions to him. For she cannot fathom the nature of her sister's relationship, and her inability frustrates her: Maddy's teasing tenderness suggests intimacy, but she does not confide in her sister, telling her that he is her "only real friend." The narrator's reaction to this description is expressed thus: "This thought depresses me (unconsummated relationships depress outsiders perhaps more than anybody else) so much that I find myself wishing for them to be honest lovers" (p. 194). The narrator thus confirms her outsider status, and exposes her ignorance about her sister's personal life.

The ellipsis is placed immediately after this admission, and in arresting the narrative progress so abruptly Munro marks the occlusion in the narrator's knowledge, as well as in her empathetic understanding. The gap creates "a tension, an expectation of remedy" that is not fulfilled.[10] Instead, the narrative returns suddenly to the primary level where it began, with Helen's assertion, an apparent *non sequitur*, that "the rhythm of life in Jubilee is primitively seasonal" (p. 194). The narrator explains that deaths occur more often in the town's long, hard winters and that "there comes time now in the summer to think about [them], and talk" (p. 194). The deictic "now" unambiguously anchors the narrative to the present, and it makes Helen "think" and "talk" about her mother's death.

A second ellipsis further accentuates the dearth in Helen's understanding of her sister, and it also draws attention to how incompletely she has dealt with her guilt. As people stop the narrator on the street to offer her their sympathy, and their recollections of her mother, she senses their reticence about speaking of Maddy and her "ten-year's vigil." She recalls the bargain she had made with Maddy, about dividing the burden of caring, a bargain the narrator had not kept when she married and moved far away. As she reflects on why her sister remained, to shoulder the burden alone, she betrays her unease: "All I *can* think about that, all I *have ever been able* to think, to comfort me, is that she *may have been able* and *may even have chosen* to live without time and in perfect imaginary freedom as children do, the future untampered with, all choices always possible" (p. 196, italics added). The previous passage is marked by a high degree of modality, illustrations of which are italicized. Modality, as it pertains to semantics and grammar, is concerned with speakers' and writers' attitudes toward the propositions they express, and it is realized by the small class of modal verbs, and also by qualifying adverbials.[11] Here, the narrator expresses possibility, and hypothesis, when she speculates on the reasons for her sister's dutiful act, desperately searching for a motive that will "comfort" her, assuage her own remissness. The ellipsis is placed after the narrator's speculation, inviting the reader to consider how plausible her speculation seems.

In a substantial piece of analeptic narration, the narrator returns to the time of her arriving in Jubilee, at her former home, having made "a twenty-five-hundred-mile trip" with her two children. On entering the house, empty because Maddy is at work, she is startled by her imagining that she hears the plaintive, "ruined voice" of her mother, calling out for her, and this auditory hallucination evokes painful memories. These are articulated in a disjointed, halting manner: "I was allowing myself to hear—as if I had not dared before—the cry for help—undisguised, oh, shamefully undisguised and raw and supplicating—that sounded in her voice" (p. 198). At the core of the fractured sentence is "the cry for help," which is somehow shielded by the dashes on either side of it. The narrator takes time to recapture the singular poignancy of this cry, trying to define the emotions that provoked it and to better understand her mother's "state of mind" and her own. The inclusion of the exclamatory "oh" intensifies the recalled experience, making it seem as though she is responding anew to "*Who's there?*" (p. 198).

More than one Munro scholar has commented on the prison metaphors in the narrator's memory of her mother's illness. Another striking feature in the description is the abundance of discrepant juxtapositions. An adverb incongruously precedes an adjective, creating the impression of hypocrisy, and a lack of spontaneity in the sisters' care, as, for example, when the narrator explains that they "had to supply five minutes' expediently cheerful conversation" in a "remorselessly casual" way. She bluntly admits that they exhibited not a "glint of pity," but remained "unfailing in their cold solicitude." These deviant arrangements of nouns and adjectives powerfully convey the perfunctory nature of the parodic love shown (p. 199). Helen Hoy has made an extensive and illuminating study of "the startling fusion of warring terms" in Munro's fiction, arguing that, especially in her early work, the technique often serves to "convey the intense emotional ambivalence of adolescence."[12] In the context of "The Peace of Utrecht," the instances of semantic discordance expose the intensity of, more specifically, the narrator's guilt, as she strives to justify the withdrawal of filial love. That she searches for some consoling justification is evident in the plea, "how could we have loved her, I say desperately to myself, the resources of love we had were not enough" (p. 199). The extensive account of the sisters' enforced solicitude of their "Gothic Mother" (p. 200) proceeds toward another gap in the narrative, prefaced by the clamorous confession, "I felt the beginnings of a secret, guilty estrangement" (p. 201).

What follows is the discovery of the history jotter containing notes on "The Peace of Utrecht," a relic from her childhood that makes the narrator acutely aware of her "old life lying around [her], waiting to be picked up again" (p. 201). Fond, "curiously meaningful" images of the narrator and her sister in their youth conclude the retrospective piece before the narrative returns to the primary level, with Maddy's admonition to the narrator, "No exorcising" (p. 202). Like the peace of the title, a treaty that proved impermanent, the narrator's rapprochement with her sister is an uneasy one.

The first sentence of section two begins in the same way as that of the first, with a present perfective verb phrase signifying past time with current relevance: "I have been to visit Aunt Annie and Auntie Lou" (p. 202). The narrator then describes her two aunts, in four successive sentences, all beginning with the pronoun "They," all consisting of clauses linked by coordination, as in, for example, "They do not go out any more, but they get up early in the mornings, wash and powder themselves and put on their shapeless print dresses . . ." (p. 202). The resulting impression is of homogeneity, order, and orthodoxy in the two women's lives, lives from which the narrator senses she is "held at a distance" (p. 203). Yet this distancing, the belief that her aunts find it impossible to communicate with her and Maddy, is another misapprehension. On this visit, Helen's Aunt Annie makes it her duty to communicate a full account of her mother's last few weeks, an account that brings the death shockingly close to the narrator. She learns that although her sister had visited her mother regularly in hospital, she would not take her home, despite having promised her that her stay would be brief. She learns that her mother had made a frantic attempt to escape, running down the street, in her bedclothes, in the freezing cold of January, toward freedom, and that when she was brought back to hospital, she had to be restrained.

The impact of this disclosure, on narrator and reader, is heightened by its presentation in italics: "*The snow, the dressing gown and slippers, the board across the bed.*" The fact that this "picture" (p. 208) is expressed in three unembellished, oddly heterogeneous noun phrases creates an eidetic image of the pitiful flight, emblazoning it on the memory. The narrator anticipates the persistence of this image when she refers to the "haunts we have contracted for," those ghosts from the past that her aunt has ensured she will not forget (p. 209).

The brief, concluding section of the story, prefaced by the last one of the ellipses, is concerned with the consequences, for the narrator and her younger sister, of the aunt's revelations. In this scene, Munro captures the sisters' reticence, in dialogue rich in formulaic politeness and hedging indirectness.

> "Where have you been?" Maddy said.
> "Nowhere. Just to see the Aunts."
> "Oh, how are they?"
> "They're fine. They're indestructible."
> "Are they? Yes, I guess they are. I haven't been to see them for a while. I don't actually see that much of them any more."
> "Don't you?" I said, and she knew then what they had told me. (p. 209)

In a gesture of concern, the narrator urges her sister not to feel guilty about how she had treated their mother, but Maddy flippantly dismisses the possibility of guilt, and swiftly tries to change the subject. This denial is spurious, as the ending of the narrative shows, for as she utters the confession, "I couldn't go on . . . I wanted my life," she drops the kitchen bowl she is carrying, sending it crashing to the floor. On recovering her composure, she reassures her older sister that she will "take [her] life," but then she plaintively asks, "'But why can't I, Helen? *Why can't I?*'" (p. 210).

In its expression of futility, and inability, this concluding sentence is apposite, for the narrative is, in the end, about the impossibility of peace: the sisters cannot communicate with each other; they have had to "look straight into the desert that is between [them]" and acknowledge that they "reject each other" (p. 190). Neither has the means to reassure or console the other; Maddy discourages her sister with the adamant imperative, "No exorcising here" (p. 191), while Helen merely offers the useless advice, "Take your life" (p. 210). Howells perceives the smashed bowl in terms of the "irretrievable damage to a woman's life," maintaining that "the story is one of a failed exorcism . . . a Gothic tale which figures primitive female fears [of] matricide."[13] The younger sister's fear and anguish are clearly evident in the story's dramatic ending, but also manifest, throughout the account of her return visits, is the narrator's cold withdrawal, from her sister, her aunts, her mother, her hometown, and her past.

"The Peace of Utrecht" marks an important stage in Munro's writing career, as she has explained, describing it as "the first story I absolutely had to write."[14] It is where she begins to tackle personal material, and where she establishes what will become hallmarks of her retrospective first-person narrative. Like Helen, the narrator of "Material," from *Something I've Been Meaning to Tell You*, similarly looks back on a past that has informed her present; in the later work, however, the narrator appears more honest in her emotions, firmer in her conviction. Unlike Helen, she is not troubled by filial guilt, but by feelings of resentment and anger, which she articulates in her narrative and gives vent to in the occasional direct appeals to more than one addressee. The instances of interaction create what Louis MacKendrick calls "a confessional intimacy" that, in his opinion, "blackmail[s]" the reader "into accepting the [narrator's] long-suffering personality and her summary judgments."[15]

MacKendrick's own judgments on the unnamed narrator of "Material" are harsh. He maintains that she is motivated by a grudge deriving from her own guilt, and describes her account as "a farrago of memory, bitterness and self-justification . . . a confession of spite, jealousy and error."[16] There is ample evidence of the narrator's fallibility, but the flaws are acknowledged and fully admitted; moreover, some of the resentment and envy seems, in a more sympathetic reading, justifiable.

What the reader would infer most of all from this story is the narrator's emotional intensity. The infrequency of temporal anachronies means that the account is focused predominantly on the narrator's present feelings, of antipathy, which are aroused by a particular piece in her former husband Hugo's short story collection. The central character in his story is Dotty, who was known to the narrator and Hugo when they were newly married and living in a rented part of "a sad grey stucco house" in Vancouver.[17] In the basement apartment lived the landlady's daughter, Dotty, described as "flat-faced, soft, doughy, fashioned for defeat" (p. 38); she had been befriended by the narrator, who found her eccentricities amusing. Much of the anger that Hugo's story provokes in the narrator stems from her belief that he has appropriated Dotty, has used her profitably for his art, when in reality, he had been dismissive of her. The narrator is aggrieved to read that in his portrayal, he has remembered certain of the woman's mannerisms, and she wonders, "when did Hugo ever talk to Dotty?" (p. 47).

It is made clear at the outset of the narrative that Hugo is a successful writer. The opening sentence, "I don't keep up with Hugo's writing" (p. 30), fulfils two purposes: it signals the contemporaneous level of narration, and enables Munro's narrator to establish Hugo's credentials as a writer, as she goes on to explain that his name is often seen in newspaper announcements, posters in the library, or on the front cover of literary journals she no longer opens. What follows is a passage of sardonic, amusing social commentary on the "conceited academic posturing" of the world Hugo moves in, a world of literary events and precious public performances.[18] It is one the narrator looks back on and despises, one where writers deliver sacrosanct opinions savored by "women, middle-aged women like me, alert and trembling" and "soft-haired young girls awash in adoration" (p. 30). The fact that she includes herself among the celebrity worshippers she derides is to her credit, and dilutes the sourness of her derision.

The piece of commentary prefaces a passage of exposition in which the reader learns that the narrator is now married to an engineer, Gabriel, whom she met after she divorced Hugo and was living in a "tiny, shabby apartment" with her daughter Clea, "Hugo's daughter too, of course, but he had to let go of her." The narrator explains that Hugo had since married twice, and fathered six more children, noting, with wry understatement, that in "such circumstances a man can't hang on to everything" (p. 31). The admission of her own fallibility, and the insertion of these understated quips, protects the narrator from the charges MacKendrick levels against her—that she is "sour and suspicious," that she "is a master at finding fault [and] has a private agenda which none can know or satisfy."[19] For as she mocks the publicity portrait on Hugo's new book, and satirizes the fulsome blurb, correcting what she thinks are exaggerations, she knowingly exposes her own defects and vulnerabilities, as the following confession surely demonstrates: "I construct somebody from this one smudgy picture, I am content with such clichés. I have not the imagination or goodwill to proceed differently" (p. 34).

This reflexivity of narration is characteristic of metafictional writing, which "self-consciously and systematically draws attention to its status as an artifact, in order to pose questions about the relationship between fiction and reality."[20] In "Material" there are several self-conscious allusions to the fictive process. The narrator's incredulity at the fictionalizing of the author profile is expressed in the recurrent appeals she makes to a narratee, inviting the reader, for example, to "Look at Hugo's portrait" (p. 35). In her querulous commentary on the script, she challenges some of the pretensions claimed: "*He has been sporadically affiliated with various academic communities. What does that mean?*" She also directly addresses the subject, with questions and scolding imperatives, as in, "Look at you, Hugo, your image is not only fake but out of date." Her anger reaches a climax in a remarkable series of clauses: "you should have shaved your head, shaved your beard, put on a monk's cowl; you should have shut up, Hugo" (p. 35). The repetition of the modal verb phrase, the parallelism of the structures, and the use of anaphora, make her observations read like a mantra.

Immediately after this stylized flourish of rhetoric, a segment of analeptic narration begins, with a sentence that is, in contrast, purely referential, free of any ornament: "When I was pregnant with Clea we lived in a house on Argyle Street in Vancouver" (p. 36). This laconic statement initiates her account of the period in her life when she and Hugo knew Dotty. It is annotated by several observations that increase the story's self-consciousness; for example, after a brief history of Dotty's various misfortunes and ailments, rendered as the character's spoken words, the narrator concludes, "I am condensing," her flippant remark confirming the act of ventriloquy. For both the narrator and Hugo, Dotty is a source of entertainment, their "harlot-in-residence" (p. 39) whose reception of male visitors intrigues them, and amuses their friends. In a piece of prescient advice, the narrator encourages her husband to "pay more attention to Dotty if he wanted to be a writer," but he seemed uninterested, as he was "writing a verse play" (p. 38).

From being a source of amusement to them, Dotty becomes the cause of conflict. The description of this conflict reveals much about the imbalance of authority and priorities in the narrator's marriage, and may explain her resentment and envy. It appears that Hugo dislikes their neighbor's piano playing, and the narrator has to go "down to the basement, of course" and ask her to stop. The adverbial "of course" is worthy of scrutiny, for its use here as a concessive conjunct "commonly expresses superficial agreement with what has preceded while at the same time hinting at a more fundamental disagreement."[21] In this instance, I would argue that "of course" implies that the narrator is reluctantly accepting her role as obedient wife, ready to conciliate in a dispute. She discloses that in this role she is careful to avoid using the word "*write*" when explaining that her husband is working, for "Hugo had trained me not to," and the prospect of his being disturbed further "made me nervous and miserable" (p. 40). The admission that she is "trained" into acquiescence to her husband's commands and wishes constitutes for me evidence of a self-image that needs bolstering. At the outset of the story, she betrays feelings of inferiority when she identifies with the middle-aged women in the audience at literary events, "who absorb the contempt of the men on the platform as if they deserved it" (p. 31).

The narrator portrays Hugo as a man who sees "the world [as] hostile to his writing" (p. 40) and who expects his wife to act as a bulwark between his work and all that deflects him from it, a duty for which she feels inadequate. Besides the piano playing, Hugo is also disturbed by the noise of the water pump that prevents the basement from being flooded. Because the narrator has become fond of Dotty, she is protective of her, believing that Hugo is unreasonable in his intolerance of the noise and in his lack of sympathy for the woman whose apartment would be flooded without the pump. When the narrator awakens in the night to discover that Hugo has turned off the machine, a petty argument ensues. Munro scripts this argument in free, direct discourse, without most of the reporting clauses; it is easy to infer the interlocutors from the context and from the character indices displayed. In its resemblance to a drama script, the conversation, which takes up more than a page, constitutes a scene, and it marks a kernel event in the narrative. The argument lays bare the couple's intransigence, and the absurdity of their peevish stances, most amusingly in this exchange:

> "Listen to me, Hugo, you have to go and turn it on, Dotty will be flooded out."
> "In the morning."
> "You have to go and turn it on *now*."
> "Well, I'm not."
> "If you're not, I am."

"No, you're not."

"I am."

But I didn't move. (p. 43)

What succeeds this verbal parrying is another passage of self-conscious, writerly commentary, rich in rhetorical schemes such as anaphora, antithesis, and bathos, and instances of stylistic extravagance. The narrator closely analyses the entire episode, speculating on hypothetical resolutions, while candidly evaluating her own weakness and omissions, for the basement did indeed flood. Admitting that she "could have" acted otherwise, and might have prevented or lessened the drama, she concludes, "I think that is what a woman of firm character would have done . . . But I did not do it" (p. 44). MacKendrick perceives the narrator's account as an attempt to "rationalize her own guilt" when she "transfers blame for Dotty's disaster in a series of 'He could haves.'"[22] His perception is rather favorable toward the male protagonist: after all, the "could haves" relating to how Hugo might have acted are discounted or countermanded by the narrator, who accepts that she must bear much of the blame herself, as her reference to a woman of character suggests. This quarrel was to have serious consequences for the narrator's marriage, for it was never resolved. That she realized its gravity is clear from her admission that "a woman who wanted that marriage to last would have" acted differently (p. 44). The confiding, self-critical quality of the narrator's analysis is sustained as she concludes her retrospective account, recalling her obduracy with the candid admission, "What presumptuousness, what cowardice, what bad faith" (p. 47).

The concluding scene in "Material" takes place in the house where the narrator now lives with her daughter Clea, her husband Gabriel, and his sons. It is a short piece of analepsis in which she relates her reactions to Hugo's story, and it explains the preceding emotional intensity. By comparison with Hugo, with his widely publicized fame as a writer, his unconventional lifestyle, and his home "*on the side of a mountain above Vancouver*" (p. 35), the narrator's present circumstances are humble and mundane. She comes home in the afternoon from the private girls' school, where she teaches history part time, to snatch and "enjoy" an hour before the family returns (p. 47). In this glimpse of a perhaps unfulfilled career, I believe that the narrator sheds light on the reasons for her antipathy toward Hugo, and in her generous praise of his fiction, she shows herself in a better light. She admits that Hugo's story (of Dotty) is "an act of magic, there is no getting round it . . . an act, you might say, of a special, unsparing, unsentimental love." She admires the way that her former husband has transformed Dotty so that she has miraculously "passed into Art," and she thinks of writing him a letter, where she will ironically remark on the different uses each has made of the same "bank of memory" (p. 48).

Mingled with her admiration, however, are resentment and envy. She likens Hugo to Gabriel, seeing both men as better able than she has been to accomplish objectives, because "both have authority [and] are not *at the mercy*" (p. 48). Sitting alone at her kitchen table with "a pile of test papers and [her] marking pencils," her domestic chores done and the family settled or in bed, she presents an appearance of resignation, even defeat. MacKendrick perceives her as "a vigorous combatant in her own arena," observing that "it is little wonder that she is left alone, bitter, to mark her papers and her life."[23] This evaluation of her fate seems severe. Munro refers twice to the "test papers" and describes her narrator as "burdened" with them, "preoccupied" with toil that is, in contrast with Hugo's rewarding, beneficent creativity, deadly dull (p. 49). The "short, jabbing sentences" with which the narrator begins her letter are given up: they were, as she acknowledges, "never planned" and do not make up "an argument to send through the mail" (p. 48). They read like emotional outbursts.

Unlike Helen in "The Peace of Utrecht," this narrator has lavishly expressed her emotions, expunging them in various ways: in her satire of posturing writers and academics; in her attack on the hypocrisy of biography; in her analysis of her own deficient reasoning. Moreover, in the tribute to Hugo's skill as a writer, and in the passages of melodramatic declamation, her zeal for the "self-conscious manipulation of language" is made apparent.[24] The first-person female narrator, often a writer, recurs in Munro's *oeuvre*. In later stories, like "Nettles" or "Family Furnishings," the character is neither as emotionally candid, nor as self-conscious about her creativity, and the uses she must make of the past, if that creativity is to flourish.

CHAPTER 2

CHANGING PERSPECTIVES

IN THE BOOKS THAT FOLLOW *SOMETHING I'VE Been Meaning to Tell You*, Munro relies less often on the first-person narrative perspective that, according to Robert Thacker, is "distinctive . . . throughout her work."[1] All the stories in *Who Do You Think You Are?*, published as *The Beggar Maid* in the United States and Britain, are told from a third-person point of view. Reference has already been made to this book's complicated publishing history, one that illustrates Munro's enthrallment to her artistic principles.

As Helen Hoy carefully explains in her essay on the genesis and publishing of *Who Do You Think You Are?*, the collection was initially announced in the *Globe and Mail* as *Rose and Janet*.[2] Two stories featuring the character Janet (as narrator) were held over for Munro's next volume, *The Moons of Jupiter*; they are "Chaddeleys and Flemings" and "The Moons of Jupiter" and are the strongest stories in the book. In these two pieces, Munro is exploring and celebrating the lives of her forebears, albeit fictively. There are three other first-person stories: "Hard-Luck Stories," which contains material originally from an extended version of "Simon's Luck," in *Who Do You Think You Are?*;[3] "The Turkey Season," whose adolescent narrator brings to mind Del Jordan in *Lives of Girls and Women*; and "Bardon Bus," whose sexually unsettled (and unsettling) female narrator, far from adolescence, confesses to a "stubborn virgin's belief . . . in perfect mastery."[4]

In *The Moons of Jupiter* there are signs of increasing boldness in both content and form. In "Bardon Bus" Munro travels beyond Canada for the first time in her work, when her narrator returns to a time spent in Australia, where she had enjoyed a passionate affair; "Labor Day Dinner" is strikingly different from previous stories because it is narrated mostly in the present tense, and its temporal and spatial ranges are narrow, claustrophobically condensed, like the characters' lives. The story "Accident" is particularly ambitious in relation to Munro's treatment of perspective and time. Its heterodiegetic narrator introduces a scene described entirely in present tenses, but the events are long in the past, and it is not until the conclusion that the reader is taken, abruptly, to the contemporaneous level of narration. Moreover, the heterodiegetic narrator shares the perspective with the subject of the focalization, Frances, one of two protagonists; the other being her lover, Ted. In the use of a heterodiegetic narrator who flaunts omniscience and who seems, at times, a mouthpiece for the community, "Accident" prepares for the polyphony and the experiments with focalization that distinguish "Fits" and "Lichen" from *The Progress of Love*. This book won the writer her second Governor-General's Award, and is one that Munro's biographer regards as "perhaps, her best collection overall."[5] Both "Fits" and "Lichen" amply illustrate Munro's desire to vary and elaborate her narrative strategies.

"Fits" is concerned with the irruption of violence in intimate relationships, in outwardly ordinary lives, and it explores how the central characters react to the irruption. The principal act of violence is the murder-suicide of an elderly couple who lived next door to the protagonists, Robert and Peg Kuiper, in Gilmore, Ontario. It is Peg who discovers the bodies: Walter Weeble shot his wife Nora, then killed himself. Peg's shocking discovery is not directly reported by the third-person narrator; the details are gleaned mostly from Robert's imaginative reconstruction of Peg's experience. The reasons for the murder-suicide remain unknown, as do other intriguing mysteries in "Fits": why Peg is so reticent about finding the bodies; why she invents details relating to the crime scene; why her partner does not know her better. The story has attracted vastly differing scholarly approaches. Virginia Pruitt argues that when "appraised from a psychodynamic perspective,"[6] the story's enigmas are less puzzling, while, in a study enriched by knowledge of the Gothic genre and horror cinema, Caitlin J. Charman concludes that "perhaps we leave 'Fits' with a foreboding sense of real terror and the 'periodic fits' that may await us outside."[7]

In her discussion of the story, Ildikó de Papp Carrington points out that what Peg witnesses is "*doubly* distanced by being filtered through the point of view of an outsider and a second-hand observer."[8] The concept of distance is relevant to an analysis of "Fits," where Munro creates protagonists who are, in different ways, out of reach: Robert is depicted as an outsider to Gilmore, not fully conversant with its geography, and its mores, but eager to explore; Peg is presented as an emotionally withdrawn, repressed, and taciturn woman. One character is anxious to know more, while the other is reluctant to tell. The gaps in knowledge and disclosure open up in a narrative whose heterodiegetic narrator has considerable authority, which is generously displayed at the outset. The opening sentences of the first paragraph are confidently referential and assertively evaluative: "The two people who died were in their early sixties. They were both tall and well built, and carried a few pounds of extra weight. He was gray-haired, with a square, rather flat face. A broad nose kept him from looking perfectly dignified and handsome. Her hair was blond, a silvery blond that does not strike you as artificial anymore—though you know it is not natural—because so many women of that age have acquired it."[9] The passage reads like an account delivered by a well-informed resident of the town, a keen, critical observer of appearances. The "you" is noteworthy, for its use helps to confirm the narrator's authority. It makes sense to think of the "you" as not the addressee or narratee, but the narrator, choosing the second-person pronoun instead of "me" or "one," both of which would be inappropriate, the former because the narration is not first person, the latter because "one" is excessively formal. The generic "you," typically an informal equivalent of "one," "retains something of its 2nd person meaning [for] it can suggest that the speaker is appealing to the hearer's experience of life in general, or else of some specific situation."[10] In this instance the narrator is faintly mocking "women of that age" who dye their hair, and is slyly inviting the reader to share the knowingness.

The narrator's authority is sustained in the panchronic summary of the protagonists' background, which begins, "Robert and Peg have been married for nearly five years" (p. 107). That Robert is an outsider to Gilmore is alluded to several times in the narrative. The reader learns that his family had never lived in the township, although they owned the arcade that Robert inherited and took over. He had eventually settled in the town, having spent many years travelling, and, in middle age, married Peg, who works in the Gilmore store. She is a native of Gilmore, and has two sons from a previous marriage. The narrator explains that Robert thrives on the challenges of the isolated country north of Toronto, "the snow belt" where "winter comes down hard"; however, the contiguous observation that "people live within the winter in a way outsiders do not understand" is another reminder that the character is not native to this "different country" (p. 110), and, regardless of his relish for Gilmore, his understanding may be deficient. The picture gradually emerging of Robert is of one who harbors an idealized perception of the wilderness beyond Toronto, and it is noticeable that the narrator seems to liken him, in this respect, to the Weebles, also city people, from Hamilton. The connection between Robert and the Weebles is subtly effected by Munro's use of reported speech. Peg discovers the Weebles' bodies because she has called at their house to deliver eggs left by the farm woman; the narrator explains that, like Robert, the couple seemed to prefer farm eggs, reporting Peg's opinion that "city people had a thing about brown eggs—they thought they were more natural somehow, like brown sugar" (p. 111). From this observation the reader infers Peg's mockery of outsiders who are easily impressed and seduced by an unfamiliar rusticity.

The heterodiegetic narrator thus establishes Robert's outsider status, a status he shares with the Weebles. Munro's textual configuration serves as another means of linking Robert and his next-door neighbors. When he leaves for work, he notices that the Weebles' car is in its carport, and, as the snow is still piled up outside their driveway, he concludes that the couple had not left their house recently. Robert becomes the subject of the focalization as his thoughts on the scene are rendered: "They couldn't have been out last night. Unless they were walking . . . it was difficult to walk along the narrowed streets with their banks of snow, but, being new to town, they might not have realized that." Because the supplementive clause "being new to town" is fronted and marked off by commas, attention is drawn to the Weebles' status—a status that would, in Robert's reasoning, make them unfamiliar with Gilmore's geography. It is an unfamiliarity that also marks Robert, as the narrator has already made clear. In the one-line paragraph following Robert's speculation, the perspective returns to the narrator: "He didn't look closely enough to see if there were footprints" (p. 111). As Robert's failure to notice the footprints is recounted in an isolated paragraph, the inadvertence is somehow exposed and the proximity of two allusions to a *lack of knowing* seems less of an accident.

An ellipsis placed after this short paragraph accentuates the inadvertence. The gap also marks a boundary between what Robert saw, and did not see, outside the Weebles' house and what he imagines his wife witnessed inside. Robert's reliability is undermined, first, because he is an incomer and does not fully know Gilmore, and second, because it is implied that his capacity for alert observation is lacking.

Unlike her husband, Peg is depicted as watchful, someone who would be more attentive to detail, for she is variously described as self-contained, unobtrusive, earnest, and conscientious (p. 108–9), keen to augment her knowledge of the world in evening courses at the local high school. As a witness and observer, Peg would seem to be the epitome of reliability, and so it is interesting that her discovery of the bodies is not directly reported, but filtered through Robert's perspective. In order to describe Peg's journey from her home to the Weebles' house, the narrator transfers the focalization to Robert, who imagines his wife's perspective, integrating what he has learned from conversations with the constable, in the diner, and with Peg, and with her workmate, Karen, in the store. Into this account the heterodiegetic narrator inserts comments that seem to correct Robert's extravagance.

Some of the precision in this scene is characteristic of omniscient narration, as in, "The Weebles' house had been built as a mirror image of the Kuipers' but the front window had been changed, its Christmas-card panes taken out" (p. 112). The past perfective aspect betokens knowledge of the place's history, and suggests attention to detail that Robert might have missed, or not known, as an incomer. Such minutiae would be unlikely to figure in the account Peg later gives to the constable, and to her husband. The account of Peg's actions, as she carries out her errand, taking the eggs to the couple, is an intriguing blend of different discourses, exemplified as follows:

> She set the eggs on the clothes dryer, and was going to leave them there. Then she thought she had better take them up into the kitchen, in case the Weebles wanted eggs for breakfast and had run out. They wouldn't think of looking in the utility room.
> (This, in fact, was Robert's explanation to himself. She didn't say all that, but he forgot she didn't. She just said, "I thought I might as well take them up to the kitchen.") (p. 113)

With its initially informative function, and the inclusion of the reporting clause "she thought," the first paragraph reads like heterodiegesis. However, the account assumes the qualities of free indirect discourse, evident in vestiges of informality and markers of modality and contingency. These make the report seem less authoritative. What follows in the narrator's interjected parenthesis confirms that it is speculative, and, along with the allusion to his forgetting, provides further evidence of Robert's unreliability. So too does the contrast between the elaborate thought processes he spuriously attributes to his wife and the banal explanation she provides, *verbatim*. The contrast hints at an errant inventiveness, manifest in the scene where Robert envisages his wife approaching the bedroom where the bodies lie.

The subject of the focalization is not Peg, for her perspective is imagined, one might say borrowed, by Robert, who has listened to her account (but invents details so the reader is informed). Peg's progress is narrated in such a way that suspense is generated, as in, "Peg walked now across the clean, pale carpet to the foot of the stairs. She started to climb. She did not call again" (p. 114), where the proximal deictic "now" brings the reader close to the scene, and the two single-clause sentences impart an urgent purposefulness to the actions. Once more, Munro arranges textual segments in such a way as to excite reader expectation. She isolates the plangent statement, "The door of that room was wide open," in a single paragraph, immediately succeeding it with an ellipsis; the urge to enter "that room" is denied by the hiatus, and narrative suspense is consequently sustained. The artifice in this imagined account is absent from the following segment, which begins, "Peg came downstairs and left the house by the kitchen, the utility room, the side door" (p. 114). Here the narrator has taken over, presenting the action, in contrast, prosaically, without any adornment, explaining that Peg continues on to the police station to dutifully report the crime. In this brief scene, enclosed by two ellipses, Peg's reporting is depicted as a perfunctory business, and the reader might recall how, early in the narrative, the critical, well-informed, and confident observer described how "[Peg] would smile in the store when she gave you your change—a quick transactional smile" (p. 108).

Peg's impassivity and reticence are evident in the scene where she prepares to embark on her everyday routines at the store, withholding details of her gruesome discovery from her colleague Karen, who learns of the tragedy from a customer. It is Karen who provides Robert with the story of Peg's unnatural taciturnity, and her incredulity is presented in the form of her reported conversation. A subsequent stretch of dialogue between Robert and Peg reinforces the impression of Peg as clamlike in her reticence. These scenes in the store reveal important character indices: primarily, they show how Peg is intent on repressing news that others would probably rush to disclose. In addition, her cool, distanced reaction to her experience provokes not only shocked disbelief from her workmate, but also disappointment. Karen is aggrieved that she was not chosen as a confidante, berating Peg with the accusation, "How come you never said a word about this" (p. 116). She is frustrated by her lack of knowing.

Robert is also disappointed with Peg, because he thinks she should have contacted him, involved him somehow. Instead, he finds her in absolute control of her emotions, far removed from "any state of collapse" (p. 117). Indeed, she is so unaffected by the Weebles' deaths that she has returned to work and looks forward to her usual lunch. In this second store scene, the narrator transfers the focalization to Robert, who notices the "long crusty smear of reddish-brown paint" on Peg's coat hanging on the washroom door and then reappraises what he sees: "Of course that wasn't paint. But on her coat? How did she get blood on her coat? She must have brushed up against them in that room. She must have got close" (p. 118). This instance of free indirect discourse conveys Robert's unease at what he suspects is his wife's prurience, but it is a prurience not so different from the curiosity he and Karen display, when each demands to know and expresses disbelief at being excluded from knowledge.

Immediately after these revelations of ghoulish curiosity, the narrator reports on how the Gilmore community in general reacts to news of the murder-suicide. Their reactions are presented in a series of questions and answers spoken by "people on the street, in the bakery and the café and the bank and the post office, talking" (p. 118). Individual opinions on the reasons for the murder-suicide are mostly expressed without reporting clauses or speech marks, in free direct discourse: "Was it a lot of money? Certainly. A lot. It was not money at all. They were ill" (p. 119). In their elliptical vagueness and randomness, the utterances read like local gossip, captured by the subject of the focalization, Robert, who "listened to all these explanations but did not believe them" (p. 119). In another piece of parenthetical comment, the narrator explains that "Robert was right about the reasons," for all the speculations about the murder-suicide are refuted: "In Gilmore everything becomes known, sooner or later" (p. 121). What follows, however, in the remainder of this parenthesis is ironic, for, contrary to what the reader might hope for, what is provided is only a list of discounted theories, no "specific clues," no solution at all (p. 122). The opportunity for an explanation is not taken: the disbelieving Robert does not know the real reason for the crime.

In the final scenes of the narrative, possible explanations emerge. First, the Kuipers are presented in the kitchen where Peg prepares a meal, and into this ordinary domestic setting the neighbors' deaths intrude. The younger son, Kevin, "another person who thought Peg should have let him know," wonders how much "blood and guck" (pp. 122–23) there was, while the older son, Clayton, asks his mother if she screamed. After the meal, Peg reveals more to her husband about what she witnessed in the Weebles' bedroom, including a detail that is, it later transpires, invented, about the man's "leg outstretched into the hall" (p. 125). The narrator explains that Peg is now telling Robert "her part of the story" (p. 126). This intriguing phrase implies that the circumstances lie outside the realm of factual testimony, and there are several factors that distance them further: the narrator has assembled snippets of Gilmore gossip about the deaths, all disproved; it has been established that the focalizer's local knowledge and powers of observance are erratic; the account of the actual discovery of the dead bodies is imagined, described from a borrowed perspective; and the one character who comes close to the aftermath of the killings is reluctant to expand on what she saw. Responding to her older son's speculation—that the Weebles had fought—Peg replies: "'We don't know that . . . We don't know if they had a fight, or what'" (p. 125). Her disavowal of knowledge is at odds with the desire for knowledge that everyone else in the community seems to possess, for "Nobody would

want not to know. To go out into the street not knowing." (p. 118). At
this point the reader might recall the narrator's wry observation, "For a
Gilmore person, Peg is reserved" (p. 108).

The reserve may be a façade, however, as the reader infers from Clayton's disclosure that his mother and her first husband used to have such
violent arguments that he feared for his life. Robert tries to explain these
irruptions of violence as "fits," or "freak occurrences," rebutting Clayton's
suggestion that the "fits" are "periodic" ones that "married people have."
This rebuttal would appear to be endorsed in the line, "'No,' said Clayton, "No, not you'" (p. 126). Caitlin J. Charman interprets this reply as
indicative of a "hesitancy" that suggests the son believes the "fits" are far
from "extraordinary, and that at any moment the ordinary might split
open and erupt into violence."[11] It is equally plausible, I would argue, to
regard the triple negative as firm refutation of any suggestion of latent
violence in the family's present home. Much would depend on how Clayton utters these words, and Munro provides no directions. Her description of Peg's expression as "fixed in steady, helpless, unapologetic pain"
(p. 126) depicts a protagonist trapped by troubling memories, and lends
weight to a reading of the periodic fits as belonging to the past.

Robert is certainly disturbed by memories of conflict with his former partner Lee, which beset him in his evening walk across Gilmore's
snowy fields. It is in this section of narrative that a connection between
the Weebles' deaths and the protagonists' past, intimate lives is clarified. Robert looks back on a time when he had argued with Lee and "all
of a sudden, the argument had split open—Robert couldn't remember
how, but it split open" (p. 127). The metaphor of splitting retrieves the
image of earthquakes and fits he employed when trying to explain to
Clayton why some couples have fierce fights. The argument is described
in sadomasochistic terms, as, recognizing "their extremity," the couple
"trembled with murderous pleasure, [and] exulted in wounds inflicted
but also wounds received" (p. 128). Immediately following this memory
runs another analepsis, one nearer to the contemporaneous level, when
Robert and Peg are together, exchanging histories. The contrast between
Robert's self-presentation and that of Peg merits scrutiny. The former is
characterized by emotive, hyperbolic language, as in, "He said he had
been an emotional spendthrift, had thrown himself into hopeless and
painful entanglements . . . all experiment and posturing." Peg's account,
expressed in free direct discourse, is, in contrast, almost entirely referential and unembellished: "We lived with Dave's parents. There was never
enough hot water for the baby's wash . . . Then Dave got another job,
he went up North, and I rented this place." Facts are tersely delivered in

coordinate clauses assembled in chronological sequence, with scarcely any other means of conjunction. With Robert as the subject of the focalization, the flashback ends on a note of speculation about why the marriage ended: "Things happen before he goes . . . There's got to be some wrenching and slashing. But she didn't say" (pp. 128–29). Both Robert and Peg, then, have come from turbulent relationships, marked by what Virginia Pruitt describes as "toxic surges of aggressive energy unopposed by love."[12]

The story moves toward a puzzling conclusion, where Robert, still the subject of the focalization, reconsiders Peg's account of her discovery and ponders on the crucial "discrepancy, a detail, in the midst of so many abominable details" (p. 130). It transpires that while Peg had described to Robert the outstretched, clothed leg of Walter Weeble protruding in the hallway, the constable in the diner had earlier confirmed that what lay there was the man's head, blasted apart by his shotgun. When Robert listened to his wife's account earlier in the kitchen, he had known this fact. The nature of the discrepancy is not instantly revealed, however, but is delayed by a passage of richly figurative description: in his walk across a sparkling expanse of snow, Robert approaches "a new kind of glitter under the trees . . . [a] congestion of shapes, with black holes in them, and unmatched arms or petals reaching up" (p. 130) that turns out to be a pile of car wrecks in a junkyard. The impression of Robert as a romantic idealist prone to exaggerate, to imagine what is not there instead of noting the obvious, is sustained in the story's ending. It is confirmed that his vision is unreliable, for what he thinks are outlandish giants are "nothing but old wrecks" (p. 131). In the description of this realization, Munro retrieves an allusion to proximity applied to Peg's discovery of the bodies. The reader is told that Robert wanted "an explanation" for the shapes, but was "not getting one until he got very *close*," that he wanted to tell Peg about "how *close* he had to get before he saw what amazed and bewildered him" (p. 131, italics added). Earlier, when Robert noticed the smear on his wife's coat, he knew that "she must have got *close*" to the bodies (p. 118, italics added).

The reprised allusions to proximity are surely not coincidental. Perhaps Munro intends the reader to reflect on how her two protagonists approach the unexpected, the uncanny: both have to get close to understand what is there, to find an explanation. There is, however, a crucial difference between how they respond to their encounters with "monstrosities." Robert's reaction is described in emotive terms, when the narrator reports that the assembly of strange shapes initially "amazed and bewildered" him, then he "felt disappointed, but also like laughing" (p. 131). He is, by his own admission, an emotional spendthrift. By contrast, Peg's reactions to the horror of her discovery are frugal, laconic: she admits that she was not frightened, that she was only "surprised." The terse statement "'He shot her and then he shot himself'" (p. 116) is as much as she tells her workmate about the deaths; other extracted details relate to how she tidily leaves the crime scene. Most of the information that the reader gleans about this act of murderous violence is mediated or imagined by the subject of the focalization, Robert, whose knowledge and skills of observation are suspect.

Both protagonists in "Fits" are weakened by distance: in Robert's case it is a distance resulting from his outsider status, his inadvertence, and his shallowness—those "errors of avoidance" that are emphasized by a double repetition. With Peg, her distance is emotional, for she is depicted as impassive and self-possessed, comfortable with unadorned facts, no matter how inexplicable. "But she didn't say, and he didn't ask" (p. 129) appropriately encapsulates one's reluctance to tell, the other's inability to find out.

In studies of "Fits," scholars tend to be far more critical of Peg's character than of Robert's. Ajay Heble believes that her "overt disinterestedness conceals . . . a morbid fascination,"[13] while Héliane Ventura goes further, maintaining that her "flawed discourse points to her moral alienation."[14] Peg's curiosity at the crime scene is described as "brutal" by Carrington, who interprets her behavior as indicative of a "frozen, rigid and deeply repressed nature."[15] Virginia Pruitt admits that the reason for Peg's invention "remains elusive," but she takes a more compassionate view of the character's actions. She suggests that the proximity to brutality reminds Peg too painfully of ferocious quarrels in her failed marriage, and so she tidies the scene in her account, and in her mind. The memory may be so powerful that "she instinctively engage[s] in the defence mechanisms of suppression and displacement."[16] The image of an outstretched leg "whole and decent in its trousers" (p. 131) would be neater and less horrifying than what she saw. Robert's unease about this solitary invented detail strikes me as ironic, in view of the fact that his entire account of his wife's discovery is a "pictured" reconstruction (p. 111).

What is undoubtedly true about what Pruitt calls this "compelling but problematic short story" is that there is, in the end, no definitive explanation, either for the murder-suicide, or for the discrepancy in Peg's testimony.[17] The reader is left with a series of questions about, for example, the extent to which one knows the other in a committed heterosexual relationship, about the contrast between knowledge and speculation, and the boundaries between knowing and prurience, between disclosure and a self-protecting deceit.

I would argue that Munro's experiments in narrative technique thicken the layers of mystery and uncertainty in "Fits." The text is much more fragmented than any before: there are nineteen segments, some no more than two or three short paragraphs in length, and this fragmentation works in conjunction with the frequent shifts in perspective to create a blurring and diffuseness of focus. Although a confident heterodiegetic narrator begins the story, control is quickly and often surrendered to the focalizer, an outsider and a careless observer, with the result that narrative authority and reliability are compromised. The reader is then unsure of where to place her trust. Additionally, Munro arranges the textual segments in ways that frustrate reader expectations; more than the customary Munrovian temporal and spatial shifts, there are overtly placed retardatory devices, such as the tantalizing withdrawal from the open bedroom door in the Weebles' house (p. 114), or the postponement of the discrepancy. And this disclosure is delayed by a passage of narration, the metaphorical and metonymic significations of which are cryptic and decidedly ambiguous.

More than any other piece of fiction Munro has published so far, "Fits" seems to confirm the truth of the narrator's statement at the end of "Chaddeleys and Flemings: The Stone in the Field," when she acknowledges that she "no longer believe[s] people's secrets are defined and communicable, or their feelings full-blown and easy to recognize."[18]

Secrecy and deception lie at the heart of "Lichen," a narrative concerned with shifting balances of power in sexual relations. In her intricate weaving of the ties that connect the characters in this story—Stella, David, Catherine, and the absent Dina—Munro explores the consequences of aging, on physical appearance, on sexual allure, and on the estimation of self-worth. "Lichen" is the description applied to the pubic hair of a young woman, Dina, photographed naked in a provocative pose. The photograph belongs to David, who shows it to his wife Stella, from whom he is now separated, in a gleeful display of his latest sexual triumph. It is in response to his boasting that Stella delivers her reductive comparison. To compound his cruelty, David asks her to keep the photograph safe, and secret, lest he reveal it to Catherine, his current lover, to whom he is unfaithful, and of whom he now tires.

As in "Fits," Munro uses techniques such as polyphony, transfers of focalization, and temporal disarrangement as she develops the dynamics in power between these characters; she also employs a central image, of lichen, but this trope plays a much more substantial role than the metaphor of splitting, functioning as both metonym for aging and as a symbol of the older woman's defensive imagination. While the noun "lichen" is significant, so too is its homophone, the verb "liken," for there are several instances of analogy in the narrative. For example, at the very outset, David, in a petulant observation to Catherine, likens Stella to a "troll" (*The Progress of Love*, p. 32). Catherine, trying hard to impress her company, likens Stella's summer cottage to "a lovely shabby house" in an "old Ingmar Bergman movie" (p. 36). But "liken" also functions ironically, when certain versions of events are revealed as specious, not what they appear to be. So it is with David's perception of Catherine's age, and her supposed feyness, and with Stella's optimistic view of the separation. In this narrative, the reader is often made aware of disparities, when a character's judgments are at odds with those of another or when they appear to be flawed.

The first three paragraphs contain several allusions to discrepancies, to differences in perception, and to shape changing. The shifting narrative perspective that is one of the story's hallmarks draws attention to the theme of transformation.

> Stella's father built the place as a summer house, on the clay bluffs overlooking Lake Huron. Her family always called it "the summer cottage." David was surprised when he first saw it, because it had none of the knotty-pine charm, the battened-down coziness, that the words suggested. A city boy, from what Stella's family called "a different back-ground," he had no experience of summer places. It was and is a high, bare wooden house, painted gray—a copy of the old farmhouses nearby, although perhaps less substantial. In front of it are the steep bluffs—they are not so substantial, either, but have held so far—and a long flight of steps down to the beach, where Stella grows vegetables with considerable skill and coaxing, a short sandy lane, and a jungle of wild blackberry bushes.
>
> As David turns the car into the lane, Stella steps out of these bushes, holding a colander full of berries. She is a short, fat, white-haired woman, wearing jeans and a dirty T-shirt. There is nothing underneath these clothes, as far as he can see, to support or restrain her.
>
> "Look what's happened to Stella," says David, fuming. "She's turned into a troll." (p. 32)

The narrative begins from a position of external focalization, where "an anonymous agent, situated outside the fabula [story], is functioning as focalizor . . . an external, non-character-bound narrator."[19] That the narrator or focalizer is external (and heterodiegetic) is inferred from the panchronic references to, for example, David's first visit there, and to his family background; also indicative of external focalization is the impression of a panoramic view of the surrounding countryside and the steep bluffs. In the identification of the figure of Stella, in her "small fenced

garden," where she "grows vegetables with considerable skill and coax-
ing," the simple present tense is more precisely termed the habitual present, for it refers to a sequence of events or actions, repeated over a period.
The combination of this kind of simple present tense and the accompany-
ing adverbial suggests that Stella's routines are deeply rooted and comfortable. The instantaneous present tenses in the succeeding paragraph create
an altogether different effect, one of commentary, and these usher in the
internal focalization of the character David. The parenthetical comment
clause, "as far he can see," confirms such a shift.

Munro begins with an external focalizer, then she aligns the perspective with an internal one, the character David, who thus becomes the
subject of the focalization. His ideologies and prejudices are revealed in
the following extract, when he considers how Stella has aged. The kind
of focalization exemplified here is what Michael Toolan calls "an involved
emotive focalization [where] scenes are represented in a noticeably idiosyncratic way."[20] "David thinks that Stella has done this on purpose. It
isn't just an acceptance of natural deterioration—oh, no, it's much more.
Stella would always dramatize. But it isn't just Stella. There's the sort of
woman who has to come bursting out of the female envelope at this age,
flaunting fat or an indecent scrawniness, sprouting warts and facial hair,
refusing to cover pasty veined legs, almost gleeful about it, as if this was
what she'd wanted to do all along. Man-haters, from the start. You can't
say a thing like that out loud nowadays." (p. 33)

What this passage clearly illustrates is free indirect discourse (in this
case, thought), betokening internal focalization. It can be recognized here
by several typical features: the retention of the tense and pronoun usage
of the narrative; markers of deixis, specifically the demonstrative "this";
vestiges of the character's idiolect ("oh no, it's much more"); reliance on
structures of equal syntactic value, exemplified in the repeated –ing form
of the verb, conveying a list of what David dislikes about "this sort of
woman"; and evidence of modality, in the auxiliary verbs that express
David's intolerance.

This early shift in perspective achieves more than one objective: first,
with external focalization, Munro is able, at the outset, to delineate the
scene and to present the main characters, implying the nature of their
relationships with each other; second, by juxtaposing the external and
the internal viewpoints, she immediately generates a tension between the
portrayal of an apparently contented and capable older woman, living
alone, and another version of her, courtesy of David, as a physically unattractive misanthropist. Munro's dexterous introduction of free indirect
discourse serves to cast suspicion on David's judgment, which appears,

at the very least, peevishly captious. The unequivocal assertions contrast with the qualifications and retractions the narrator alluded to earlier when explaining the disparity between David's expectations of "the summer cottage" and its reality, devoid of the "charm" and "coziness" he imagined. An urban upbringing had not prepared him for the rural setting to which Stella was accustomed, and by presenting David as "a city boy, from what Stella's family called 'a different background,'" the narrator hints at a difference in social status between the two. The epithet "cottage" is, it is acknowledged, an inappropriate description of a building that is more accurately an old farmhouse. But the cottage is merely "a copy" of the nearby farmhouses, and is described as less substantial. Even the bluffs on which the cottage stands belie their appearance, for they are "not so substantial either," the clause "but they have held so far" suggesting their possible future collapse. These indicators of disparity and uncertainty are too closely juxtaposed and numerous to be dismissed as accidental. They foreshadow the processes of undermining that take place in the subsequent narrative, as each character's knowledge of himself/herself and of others is revealed as insecure.

Magdalene Redekop describes "Lichen" as "a story about deceit and betrayal," and the principal deceiver is David.[21] The reader learns that he treats his wife of twenty-one years as a reluctant confidante, telling her about the younger women he falls in love with and to whom he eventually delivers the "coup de grâce" (p. 43). He makes a point of informing Stella that he is going to end his relationship with Catherine, in whom he once detected "many remnants of girlishness" (p. 34), but whom he now considers "stale" and overdependent on him. His description of her as "inclined to be fey" (p. 40) is one that Stella reminds him of, and later seeks to disprove when she entertains Catherine on her own, and finds out that she possesses more commonsense than David credits her with. Stella learns, too, that, unknown to David, Catherine fortifies herself with drugs, which enable her to shed "several layers of wispy apology [and] tentative flattery" (p. 44). In the section of the narrative where David is absent from the action, Munro transfers the focalization to Stella, thereby entrusting to her character the authority that David was initially accorded. Stella's "involved and emotive" attitude can be inferred from statements such as, "Catherine doesn't seem to mind being interrogated, or even to notice that this is an interrogation" (p. 45). Her questioning exposes David's ignorance of and misjudgments about women; moreover, in the process, Stella forms a solidary relationship with the woman she knows will soon, like she did, experience rejection.

David intends to leave Catherine for the "little witch" Dina (p. 42), whose nude photograph not only provides the image in the title, but also constitutes what Munro calls "that kernel . . . in the centre of the story."[22] This photograph is accorded great significance in the text: when David and Stella meet a retired couple, Ron and Mary, at the liquor store, David furtively invites only the male to look at "one of my interests" (p. 39). Munro inserts an ellipsis immediately after this invitation, so that the disclosure of the photograph's nature is postponed. The ellipsis placed after David's trophy display enables the narrative to move forward to a time when David asks Stella if she wants to see the photograph, but she declines. Another ellipsis prefaces the scene, in Stella's kitchen, where he eventually foists it upon her, "before she can turn her head away" (p. 41), and he can witness her reaction. Munro prepares for the injurious impact of this photograph on Stella by adjusting the pace of the narrative and thereby accentuating the repeated allusions to it. These ellipses, the principal means by which narrative speed is quickened, generate suspense, whetting the reader's appetite for disclosure; they also alert the reader to certain character indices, namely, David's sadism, and Stella's vulnerability.

In the scene where the nature of David's Polaroid photograph is at last revealed, the narrator articulates a crucial disparity in perception, made apparent in two consecutive paragraphs: "'That's my new girl,' he says. 'It looks like lichen,' says Stella, her paring knife halting. 'Except it's rather dark. It looks to me like moss on a rock'" (p. 41). Stella's response is a cryptic one; it is syntactically anomalous, for the neuter pronoun is incongruent with the gender marking in David's statement. There is no coreferent for "it." The subsequent description of Dina's naked body, delivered from Stella's perspective, is irreverent and dehumanizing: the legs are likened to "fallen columns," the pubic hair to "moss, or lichen," or more "like the dark pelt of an animal . . . some unlucky rodent" (p. 42). Stella dispassionately derogates the young woman's physical appearance in a defensive reaction to the tones of "tender disparagement" (p. 40) David adopts when he speaks to his former wife of his latest loves. There is a marked disparity between David's concupiscent portrayal of Dina as "the little witch" who "torments [his] soul" (p. 42) and Stella's reduction of her to a lifeless and animal state.

Carrington adjudges Stella to be a robust character, believing that "her ability to accept the inevitable effects of aging distinguishes Stella . . . from David."[23] It is clear, however, that David's actions and words cause his former partner some pain: that Stella has been discarded by her husband for younger women, and that she continues to be reminded of his fondness for such companions, are not matters of indifference to her. By skillful juxtaposition and structuring, Munro shows the effects that David's cruelly intentioned confidences have on Stella: "'You know, there's a smell women get,' says David, standing in the living-room doorway. 'It's when they know you don't want them around anymore. Stale.' Stella slaps the meat over" (p. 40). Stella's reflexive reaction to David's misogyny is expressed in a simple sentence, isolated in a single paragraph. The successive alveolar sounds and the onomatopoeic verb "slaps" combine to convey the impression of anger, perhaps even of vicarious violence. Moreover, it is not fanciful to argue that the noun "meat" is, in this context, colored by its *coarse slang* meaning, listed in the *Oxford English Dictionary*, of "the human body regarded as an instrument of human pleasure." In the story's opening scene, after all, the reader is provided with ample evidence of how David objectifies women, speaking of them as commodities that degenerate with age.

There is further evidence to suggest that Stella does not enjoy being the recipient of all David's sexual secrets, and that she finds the confidences painful to keep. When she reminds him that he had formerly described Catherine as "inclined to be fey" (p. 40), she does not elaborate on information he divulged to her, telling him that she cannot remember, when in fact she lies: "Of course she remembers. She remembers the exact tone in which he said 'inclined to be fey.' The pride and irony in his voice. In the throes of love, he can be counted on to speak of the woman with tender disparagement—with amazement, even. He likes to say that it's crazy, he does not understand it, he can plainly see that this person isn't his kind of person at all. And yet, and yet, and yet" (p. 40–41). The disparity between the vagueness of her feigned nonchalance and the fine detail of her recollection is exposed by the free indirect discourse, illustrated by, among other features, parataxis, informality, and, in the last line of the previous quotation, the idiolectal repetition that powerfully expresses Stella's sad resignation.

In a passage of analeptic narration near the end of "Lichen" the reader might gain some insight into the reasons for this resignation. Once more, Munro's use of anachrony *delays* disclosure and invites the reader to reappraise the protagonists' relationship in the light of new evidence. The setting of the penultimate section is the nursing home where Stella and David visit Stella's father. To make this annual visit is ostensibly why David returns to the summer cottage. In the presentation of this scene, Munro effects several shifts in focalization: sometimes the narrator takes command, at other times the subject of the focalization seems to be Stella or David. In one particular section, where David is, I shall argue, the focalizer, Stella's vulnerability is once more made manifest, and David's deception is shown to be of long standing. The analepsis is introduced by the narrator, who describes how Stella "seemed to have regained some sleekness and suppleness of former times" (p. 52); this allusion to a younger Stella initiates David's perspective, where he "saw her coming across the lawn at a suburban party, carrying a casserole" (p. 53). In her essay on "Lichen," in which she convincingly argues that Munro's story deconstructs the Renaissance *blazon*, Marianne Micros shows how both protagonists think and speak of David's women in dissociated parts; David himself does so by "isolating a physical feature of a woman and highlighting its imperfections,"[24] while Stella reduces Dina's body to stone, moss, and rodent's fur. Micros reads the piece of analeptic narration as deriving from Stella's perspective, arguing that the character's memory of the suburban scene is dominated by her recollection of her husband's infidelity, for at the time he was having an affair with Rosemary, "a shrill trite woman" (p. 53). The description of his stroking Rosemary's leg is further evidence, Micros points out, of how Stella "controls her reactions to [David's] women by containing them through image and metaphor."[25]

I prefer to interpret David as the subject of the focalization in this analepsis. The scene once more illustrates his deception, and it also provides examples of the disparities that permeate the narrative. There are unambiguous indicators of the free indirect discourse that characterizes periods of internal focalization; in the following example, one can find deictic markers, modality, parataxis, and idiolectal features: "She was wearing a sundress. She always claimed in those days that she was too fat for pants, though she was not half so fat as now. Why did this picture please him so much? Stella coming across the lawn, with her sunlit hair . . . crying out greetings to her neighbours, laughing, protesting about some cooking misadventure" (p. 53). The affectionate wistfulness of David's image is abruptly dispelled by the bathetic revelation that "at that moment, with his bare foot, he was stroking the cold, brown, shaved and prickly calf of another neighbourhood wife." This description is, for me, incontrovertible proof that the episode is imagined by the male character, for how else can one account for the recollected physical sensation? It is only by interpreting the orientation as David's that one makes sense of the relational reference, "another neighbourhood wife," the sexism of which is intensified by the appositive noun phrases, "His first, that one, the first while married to Stella" (p. 53).

In this scene the reader encounters yet more deception and disparity: David deceives his wife; he also deceives himself, thinking that she would condone his infidelities, when "that did not turn out to be a notion Stella shared at all" (p. 53). Another errant notion that the male protagonist possesses is of Stella as someone strangely empowered by her knowledge of "all his ordinary and extraordinary life" (p. 54). Rather than "a woman . . . bloated with all she knew," it appears that she is, in contrast, a reluctant repository for the sexual secrets he relishes telling her, "with a deliberate cruel sweetness" (p. 42). The disparity between David's estimation of Stella's power over him and the evidence of her pained forbearance is clearly discernible. Munro's use of shifting focalization lays bare the chasm in understanding that each character has of the other.

In one remarkable scene, Munro exploits the dramatic and ludic qualities of mimesis to expose yet another disparity, that between David's sexual fantasies and the mundane reality he experiences, where he is a civil servant, dyes his hair to conceal his aging, suffers from "digestive sensitivity" (p. 54), and spends "boring lunch and coffee breaks" (p. 52) discussing cars. In the telephone booth where he tries in vain to contact Dina, the entire dialogue between David and the operator is relayed, its presentation made more detailed by the abundance of instantaneous present tenses, which fulfill the function of commentary, as in "David . . . begins to dial Dina's number. Then he remembers it's long distance . . . He dials the operator" (p. 46). As well as the direct speech of David and the operator, Munro incorporates into the scene snatches of free indirect discourse, as in "No, he does not have a street address" (p. 47), in response to the operator's request. Other voices, too, are imagined and articulated by David as he awaits the answering of the telephone, and these serve to make him look foolish, desperate in his quest: "Perhaps he could do a woman's voice, squeaky. Or a child's voice, a little-sister voice. *Is Dina there?*" He even mimics the voice of an imaginary, outraged respondee, uttering "'What are you phoning me for?'" and he recalls Stella's chiding voice, telling him that all he is interested in is "being a big bad boy" (p. 49).

In summary, different types of speech and thought representation in fiction are illustrated in this scene, and it is by weaving all these discourses and the various impersonated voices that Munro successfully evokes "the desperate, furtive nature of [David's] quest" (p. 48) and also of his sexual desire.

The futility of the quest is finally acknowledged in the assertion "of course she has betrayed him"; the self-deceptions are recognized, too, in the admission that the pursuits of younger women "aren't real love" (p. 49). Redekop maintains that in "no other story by Munro does the battle between the 'watcher' and the 'keeper' reach such intensity."[26] She relates her comments specifically to Stella's acts of beholding the Polaroid photograph; however, an equally keen struggle between watching and keeping occurs at the end of the telephone booth scene, when David recognizes that his "interests" are desperate and futile, but cannot imagine relinquishing them, for "he knows all this and observes himself, and such knowledge has no effect at all on his quaking gut, zealous sweat glands, fierce prayers" (p. 50). The telephone operator's polite inquiry, "Sir? Do you want to keep on trying?" is ambiguous, for not only does it refer to David's attempts to contact Dina, but it could also apply to his constant search for "bouts of desire and dependence and worship and perversity" (p. 49). It is a question that remains unanswered, and, by inserting an ellipsis immediately afterwards, Munro makes salient the absence of any reply.

It is plain that David will keep on trying, for in the previous passage of internal focalization it is admitted that "he knows that sooner or later, if Dina allows her disguise to crack, as Catherine did, he will have to move on" (p. 50). By admitting his enthrallment to pretences, disguises, and wild fantasies in his relations with women, he reveals a candor more endearing than qualities shown earlier in the narrative.

At the conclusion of "Lichen" the reader is left with the impression of two characters for whom deception and pretense have become reflexive. The photograph of Dina is left on the cottage windowsill, where David has placed it, hiding it from Catherine, but not very well; that it is positioned purposefully is suggested by the detail of its location "at the spot where you stand to get a view of the lighthouse" (p. 55). (The attentive reader will recall that, early in the narrative, Stella informs David and Catherine that she is writing about the lighthouse for the historical society.) The reaction the photograph provokes from Stella the second time is much more restrained. She notes that the analogy she first used seems accurate, for the "black pelt in the picture has changed to gray," but then she qualifies her assertion, reminding herself, "She said it was lichen. No, she said it looked like lichen," adding, "But she knew what it was at once" (p. 55). The negation, and the contradicting "but" cancel out the first certainty; in addition, in her reappraisal Stella replaces the metaphor with a simile, which "proposes the transference," rather than assuming it "is possible or has already taken place."[27] These qualifications are in keeping with the deceptions and disparities that characterize the story, right up to its conclusion.

With Stella as the subject of the focalization in the final scene, which takes place in the summer cottage that is specified as her "domain" (p. 33), it is tempting to believe greater narrative authority rests with her. However, such a belief may be unfounded. As I have argued, Munro's use of an alternating point of view reveals how complex are the relations involving Stella,

David, and the women he delights in describing to her. The last image the reader has is of Stella looking at the photograph, thinking that "her words have come true," but scrutiny of the closing paragraphs suggests that the truth is a small consolation: "Stella's words have come true. This thought will keep coming back to her—a pause, a lost heartbeat, a harsh little break in the flow of the days and nights as she keeps them going" (p. 55). Here one can detect a telling disparity between self-congratulation and regret. The image Stella invents may be quirkily apposite, confirming her "funny way of looking at things" (p. 53), but it also reminds her, once more, of the transformations wrought by aging.

In her stoical responses to David's taunting, Stella has shown a degree of control over her emotions, but at some cost to her integrity. She may have "held on," but by lying and by deceiving herself. The story's conclusion illustrates another deception: Stella believes that the fact that her words have come true illustrates her prescience, when all it shows is time's transfiguration. Stella notes that the "outline of the breast" has gone; the hair color is now gray, its texture rough and dry; the legs look nothing like legs. The processes that fade the Polaroid seem very much like female aging itself.

Carrington reads "Lichen" as primarily concerned with the effects of aging on both men and women, but she thinks that the female protagonist emerges as the stronger. She argues that, while Munro assigns "a similar self-critical lamentation to both characters," the allusions to Stella's busy social activities suggest she has "the control that the desperately struggling, self-deluding David lacks."[28] Unlike David, Stella has more readily accepted the "natural deterioration" of aging: at the start and at the end of the narrative, she is portrayed as someone at home in her surroundings, leading a contented, purposeful, and self-sufficient life. These indications of domestic comfort and well-being will sustain her "in the days and nights as she keeps them going" (p. 55).

But a jarring note in the last line of "Lichen" qualifies the affirmation that such a picture conveys. Stella knows she will be brought up sharp by "this thought" of the "harsh little break" that ruptures the flow of her days and nights. The demonstrative determiner "this" indicates that it refers to the immediate precedent, namely, the fact that "her words have come true" about the lichen in the photograph. But a closer inspection of her truth-telling utterance reveals her own acknowledged self-deception: "No, she said it looked like lichen. But she knew what it was at once" (p. 55). Again, we note a disparity between what Stella sees and says: the pleasure she feels at her prescience is muted by her knowledge that her description is, like the lichen itself, merely a cover, a protection.

In a sophisticated, densely allusive essay on "Lichen," Héliane Ventura posits a much more positive interpretation of Munro's imagery.[29] She argues that in the textual descriptions of the Polaroid photograph, Munro revisions a famous painting by Gustave Courbet, entitled "L'Origine du Monde," in which female genitalia are starkly objectified. In Stella's analogy to "lichen," Ventura believes that Munro subverts the conventions of feminine portraiture; where before, Dina's naked body was vulnerable to David's salacious gaze, offered as a source of prurient excitement to other men, now it is recategorized, metamorphosed into vegetable matter that, in the narrative itself, is described as "mysteriously nourished on the rocks" (p. 55).

If the presentation of Stella's reasons for her analogy were different, this reading of the transformation might be more persuasive. However, as I have previously argued, Munro depicts Stella as a woman who retains a "wifely" interest in her former partner (p. 38), perhaps harboring hopes of his future return to her. Such an inference can be gleaned from early in the narrative, when David and Stella meet the retired couple, Ron and Mary. David is plainly the subject of the focalization during the exchanges of dialogue: Ron's teasing question about when he is going to retire and join them by Lake Huron "makes David wonder what Stella has been telling them about the separation" (p. 38). At the summer cottage, minutes after Stella has been introduced to Catherine, she reminds the younger woman of her proprietary claim: after David has scolded Stella for not clearing the driveway, she jokingly tells Catherine, "Listen to him, still sounding like a husband" (p. 34). Unfortunately for Stella, however, David does not sound or act like the kind of husband she would surely prefer.

Stella constructs several defenses against the hurt of rejection, and her derogation of a rival's body is one of these defenses. She uses the same strategies when she comments on Catherine's unfocused eyes, or makes fun of her inappropriate dress, and her drawling accent, which she imitates with a "certain viciousness of tone" (p. 42). When Stella first likens Dina's pubic hair to lichen, a plant belonging to the Fungi kingdom, her comparison is not well-intentioned, but understandably mean spirited. The pleasure at what she later thinks is her clairvoyance is pathetically misplaced, but it might serve as some consolation.

The relations between the main characters in this story are in constant flux. The positions of authority appear initially clear cut: the philandering David holds the critical, disparaging gaze, with Stella, Catherine, and Dina all objectified by his reductive estimation of female beauty, one that depends on the worship of youth. However, the sexual dynamics change; the authority of each of the characters waxes and wanes, as Munro transfers the perspective from external to internal focalizer, varying the types of discourse presentation in order to exhibit particular character indices. David's ability to objectify is diminished by his fear of aging, mercilessly exposed in the telephone booth scene. Catherine, whom the reader encounters as "frail" and "drooping" (p. 33), draws some strength from her meeting with Stella, where the observations she delivers reveal greater insight than David credits her with; even Dina exerts vicarious influence, in her nude pose, and by her absence.

In Stella, Munro creates an older woman whose authority and self-confidence fluctuate enormously. The narrator presents her as an empathetic, astute observer of human nature, capable and contented in her domain. Yet, perversely, she allows herself to be humiliated, willing to be burdened with her former husband's sexual secrets. This puzzling ambivalence contributes to the indeterminacy that characterizes *The Progress of Love*.

In her next volume of stories, *Friend of My Youth*, Munro makes more conscious use of different narrative levels in her fascination with what is ambiguous, insecure, and provisional in her characters' experience. The title story resembles that of *The Progress of Love*, insofar as its first-person narrator tells a transformative story her mother has told her; in this later work, however, the retelling is much more extensive, and the mother's voice much more clearly audible. The embedded story vies with its host for a stronger claim to narrative authority. In their final depictions of Flora Grieves, the principal character in the embedded story, the narrators—mother and daughter—are at odds, creating a tension that is unrelieved by the coda. This idea of competing versions, competing testimonies, is explored in much greater depth in "A Wilderness Station," from *Open Secrets*, a work also discussed in the ensuing chapter. In the two pieces examined, I argue that Munro's experiments with narrative level and voice represent another of her determined strategies of disarrangement.

CHAPTER 3

COMPETING TESTIMONIES

DEBORAH HELLER OBSERVES THAT THE STORIES IN *Friend of My Youth* represent "new departures" for Munro, who returns to "familiar situations, structures and concerns" but "develops them in fresh ways."[1] Among fictive situations familiar to readers of Munro's fiction will be the female protagonist's adolescent crush on an older girl, something that links Joan in "Oh, What Avails" and Rose in "Privilege," from *The Beggar Maid*; like the adult Rose in "Mischief," too, the adult Joan plans a risky extramarital adventure, feeling herself "loosed, in jeopardy" at the prospect (*Friend of My Youth*, p. 200).

In narratological terms, *Friend of My Youth* illustrates several strategies used with such dexterity in previous collections: temporal dislocation, the spanning of three generations in one narrative, and the seamless transfer of focalization. In this, Munro's sixth collection, however, relations between narrative levels are sometimes more intricately developed; in addition, a variety of different voices and discourses is blended into the primary narrative, noticeably when the writer is delving "into Canadian colonial history and the Scots-Canadian cultural inheritance," in, for example, the stories "Meneseteung" and "Hold Me Fast, Don't Let Me Pass."[2] In the title story, Munro's willingness to experiment is particularly salient. The writer takes the figure of the narrator's mother, prematurely stricken by a fatal illness, as she was in "The Peace of Utrecht" and "The Ottawa Valley," and now gives this character the power to narrate. The mother does so in an embedded story framed by dreams described by her daughter, who narrates the host story. In these dreams the mother appears in good health, "light-hearted [and] moving rather carelessly out of her old prison" (p. 23). Her transformation partly consoles the daughter, but also disconcerts her, for the new image subverts and contravenes long-held, obdurate assumptions. How the narrator would staunchly oppose her mother in her youth and early adulthood is revealed as she delivers her mother's tale concerning events in her life as a young teacher in the Ottawa Valley. The daughter narrates this tale with occasional suspicion, relishing the irreverent revised codas she offers as alternatives.

The opening paragraphs of "Friend of My Youth" establish the narrator's awkward ambivalence toward her mother, inviting the reader to wonder why she now mediates this tale. She explains that the image of her mother in the recurrent dream is too positive, too "easy in its forgiveness," and it presents engaging qualities the narrator had forgotten, choosing instead to keep a "bugbear in my mind" (pp. 4–5). An ellipsis abruptly signals the end of the framing segment and demarcates the narration of the present from that of the past. The analepsis begins, "When my mother was a young woman with a soft, mischievous face and shiny, opaque stockings on her plump legs (I have seen a photograph of her, with her pupils), she went to teach at a one-room school, called Grieves School, in the Ottawa Valley" (p. 4). The wistful tenderness in the sentence that initiates the ensuing anecdote is at odds with the idea of a "bugbear," and consolidates the impression of ambivalence. The reader soon realizes that the innocence suggested in this picture is no reliable portent of the tragedies and treacheries uncovered in her mother's Ontario Gothic tale.

Recounted in this tale are the circumstances and the history relating to the Grieves farmhouse where the narrator's mother lodged. At the time of her stay, the farm was owned and occupied by two sisters, Flora and Ellie. Also living there was Robert Deal, the husband of the younger sister, Ellie. He had been engaged to Flora, but after impregnating the younger sister, he had to marry Ellie. Ellie's pregnancy resulted in a stillbirth, and despite many painful, debilitating attempts, she bore no live children, spending most of her days in her sickbed, faithfully nursed by her devoted, magnanimous sister. After the narrator's mother left the Ottawa Valley to start her married life, she is informed by scandalized friends that Robert had once more disappointed Flora, choosing, after Ellie's death, to marry the nurse employed to look after his dying wife. The conclusion of the mother's tale is partially gleaned from her correspondence with Flora, who might be the "friend of my youth" she addresses in an unfinished letter the narrator finds. Flora eventually moved out of the Grieves farmhouse, into town, saying little of how she felt about her destiny. The ending does not satisfy the daughter-narrator, however, who admits, "I had my own ideas about Flora's story," and who then delights in taking a "different tack" (p. 20). Her versions, depicting a Flora entirely different from her mother's saintly, selfless heroine, compete with the embedded story for credibility and authority.

As Gérard Genette notes, there are several kinds of relationships between a second-degree narrative, which he calls metadiegetic (or hypodiegetic), and the first narrative into which it is incorporated.[3] The most common of these relationships is an explanatory one, where the embedded story sheds light on events in, or on, the context of the primary narrative. The meta-diegetic narrative in "Friend of My Youth" serves this type of function, for, by the conclusion, the narrator has shown her true hand: in her remaking of her mother's story of Flora Grieves, the self-denying Cameronian, the subject of her mother's tale has become the mother herself, and the narrating act has, perhaps, become for the daughter an attempt at reconciliation.

The daughter takes care to attribute the provenance of the narrative to her mother, as she depicts the setting, from her mother's perspective, mentioning the "well-drained fields" and peculiar wooden buildings of the Ottawa Valley, with walls that "had never been painted but left to weather" (p. 4). The mother's native knowledge of the landscape is established in the following text, which immediately follows the previous description: "And when wood weathers in the Ottawa Valley, my mother said, I do not know why this is, but it never turns gray, it turns black. There must be something in the air, she said. She often spoke of the Ottawa Valley, which was her home" (p. 4). Munro effects a smooth transition from narrative diegesis to the free direct discourse that presents the mother's voice. Two reporting clauses are inserted in order to distinguish that voice, echoed in the indirect discourse of the last sentence. The adverb "often" conveys an impression of the mother's fondness for reminiscence. That her daughter would not always welcome these anecdotes about her mother's home territory is inferred from the assertion, "Of course I was disappointed when I finally got to see this place" (p. 4), where a reflexive antagonism is discerned.

Indicators of the mother's voice permeate "Friend of My Youth," most obviously in the countless reporting clauses, for example, "my mother thought" (p. 6), "my mother said" (p. 8), that remind the reader that it is a mediated, ventriloquized tale. The noun phrase "my mother" is ubiquitous, the frequency of its use accentuated when it begins a sentence, as it does several times: "My mother could not say who the Cameronians were or why they were called that" (p. 5); "My mother slept now on clean sheets" (p. 7). The mother's presence comes across in the many verb phrases that express her agency, when she "envied" Flora's slim figure, "heard" rumors of the younger sister's illness from people she "knew," but "did not feel" she "was listening" to gossip (p. 8). Her habituation to Ottawa Valley routines is suggested in modal verb phrases such as "would wake up" (p. 7) and "might invite herself along" (p. 12), when the narrator explains how her mother became accustomed to the Grieves household. The narrator is keen to distinguish certain ideological and emotional stances, incorporating her mother's idiolect into the account, as, for instance, when she describes how Flora liked to ride to town in the cutter, standing erect, wearing a black hat: "Almost ridiculous but not quite. A gypsy queen, my mother thought she looked like" (p. 8). When the narrator reveals the surprising twist in the tale—Robert's marrying Ellie instead of Flora—she simulates her mother's animation: "No cake, no new clothes, no wedding trip, no congratulations. Just a shameful hurry-up visit to the manse. Some people, seeing the names in the paper, thought the editor must have got the names mixed up. They thought it must be Flora. A hurry-up wedding for Flora! But no—it was Flora who pressed Robert's suit—it must have been" (p. 10). Here, Munro fuses two voices, that of the mother and that of the collective community, incredulously reacting to the scandal. The free direct discourse reproduces the idiomatic expressions, fragmented sentences and emotive reformulation that characterize these voices. Also noteworthy in this passage is the way that Munro enriches the polyphony by blending in a faint flavor of the primary narrator's response to the secondary tale. In the emphatic negation, "But no," and the assertiveness of the modal verb phrase "must have been," one can imagine the mother's obviating her daughter's assumption.

There are overt examples of interaction between daughter and mother. The narrator's comments on her mother's tale increase in number and substance as the opportunities for her invention present themselves. Describing the periods when Ellie "was constantly pregnant," suffering illnesses that resulted in "agonizing" miscarriages and stillbirths (p. 11), the narrator explains that her mother would keep Flora company when she read to her sister, in the evenings. The narrator's curiosity is evident in the questions she poses: "What did Flora read? Stories about Scottish life—not classics . . . She would pick up another old book, an old book written by some preacher of their faith. There was such stuff in it as my mother had never heard. What stuff? She couldn't say" (p. 12). She tries to fill the gaps in her mother's account, informing the reader that the "stuff" would probably relate to the "configuration of the elect and damned" (p. 12) that the Grieves' Cameronian religion entailed. It is at this point that the narrator's delivery of her mother's tale takes on a carping tone: the reactions illustrated previously read like impatient questions her mother cannot fully answer. Parenthetical comments on missing or scant information read like accusations, as when the narrator wonders why her mother found Flora's stories, recited mostly in Scots, difficult to understand: "(But wouldn't it be the way Robert talked? Perhaps that is why my mother never reports anything that Robert said, never has him contributing to the scene. He must have been there, he must have been sitting there in the room)" (p. 12). In the repeated allusion to what her mother neglects to include, and her dogmatic insistence on the validity of what she imagines, the narrator seeks to invalidate her mother's presentation of events. She quotes her mother's disapproval of these religious readings ("But what sort of thing was that, she asked (silently), to read to a dying woman?") and provides her own reply: "The answer—that it was the only thing, if you believed it—never seemed to have occurred to her" (p. 13). Here, the contemporaneous narrator points, somewhat smugly, to a deficiency in her mother's narration, and comprehension. The aside in brackets implies some degree of timidity, even hypocrisy, on her mother's part.

Andrew Hiscock notes that the narrator takes great pains to "piece together irregular fragments from her mother's past into a coherent jigsaw formation," daunted as she is by "frustrating reading experiences and inadequate knowledge."[4] He identifies as sources of frustration the puzzling stories the mother hears Flora read, and all the "stuff that was in their monstrous old religion" (p. 12). In her mediation of the tale, the narrator does impose coherence, for events are linked by chronology, and causality; however, the regular structure is already extant in the mother's account, and is manifest in the indicators of her voice and her narrative agency. The inadequacies of knowledge relate, in the main, to the Cameronian religion, to the shadowy figure of Robert Deal, and to Flora's state of mind about her treatment by him. Flora's final letter to the narrator's mother is described as an "unsettling letter, leaving so many things out" (p. 24), merely explaining that she left the farm and moved to town, where she works part time in a store. This news offers the reader a kind of conclusion, but it is not one the narrator desires, for there is no mention of what Flora thinks, or believes. The omissions and deficiencies are the catalyst for the emulous daughter's narrative powers: she is at liberty to address what she thinks are weaknesses in her mother's tale, fill in gaps, and offer alternative characterizations and interpretations, and she does.

The impetus for the daughter's subversive opposition is her mother's attitude toward the central figure, Flora, and to the fates that befall her in the Grieves' farmhouse. As Mark Nunes observes, "what the mother sees as saintly patience, the narrator sees as guilt-inducing manipulation."[5] In her recounting of events in the Grieves' household after the arrival of Nurse Atkinson, the daughter exaggerates her mother's subjective views, explaining that she "caught a whiff of the cheap life" about the nurse, "which Flora was too unworldly to notice" (p. 14). The mother's anger at what she considers the nurse's usurpation is expressed in a letter she writes to Flora, long after she has left the Ottawa Valley and has settled into married life. In this letter she "offered sympathy and showed outrage, and said blunt disparaging things about the woman who had . . . dealt Flora such a blow." The narrator regards her mother's gesture as ill judged, believing she had acted impetuously "perhaps in a flurry of importance due to her own newly married state" (p. 19). In her instant reply, Flora dismisses these grounds for pity, tartly advising her correspondent to concern herself with her own life. Traces of the daughter's tendentious narration, discernible earlier as I have suggested, are now more firmly imprinted on the original account, as she recalls how, in her later years, her mother told her that she wished she had been a writer and could have written the story of Flora's life, entitling it "'The Maiden Lady.'" This memory excites the narrator's sardonic, resentful response: "*The Maiden Lady.* She said those words in a solemn and sentimental tone of voice I had no use for . . . I was fifteen or sixteen years old by that time, and I believed I could see into my mother's mind" (p. 19). The bitter mockery conveyed by the italics contrasts with the wistfulness of the mother's aspirations, when she "sometimes talked about the things she might have been, or done" (p. 19).

The older narrator remembers the adolescent antipathy to what she perceives as her mother's sanctimony, recalling the contrasting version of Flora Grieves's life that she herself would have written. She would "take a different tack," casting Flora as an avenging "Presbyterian witch, reading out of her poisonous book" (p. 21). She understands, now, the reasons for her distorting vision, acknowledging that the stoical, self-denying virtuousness of her mother's Flora was anathema to someone excited "with the thought of a man's recklessness and domination." In her maturity she realizes she and her mother were not so different, in that both were favorably disposed toward progressive "notions of our times" about female sexuality (p. 22). Deborah Heller believes that by acknowledging this affinity with her mother, the narrator shows "remarkable generosity and humility, which enable [her] to transcend mother-daughter competition for narrative authority."[6] The empathy is, however, short lived. Had Munro's story ended at this point, it would have ended with equilibrium poised between the two tales, the primary and secondary narratives. But the narrator has not finished with Flora, and seeks to wrest her from not only the fixed presentation in her mother's tale, but from the tale itself.

The narrator intends to eclipse the tale, with competing versions in which she is an actor. So far, she has intruded in her mother's story with comments and additions that resemble editorial annotation: finally, she wants a part in the action of the embedded narrative. Such transitions across narrative levels are called metalepses and they confirm relations between the host and the embedded narrative.[7] Having "lost interest in Flora" after her adolescence, she now resurrects her, wondering what kind of store she works in. Her imagination constructs a woman who escapes from the confines of religion, duty, and saintliness, to move into a modernity where she might have to learn about "food blenders," apply "cosmetics," "visit a city," "go on holidays," "even meet a man" (pp. 24–25). Spinning what Heller calls "this fantasy of open-ended possibility,"[8] the narrator envisages entering the store to meet the emancipated Flora, but it is here that her quest loses its momentum and her control over her mother's narrative falters.

She begins to envision her meeting with Flora, but her attempt is tentative, demonstrable in the self-correction, the qualifying modality, and appeals to an addressee: "I might go into a store and find her. No, no. She would be dead a long time now. But suppose I had gone into a store— perhaps a department store . . . Suppose a tall, handsome woman, nicely turned out, had come to wait on me" (p. 25). The narrator's fantasy, of meeting a woman with "sprayed and puffed hair . . . pink or coral lips and fingernails" (p. 25) is plainly absurd: Flora would be long dead, as she acknowledges, and in any case, the transformation is based on her subjective, distorted imagining and is not a plausible outcome for the kind of character constituted in her mother's account. The imagined Flora, metamorphosed into someone unrecognizable from the "real Flora" (p. 23) smiles with "a degree of mockery, a faint, self-assured malice," wearily reproving the narrator for presuming to know her. And in her gentle mockery, she becomes the figure of the mother, as she appeared in the dreams that initiate the story. "Of course it's my mother I'm thinking of," the narrator suddenly accepts, recalling how "disconcerted" she was to see her "moving rather carelessly out of her old prison" (p. 26) in those dreams. The narrator may have thought she could free Flora from her status as "The Maiden Lady," but she struggles to dislodge her from the original depiction; the passage into her mother's narrative territory is attempted, but it is not successful. Flora belongs to her mother's story.

Just as the narrator cannot know Flora, she finds it hard to recognize the new dream version of her mother, healthy and carefree, and admits to feeling "tricked, cheated by this welcome turnaround" (p. 26). Why would she feel cheated? Munro has certainly connected two "unreal" figures—the imagined Flora and the mother in recurrent dreams—and has drawn attention to how they both resist the narrator's erroneous perception. The narrator's presumption, that she could reconstruct Flora, and could reliably estimate her mother's "options and powers," is misplaced. Gayle Elliott believes that the narrator experiences here a kind of epiphany, arguing: "In recognizing Flora as a fictional character, the narrator realizes that she, too, has been living with a fiction of her mother."[9] Maybe she feels "offended" because her faith in her inventiveness and acuity of judgment is weakened.

There is, as Elliott observes, "no single truth about the Grieves sisters."[10] The original story incorporates gossip, speculation, and legend circulated in the Ottawa Valley community and relayed to the teacher in her stay at the farmhouse. The narrator repeatedly refers to how local people contribute to the account, to "what people told my mother" (p. 5), to "what people would say" (p. 25); information is also passed to her mother in letters, for "the post-office friend had written, and so had others" (p. 17). Flora's own letters would seem to confirm the impression of an unnaturally stoical, forgiving, self-denying woman, a strict adherent of a punitive religion, but this outward appearance of saintliness may have been a pretense, a matter of "leaving things out" (p. 24).

The final paragraph, in which the narrator provides information she has researched about the Cameronian sect, confirms her continuing preoccupation with her mother's tale. The anecdotes she leaves the reader with illustrate qualities associated with the religion—fervor, violent bigotry and intolerance—but it is the last detail that is especially revealing. The narrator tells of one minister who rejoiced "at his own hanging [while he] excommunicated all the other preachers in the world" (p. 26). Perhaps, as Elliott suggests, this particular image should serve as a "cautionary tale," representing as it does the dangerous lunacy of adhering "to any single reality [and] uncompromising belief in a monolithic and unitary truth."[11] The account that the daughter undertakes gives her the opportunity to test and compete with her mother's power to narrate; in the process, she comes to recognize why she needs and wants the rivalry.

By using more than one level of narration, Munro offers her reader different perspectives on characters and events in "a scrambled, disarranged sort of country, with no easy harmony about it, not yielding readily to any description" (p. 5). In "A Wilderness Station" from *Open Secrets*, Munro turns her attention from levels of narration to focus on narrative voice. A hallmark of this story is the skilful juxtaposition of several disparate voices—public and private—that comprise a social history of Huron County, Ontario, in the mid-nineteenth century. It is an exciting and rewarding story for someone interested in those narratological approaches to Munro's work that are feminist in their sympathies.

In her essay, "Toward a Feminist Narratology," the American narratologist Susan S. Lanser writes: "in narrative there is no single voice"; indeed, often "voice impinges upon voice."[12] She illustrates narrative polyphony in her scrutiny of a nineteenth-century letter purporting to be a young wife's self-effacing eulogy of her husband, and of the institution of marriage; a decoded subtext, however, yielded by a reading of the document's alternate lines, reveals a bitter attack on the man's deficiencies and an anguished lament for her situation. Lanser suggests that the letter is written for two readers, the censoring husband and an intimate female friend, and she argues that this "double construction" is a device frequently found in female-authored narratives that operate on two levels, the public and the private.[13]

Lanser defines public narration as that which is addressed to a narratee "external to the textual world, and who can be equated with a public readership."[14] Private narration, in contrast, is intended for a specifically designated narratee within the textual world. In the letter that is the subject of her scrutiny, Lanser discusses the salient differences between the public voice of the young bride, one which she describes as "a discourse of the powerless," and the voice of the subtext, which is assertive and direct.[15]

"A Wilderness Station" is an epistolary narrative consisting of twelve letters, the first dated January 1852, the last July 1959, collected by an historian researching the life of a politician from Huron County, Ontario; each letter sheds light on the remarkable experiences of Annie Herron (McKillop), the central figure in the narrative.[16] The story is constituted by the distinctive discourses of six characters, the writers of the various letters. Those written by characters other than Annie are identified by provenance and named addressee, and the reader understands that all letters reach their intended destination. All those emanating from Annie, however, do not reach their designated addressee, Sadie Johnstone, a character who inhabits the textual world, but never materializes in it. The distinction between public and private narration may seem, initially, inappropriate in an analysis of fictive letters assembled for an extratextual audience, Munro's contemporary reader. But there are certain features of Annie McKillop's third letter that clearly differentiate it from the other discourses in the epistolary narrative and encourage one to read the testimony as private narration. It is an unsolicited, confiding account to an absent friend in which Annie relates events following the death of her husband, Simon Herron, and the changes in her circumstances that are occasioned by the death. It is unlike all the other letters in that it is not read by any character within the text. As Carrington observes in her essay on Munro's story: "Annie's letter never resurfaces intratextually. No-one ever seems to receive it, read it, or respond to it except, of course, the extra textual readers of *Open Secrets*, and the *New Yorker*, where the story was originally published in April 1992."[17]

The death of Annie's husband, the kernel in the epistolary narrative, is based on an authentic incident in the lives of Munro's ancestors, on her father's side. Several Munro scholars have referred to this historical detail in their work, citing the tragedy as one of many hardships endured by early pioneers in the Huron Tract. In his interview with the writer, Chris Gittings discusses Munro's ongoing interest in her father's Laidlaw family history, an interest she has apparently developed into a nonfiction project, and about which she writes in *The View from Castle Rock*. Munro confesses: "I've found it difficult . . . keeping oneself within the bounds of fact instead of taking that fictional germ and doing something with it."[18] What Munro has done in "A Wilderness Station" is use the fictional germ—the young man's death in the woods—to create a narrative that centers, predominantly, on the female experience of a hard, punishing pioneer life.

This transformative reworking of the past brings to the fore the testimony of a female character whose voice is deliberately muted until midway through the narrative. Her story is first articulated by others, whose letters respond to specific inquiries and reach their destinations. Annie's three letters are clearly differentiated from the others because, first, they are unsolicited, and second, they are not read by the intended narratee; the function and purpose of all three are not proclaimed. The archival status of the third letter, in which Annie recounts the circumstances and consequences of her husband's death, is uncertain, for how (indeed, if) the historian acquired it is not explained. The third letter is a contesting text that challenges the discourses of authority that, in the narrative configuration, precede it. The voices the reader first hears are those legitimated by the state: they are represented by the matron of the state orphanage where Annie is procured; the patriarch of the family that is the subject of the historian's research; the Free Church minister, who considers Annie to be a soul in his charge; and the Clerk of the Peace, who grants the woman shelter in his gaol.

Annie Herron's account invites the contemporary reader to reappraise various official versions of events in Huron County's history, those that are sanctioned by the church, the legislature, the judiciary, and the media. The reader of "A Wilderness Station" is encouraged, as Gittings asserts, to consider alternatives to the "constricting mononarrative of a Scots-Calvinist based truth," one enacting "a patriarchal historiographic process" that marginalizes and threatens to obliterate Annie from its world.[19] It would seem that Munro elevates the authority of her central character's testimony over other characters' accounts. She does so by selecting particular narrative strategies of arrangement and transmission, and by creating an array of discourse styles that are reflective of ideologies current at the time. Many, or at least some, of the ideologies illustrated in letters written by characters other than Annie appear rebarbative. I believe that Munro sets out to make them so, thereby discrediting their accounts. I disagree with Carrington when she maintains that Annie's confession is "problematic" and that Annie "delud[es] and torment[s] herself in the wilderness of her own mind."[20] Annie's third letter, containing her testimony, does not sound like the delusions of a crazy woman: the repeated insistence on the distinction between reality and fantasy, madness and sanity, suggests clarity of purpose. The letter is addressed Finder Please Post, and ends on a declaration of trust in some unknown person with a sense of decency. The eventual recipient of the letter is none other than the extratextual reader. I argue that the contemporary reader should approach Annie's testimony in much the same way that feminist academic Patrocinio Schweickart advocates in "Reading Ourselves: Toward a Feminist Theory of Reading," that the reader should treat the reading experience as "an intersubjective encounter" in which the audience must connect with the female writer, and with a larger community of women.[21] In "A Wilderness Station," Munro facilitates such an encounter, creating a female protagonist whose story compels and moves the modern reader. In Annie's desperate appeals to her friend Sadie, and in Christena Mullen's affectionate reminiscences, Munro alludes to a larger community of women, the potential of which is not realized in the text.

Carrington vigorously discourages an empathetic response to Munro's female protagonist, arguing that the character of Annie is portrayed as an outrageous, "malicious" liar and hoaxer, whose "solipsism" and "confused perception" cause trouble for others.[22] Elsewhere in her work, Carrington is at pains to discourage feminist readings of Munro's fiction: in her influential book on Munro, *Controlling the Uncontrollable*, she discusses what she believes to be the writer's "satire of feminists,"[23] arguing that Munro's "emphasis on female humiliation does *not* make her a feminist 'injustice-collector.'"[24] The epithet "feminist" is perhaps not always applied to Munro's work, but her fiction has undoubtedly attracted feminist scholarship; for example, in the collection *Critical Essays on Alice Munro*, edited by Robert Thacker, three of the eleven pieces are avowedly feminist. Among book-length studies that one can accurately call feminist are *Mothers and Clowns* (1992), by Magdalene Redekop, and *Dance of the Sexes: Art and Gender in the Fiction of Alice Munro* (1990), by Beverly Rasporich.[25] To affirm that Munro's work is conducive to feminist readings is neither fanciful nor tendentious. It is true, furthermore, that, noticeably in her later work, Munro writes stories in which women break loose from their conventional roles, shake off their customary or expected passivity, as they do, memorably, in "White Dump" and "Lichen" (*The Progress of Love*), "Oranges and Apples," "Wigtime," and "Meneseteung" (*Friend of My Youth*), and "Chance" from *Runaway* (2004). In "A Wilderness Station," Munro creates a female protagonist who, in her waywardness and her eccentricity, adopts "a conscious policy of resistance to male authority and violence."[26] At the beginning of the epistolary narrative, Annie McKillop's voice is muted, or articulated by various ventriloquists who claim the right to speak on her behalf. Eventually, however, she gets to tell her own story, and it is one that Munro encourages her reader to believe.

The letter that initiates the narrative is the earliest document in the archive that the reader imagines is collected by the historian, Leopold Henry. Dated 1852, it is written by the matron of the House of Industry where Annie McKillop was placed as an orphan. In this letter the matron responds to Simon Herron's request for her recommendation of "any girl of marriageable age," a request that, it seems, is common, but is legitimated only by "an endorsement from [a] minister" (p. 190). The church's role in the procurement of young women for marriage is thus exposed early in the narrative. That the matron is complicit in the transactions between male pioneers and the church is confirmed by her assertion that she is "happy to reply," and by the detailed information she conveys. In her comparative evaluation of two eighteen-year-old girls, Sadie Johnstone and Annie McKillop, who might suit Simon Herron's needs, the matron offers a glimpse of ideologies prevalent at the time: she stresses the legitimacy of their births and the respectability and Christian nature of their lineage. Extolling the virtues of the hardier, but not quite so comely Annie, the matron reassures Herron that the young woman's dark complexion and eyes are "no indication of mixed blood" (p. 191). In her advocacy, the matron both obviates and expresses the principal anxieties of the pioneers who settled in Ontario in the mid-nineteenth century; her letter adumbrates the "Presbyterian narrative of moral and spiritual uniformity" that subsequently issues from the Reverend Walter McBain, the minister who endorses Simon Herron's request.[27]

Before his first letter, Munro places the "Recollections of Mr. George Herron," dated more than a half century later, a letter contributing to the fiftieth anniversary edition of the Carstairs *Argus*. This is an account of the Herron brothers' experiences as young pioneers setting out in 1851 to "try [their] fortunes in the wilds of Huron and Bruce" (pp. 191–92). In his account, the younger brother documents the hardships the men endure in their struggle to establish a settlement on the Crown land. Three elements in George Herron's narrative merit closer scrutiny. First, there is clear evidence of conflict between the brothers: there is more than one reference to Simon's dismissal of his younger brother's opinions and wishes, and to acts of stubborn willfulness that exacerbate the hardships they already endure. The second significant element is George's account of why and how his brother sought a wife. In mitigation of what he acknowledges must seem "a strange way to go about things," he explains that his brother had not "the time or the money or the inclination" (p. 195) for courting, and he cites the minister's endorsement of the transaction as moral justification. The minister's support extends far beyond merely endorsing the letter, as is clear from the revelation that McBain helped write the original request and personally vouched for Simon Herron. The minister's patronage of the brothers is expressed in more fulsome terms in his own letters, which succeed George Herron's reminiscences.

A third significant aspect of these reminiscences is the younger brother's description of Simon's death. The vagueness of detail and the lack of affect here are noteworthy. George writes: "We were chopping down a tree where Simon wanted, and in some way, I cannot say how, a branch of it came crashing down where we didn't expect. We just heard the little branches cracking where it fell and looked up to see and it hit Simon on the head and killed him instantly" (p. 195). There are some weaknesses in the testimony. There is no hint of the inclement weather that might account for the sudden breaking and falling of a branch; the lack of any explanation for its "crashing down where we didn't expect" seems like evasion. Furthermore, the degree of syndetic coordination in the last sentence is excessive, and would be regarded by grammarians as stylistically marked. The repeated use of "and" to link consecutive clauses is fairly common in unsophisticated writing of the kind exemplified here; the last sentence, then, may appear unremarkable, considering the general abundance of polysyndeton in Herron's account. However, in this instance, the cumulative effect of the coordinate clauses makes his statement sound faltering, devoid of any causality, or, for that matter, of logical sequencing. In his description, the branch has fallen before the two look up to see its flight downward: "We just heard the little branches cracking where it fell and looked up to see it" (p. 195). In addition, the younger brother exhibits no emotion whatsoever in his narration of Simon Herron's apparently instant death. Describing his efforts "to drag back the body to the shanty through the snow," he emphasizes the "wearying" nature of the task, conveying an impression of a self-centeredness that is confirmed later in the account by the petulant complaint that he "was left to chop and clear by [him]self" (pp. 195–96).

In his letter to the Carstairs *Argus*, George mostly refers to the central character, Annie, in patronymic terms, as "a wife" (p. 194), "his [Simon's] wife" (p. 196), "my brother's wife" (p. 197). Only when he describes the burial of his brother does he use the woman's forename. It is worth noting, too, that George confesses that he has forgotten Annie's name. Except at the outset, when he has to introduce "Annie Herron," the minister uses the same relational terms of address. Alerting Mr. James Mullen, Clerk of the Peace in charge of Walley Gaol, to the possible arrival of Annie McKillop, he names her as a "widow and one of my congregation" (p. 197). Annie is thus defined phallocentrically, in her relation to a dead man, and in relation to a cornerstone of patriarchy, the church. As he elaborates on Annie's history, he employs several referents rather than use the woman's forename: "bride of the young man Simon Herron," "Presbyterian female," "young widow" (p. 198), "child of the Free Church" (p. 199). The avoidance of the forename is made more prominent by the plethora of third-person pronouns in the minister's discussion of Annie's circumstances. Lengthy paragraphs, each one consisting of several multiple sentences, are littered with subjective, objective, and genitive pronoun forms, but contain not one nominal coreferent (p. 198–99). The refusal to name the woman reduces her individuality, and sets her off at a distance from the narrator of the account. In contrast, the references to the Herron brothers, as "these two young lads" (p. 198) are familiar, even affectionate. The minister's discourse style is otherwise formal, distant and stilted, as illustrated in the following: "It is a fault of mine that I am not well-equipped to talk to women. I have not the ease to win their trust" (p. 198). His aloofness with regard to women seems to prevent his showing much compassion for the character of Annie McKillop, whose value he estimates as a member of the Free Church, and therefore as "a soul in [his] charge" (p. 199).

The reader learns more about Annie from the letters of James Mullen, with whom McBain corresponds. He is presented in a positive light, as a compassionate man, slow to censure, and willing to understand, as these statements of his suggest: "As you may know, we have a very fine new Gaol here where the inmates are . . . treated with all humanity" and "I am in perplexity about her [Annie]" (p. 202). The most significant aspect of Mullen's first letter is the disclosure of a second version of events surrounding the death of Simon Herron. This version, in which Annie strikes her husband dead with a rock, is, it is reported, delivered by Annie on her arrival at Walley Gaol. It is an account that is discounted by Mullen, for reasons that are well substantiated: he believes she is physically incapable of murder, and doubts whether a convenient rock would be found in the snow. The doctor who later examines the woman shares this skepticism.

As a feminist scholar, what I find particularly interesting in Mullen's letters is the profusion of instances where Annie McKillop's statements are mediated by others. Munro employs several kinds of speech presentation in order to demonstrate this ventriloquizing of her central character's voice. She is introduced in Mullen's letter as the subject of the minister's correspondence, and her account of the death of Simon Herron is conveyed via a mixture of different representations of speech. There is evidence of the report of a speech act, in Mullen's assertion, "I got all the particulars I could" (p. 200), where the reader infers Annie's responses to his questions. Indirect discourse is manifest in several reporting clauses, such as "she said" and "she says," which remind the reader that the central character is not yet the narrator of her own story, but is written of in the third person by others. Connections among the principal male narrators, Mullen, Herron, and McBain, are consolidated by Mullen's enclosed letter to George, in which he is asked for his opinion on Annie's version of events. Various arbiters of legitimacy—the Clerk of the Peace, the Free Church minister, Annie's brother-in-law, the doctor at Walley Gaol—pass judgment on the worth of the protagonist's testimony before it emerges in first-person form to the reader.

Toward the end of Mullen's second letter to McBain, Munro begins to prepare the reader for the textual entry of the main character's voice, using, first, free indirect discourse, followed by free direct discourse. Mullen explains that the prison doctor had asked Annie, "did she not fear hanging?" and he recalls that "she replied, no, for there is a reason you will not hang me" (p. 205). That Munro chooses to render part of the prison doctor's dialogue with Annie via snatches of free direct and free indirect discourse is worthy of discussion: such representation is in keeping with the polyvocal density of the epistolary narrative; it also offers the reader a clearer envisaging of a character who has been obliquely shown. The narratologist Michael Toolan believes that free indirect discourse often serves as "a strategy of (usually temporary or discontinuous) alignment, in words, values and perspective, of the narrator with a character."[28] In Munro's narrative, the free indirect discourse ushers in the voice of the female protagonist, and suggests a degree of empathy between this central character and the narrator, James Mullen. The reader is encouraged to trust the judgment of the Clerk of the Peace, who is portrayed as a decent man.

Two brief letters written by Annie precede her account of the aftermath of Simon Herron's death. Each of these might persuade the reader to react favorably toward the protagonist. In her communication with Sadie Johnstone, her former companion in the House of Industry, Annie appears stoical, diligent, loyal, and considerate. It is also obvious that she is no fool, for she correctly anticipates that her letters will be examined. The protagonist's full testimony is thus prefaced by these short, poignant pleas for some contact with her friend. Munro's narrative configuration serves a dual function: it creates reader sympathy for Annie, and differentiates her accounts from the public narration of the other letter writers. Carrington asserts that these short notes furnish evidence of Annie McKillop's caution and disingenuousness; she points to the date of the second brief letter, April Fool's Day, regarding it as an ominous foreshadowing of "a hoax, of concealing rather than revealing." Instead of revelation, Carrington argues that the reader then encounters a "problematic confession" that results from Annie's "distorted perception."[29] I disagree with Carrington's negative evaluation of the character of Annie McKillop, which, judging by qualities evinced in the first letters, is positively portrayed. I do not read her confession as at all problematic, and argue that her view of events is presented as plausible.

Munro has taken pains to postpone the emergence of her central character's voice, prefacing it by various discourses of authority whose certainties the reader is expected to question. For example, does the contemporary reader accept that "there was no order imposed on [Annie's] days" (p. 199) after the departure of her brother-in-law, George Herron? And what of the doctor's assessment of Annie's state of mind, as being unhinged by "the sort of reading that is available to these females" (p. 205)? By conveying her protagonist's words via others' distorted perceptions, Munro casts doubt on their claim to speak for the young woman. Annie's speech is mediated for long periods by ventriloquist characters, so that when her own words eventually break through, they seem especially clamorous.

The reader's attention is swiftly caught by the technique of *in medias res*. In the case of Annie's letter, it is the witnessing of her husband's body, being dragged toward the log shanty by his brother. There follows a vivid, meticulously detailed account of how Annie prepares Simon Herron for burial, during which she realizes that her husband has been murdered. Munro conveys this startling discovery in a sentence of unbroken monosyllables: "And then I saw, I saw where the axe had cut" (p. 209), the force of which is enhanced by the rhetorical scheme, anadiplosis, which amplifies the shock.

Whether George Herron killed his brother or not is a matter of considerable debate. The conflict between the brothers has been made known to the reader, who might accept that the younger man would eventually strike out at his unyielding, domineering older brother. Furthermore, George Herron's version of the incident in the woods is not convincing. The detail, candor, and assertiveness of Annie's testimony are, for me, compelling, and, in conjunction with the textual evidence discussed previously, persuade me of the plausibility of her account. Munro's love of minutiae in description is manifest in the mention of the "one little piece of hair" Annie cuts from her dead husband's head; the "eyelet petticoat" (p. 209) used in her sewing of the makeshift shroud; the "tea from catnip leaves" (p. 210) she makes for George, in her efforts to console him. The simple exhortations she issues are made starker because Munro renders them in staccato, predominantly monosyllabic utterances, the particular indentation of which creates the impression of a list, a mantra: "You didn't mean to do it. It was in anger, you didn't mean what you were doing. I saw him other times what he would do to you. I saw he would knock you down for a little thing and you just get up and never say a word. The same he did to me. If you had not done it, some day he would have done it to you. Listen George. Listen to me" (p. 210).

Annie's attempts to shake her brother-in-law from his apparent emotional torpor are futile. When she resorts to reading from the bible, urging George to seek forgiveness for what he did, she reveals an understanding of the scriptures that Carrington argues is indicative of her ability to "change her diction just as readily as she reverses her story."[30] Rather than illustrating duplicitousness, Annie's desperate ministrations can be interpreted as borne of compassion for a fellow victim. Annie's desire to reassure and comfort George extends to her putting him to bed, and trying to warm him, using heated cloths and the proximity of her own body. These resuscitative efforts can be read as acts of human kindness that one might perform for a person who is in shock or despair, as George Herron appears to be.

Carrington perceives this episode in a much more sinister light, arguing that Annie's solicitous acts amount to predatory sexual advances on "her *fourteen-year-old* brother-in-law."[31] She justifies this claim by pointing out the various references to heat in Annie's account, "both literal heat and the heat of sexual arousal," and to the fact that Annie pulls George to the "marital bed," not, presumably, his own. The self-inflicted bruise on the back of Annie's hand Carrington speculates may have been the result of the woman's determination "to prevent George, the auditor in the other bed, from hearing the sounds of intercourse."[32] How then does the reader interpret the bruises on Annie's legs and arms? These are presumably the consequence of Simon's rough treatment, either in or out of the marital bed. Why is George's youth of such concern to Carrington? In his letter he describes himself as "a husky lad" (p. 192), who has the physical and mental strength to set out as a pioneer in the Huron County wilderness—he is hardly a vulnerable mite.

I cannot agree with the estimation of Annie as a "female devil or Lilith" intent on seducing the younger brother, and dismayed by his inertia.[33] If I do, I dismiss the impressions formed during Munro's characterization; I thereby discount the importance of reader empathy, and my own affective responses. These persuade me to believe Annie's version of events. The emotional denial of her brother-in-law, which Annie documents so meticulously, is suggested by his own terse description of Simon's death; the futile solicitousness she engages in after his burial seems entirely sincere and believable in a character whose pathetic quest for her friend Sadie the reader already knows of. Annie's third letter, her testimony, is, as Carrington points out, more articulate, and much more substantial than the terse notes she initially sends to her absent friend. But Annie composes this final letter after she has been able to reflect on past events, when she has spent some time in the comfort of the prison, having lived like an outcast in the wilderness.

Toward the conclusion of this letter, Munro inserts the sentence, "And I would like for that yelling to stop" (p. 218). This simple assertion is noteworthy. Its significance is heightened by its separation in a paragraph of its own, and its contiguousness to Annie's child-like pleading for Sadie to come and visit her. I read the statement as a reference, not to Annie's troubling memories, her "terriblest dreams" (p. 225), but to the wretched cries of Annie's fellow inmate in the gaol, the "insane female" whom James Mullen wrote of, a rape victim whose "screams . . . resound sometimes for hours at a stretch" (p. 206). The effect of this cursory and seemingly random reference to the "yelling" is manifold: it serves to illustrate the densely cohesive nature of Munro's rich narrative, and it enlivens her depiction of Ontario prison life in the mid-nineteenth century. It also conveys a vestige of the suffering that Annie herself endured, hence her marked aversion, and, in so doing, it increases the reader's sympathy for the central character.

Susan Lanser argues that the veracity of the coded letter examined in "Toward a Feminist Narratology" relies, largely, on the reader's warmhearted response to the female victim, who is imprisoned in a loathsome marriage. Lanser observes that there are three readers of the woman's letter: as well as the husband and the friend, there is, of course, the third, the extratextual reader, "who brings to it particular kinds of knowledge" and "interpretative possibilities."[34] I would add that the reader might bring, in addition, a particular understanding, and compassion, in the same way that she or he might to Annie McKillop's account. The final letter in Munro's epistolary narrative ensures that, in the words of Coral Ann Howells, "Annie's life story has a happy ending."[35] It is Mullen's granddaughter, Christena, who provides the epilogue, wherein she affectionately recalls her memories of Annie, who lived on with the Mullen family, as their seamstress. This last letter is structurally crucial, since it provides the justification for the letters that precede it; it furnishes the reader with yet another substantial piece of settler history and further illuminates the remarkable character of Annie McKillop, whose imagination, eccentricity, and candor are all illustrated in Christena's account. There is also ample evidence of Annie's notorious storytelling, about, for example, a suitor driving up in a carriage, and a baby born from a boil on a stomach. But these absurd inventions are surely told for dramatic import, and Munro is careful to incorporate in Christena's letter the many allusions to Annie's competence, which counteracts her outrageousness: she pinpoints exactly where her former shanty stood; she designs beautiful gowns for her employer's children; she appears to make George Herron finally listen to her version.

The reader is not privy to what Annie says to George, but it is clear from Christena Mullen's recollection that the old woman enjoys her narration. She would have told her story without interruption or contradiction, since George Herron had lost the power of speech. For Annie McKillop, telling her story is as desirable as writing it, "as if to tell were in itself to resolve, to provide closure."[36]

The same desire for resolution persuades Phemie, in "The Progress of Love," to believe what appears to be a fallacious version of an incident in her mother's life. The narrator's mother once burned money bequeathed by her father, an inheritance that would have relieved the family's dire poverty: she did so because she had hated him so much. Phemie grows up believing that her own father had not protested at his wife's profligacy, and had watched in silence as the notes burned on the stove. However, it is later revealed that events had not happened in this way, for her father had never known the money had been given to the family. Yet the narrator does not want to relinquish the false version; indeed, she confesses that she will go on believing it, because it deserves to be the truth. It sustains "the progress of love," and it affords her a comforting memory.

In his review of *Open Secrets*, George Woodcock remarks: "We end up never quite knowing who is telling lies about the death of Simon Herron."[37] I maintain that the reader is persuaded to believe Annie's account of events in her "wilderness station," and I have argued that there are several reasons why the reader should accord status to Annie's testimony, the principal one being because "it seems so much the truth it is the truth" (*The Progress of Love*, p. 30).

There is a solid authenticity about the testimony, a quality that, according to Val Ross, gives Munro's fiction "its miraculous believability."[38] Several qualities make her work believable, not the least of which is the writer's deep and sustained knowledge of her own terrain—the Huron County landscape, its people, and its history. But there is another reason why one account, and not the others it competes with, can read like the truth, and it pertains to an eidetic image or revelation that emerges in the narrative, usually, but not always, toward its conclusion. In Annie McKillop's letter, it is when she writes: "And then I saw, I saw where the axe had cut." That sentence strikes me with the same force as the narrator's confession, in "Friend of My Youth," that the dream of her mother, restored to health, could change "the bitter lump of love" she has carried. A startling trope or juxtaposition, an unexpected pattern of syntax, the recurrence of certain words—such defamiliarizing strategies indicate that something momentous and transformative is being disclosed that will affect the narrating and the reading experience.

Eleanor Wachtel ventures to suggest to Munro that such instances exemplify a sudden "insight [or] epiphany," a "moment of accidental clarity" that occurs in many of her stories.[39] Munro herself uses the phrase "queer bright moment" to refer to the phenomenon I discuss in the next chapter: it is the moment when her narrator recognizes a particular truth, or an evasion of truth.[40] For the character, it is accidental, but, in terms of Munro's narrative design, it is, of course, far from being so.

CHAPTER 4

THE "QUEER BRIGHT MOMENT"

IN HER REVIEW OF *OPEN SECRETS*, IN the *New Republic*, Wendy Lesser acknowledges that a piece such as "A Wilderness Station" represents "the kind of serious, exploratory work [Munro] is doing at its highest level," but she is of the opinion that the stories generally lack "the intense visceral solidity of most of [her] earlier work." She is disappointed with the title story, which she deems to be "a pale evocation of all the usual Munro elements," and is also critical of "An Albanian Virgin," labeling it "definitely the weirdest story in the book [and] unlikely to win the heart of the true Munro fan."[1]

Munro herself anticipated, and became aware of, some readers' reservations, telling Boyce and Smith, of the Australian journal *Meanjin*: "*Open Secrets* is not a good introduction to my work. These stories don't close in the way people expect or want them to." She adds that readers may find them "disconcerting."[2] There are surprising innovations in *Open Secrets*, it is true, for some of the stories take the reader on unfamiliar journeys—far from Canada ("The Jack Randa Hotel"), into the paranormal ("Carried Away"), and out of the terrestrial ("Spaceships Have Landed"). It seems to me that the "disconcerting" elements reside mostly in the *degree* of ambiguity and uncertainty in the narrative. As I suggest in my previous chapter, critics and readers will be divided over the reliability of Annie Herron's testimony; they may believe that Millicent's lie, in "A Real Life," either robbed her friend of an expected life of seasonal routines, or thankfully protected her from this very destiny. In *Open Secrets*, the reader has to work harder for answers to mysteries. What kinds of tricks *are* being played on Louisa in "Carried Away"? Why does Liza, in "Vandals," so fervently believe Bea can spread safety? And in the title story, why does Maureen not act on what she sees from her window? As Andrew Hiscock asserts in his essay on the "Culture of Loss" in Munro's work, "reader, narrator and character [are] locked in a search for clues," hidden in stories that have become increasingly more complex, elusive and thickly layered.[3] The title story of *Open Secrets* does not end with a neat resolution, but it certainly contains several clues for the curious detective. Judith Maclean Miller believes that "Alice Munro . . . writes mystery stories [but] no-one pulls all the clues together at the end." She explains: "There are not even really clues, just bits and pieces of information that appear here and there, floating through the telling of the story, many of them unspoken, coded, implied, resonating through silences."[4] Her fiction is characterized by qualities that generate and deepen mystery—indeterminacy, indirectness, multiple layering, opaqueness, and the withdrawal of closure. Several stories in *Open Secrets* and *The Love of a Good Woman* are disturbingly cryptic because at the heart of the piece lies an unsettling secret, the provenance of which is an instance of injustice, an act of malice, even violence. I would argue that in these mystery stories the various "bits and pieces" direct a path to the "queer bright moment," the instance of sudden clarity that sheds light on puzzling incidents and themes in the narrative.

Munro uses this striking phrase in her introduction to the 1986 edition (Canadian and American) of *The Moons of Jupiter*, where she writes about "The Turkey Season," considering what the story is really about. She explains that she always thinks of a scene near the end of the story, when the narrator and her two female coworkers come out of Turkey Barn into the snowy evening, link arms, and start to sing. In this affirmative ending, Munro captures her adolescent narrator's simple pleasure, in solidarity. Munro explains, "I think there should be a queer bright moment like that in every story" (*The Moons of Jupiter*, p. xv). In that moment, the core of her narrative—a crucial scene, or image, or narrative comment—is made salient and memorable; it will often throw some light on a mystery, although it will not entirely unravel or resolve it. The adjective "queer" seems appropriate because it suggests the strangeness and obliqueness of the insight, or illumination.

The core mystery in "Open Secrets" is the disappearance of Heather Bell, one of a group of Canadian Girls in Training taking part in a hike by the Peregrine River near Carstairs. People in the community have differing views on what has happened to the girl: she may have drowned in the falls; she may have run away from home; she may have been abducted. The police question an eccentric old man who has acquired a suspicious reputation, but they learn nothing of value from him. The mystery is the subject of a ballad poem, sections of which are interspersed throughout the narrative, which is initiated by the poem's first stanza:

It was on a Saturday morning
Just as lovely as it could be
Seven girls and their leader Miss Johnstone
Went camping from the CGIT. (*Open Secrets*, p. 129)

By choosing to begin the story in this way, Munro invites the reader to wonder who has written the ballad, and what authority it has. In its lack of sophistication, it could be the collective work of the missing girl's companions, or it might have been composed by Frances, the character who speaks first, when she recites it, and shares what she knows about the incident with her employer, Maureen Stephens, for whom she cleans. Maureen is the subject of the focalization in this third-person narrative, but it is not through her perspective that the reader is introduced to events. Frances is the bearer of the news, and her theories about the girl are proclaimed when she insists: "They will try to make out she was some poor innocent, but the facts are dead different." She believes that the missing girl had arranged to meet a man, to which Maureen replies, "I think that's pretty farfetched."

In the opening scene, customary anchors of narrative certainty and reliability are loosened: the story begins with an anonymous poem; the chief source of information is, the reader learns, prone to gossip and "wild, uncharitable, confident speculations" (p. 130); instead of imposing control at the outset, the narrator establishes the context via the free indirect discourse of a secondary character, who relates a second-hand version of how the girls behaved: "Frances said that Mary Kaye said that Heather Bell had been the worst one, the boldest" (p. 130). The reporting clauses convey how indirectly the information is obtained. Maureen listens to but does not encourage Frances's outrageous ideas, as she "could not be a gossip, because of her husband's position" in the community (p. 133). Described as "intelligent and dependable" (p. 138), she is nonetheless constrained by what she fears is seen as a "lucky marriage" to a much older man, the retired Lawyer Stephens, in whose office she had worked (p. 134). He is admired for his legal probity and the gravity of his demeanor, but these outward signs of respectability belie a less attractive nature. Since a stroke that slurred his speech, Stephens struggles to make his words understood, and Maureen acts as his interpreter when people, mostly loyal former clients, call. For them he makes more effort, reserving a "testy and complaining" tone for his wife, issuing terse reproofs when he "did not care" for what he heard (p. 137). Maureen is able to cope with her role as interpreter and housekeeper, as she has the imagination to daydream, to return to times when she had been a noisy "shrieker, a dare-taker" on

CGIT expeditions, before developing "the qualities her husband would see and value when hiring, and proposing" (p. 139).

In the first section of "Open Secrets," credibility and trustworthiness are consistently undermined. The reader might justifiably ask: Whom do I believe? Who is the most reliable—the poet, the narrator, the subject of the focalization, the character with the far-fetched theories? There is further obfuscation ahead before the reader can recognize the instance of sudden insight or epiphany.

At the end of the first section, the narrator describes Maureen's view from her house, way beyond the copper beech trees on their lawn, toward the "unruly trees along the river." The description is full of foreboding: "A ragged sort of wall with hidden doorways and hidden paths behind it where animals went, and lone humans sometimes, becoming different from what they were outside . . . and there was always the other person on a path to intersect yours and his head was full of plans for you even before you met" (pp. 139–40). What Maureen sees denotes concealment, and connotes premeditated menace. This sense of approaching unease is sustained into the story's next segment, one clearly indicated by marks of ellipsis that serve to heighten the impact of the first sentence: "On Tuesday morning, while Frances was getting breakfast and Maureen was helping her husband to finish dressing, there was a knock at the front door, by someone who did not notice or trust the bell" (p. 141). The reader is alerted to the ominous nature of the visit, since the day and time are specified; moreover, by postponing the identity of a visitor who is impatient and determined, narrative suspense is generated.

What unfolds during the visit is accorded a great deal of textual space: a third of the story's thirty pages. The visitors are Marian and Theo Slater, who have come to see Lawyer Stephens. The woman is presented in such a way as to suggest that she is acting out a part, and is unaccustomed to her role. On a hot day, she wears inappropriate clothing, a heavy suit, hat and gloves, and her normally "rambunctious" manner is "toned down" (p. 142); she had also put on so much makeup that Maureen did not immediately recognize her. Her husband appears uncomfortable and incongruous, awkwardly attired in a cheap suit with "too much padding," and looking strained and bewildered (p. 142). All these details are viewed through Maureen's eyes, for she is the subject of the focalization for most of the narrative. Studying Marian thoughtfully, Maureen concludes that the woman is trying to put on a confident performance, to demonstrate that "she knew what was expected" (p. 143).

Marian and Theo Slater have come to tell Lawyer Stephens about the bizarre behavior of Mr. Siddicup, an eccentric widower who lives near their farmhouse. Marian embarks on a long, rambling tale of how this old man, unable to speak since a throat operation, had appeared at her back door, in an agitated state, and desperately tried to tell her something, making frantic gestures and sounds that she could not follow. She was alone at home, ill with a headache, and her husband had, she said, gone out with the truck. The account contains a wealth of supernumerary detail, and features an energetic imitation of Mr. Siddicup's actions that the narrator calls a "display" (p. 149), a word conjuring the idea of something staged. The narrator strengthens this impression by describing how, during "her antics," Marian keeps her eyes fixed on her husband Theo, compelling his attention, and "her look said, Hold on. Be still" (p. 148).

The woman explains that, sometime later, she remembered that Miss Johnstone and her party had called at the farmhouse on Saturday, asking for water, and how the girls had behaved boisterously; then "it all came back to her" about Mr. Siddicup and his odd behavior. She and Theo had eventually decided that they needed "to go and talk to Lawyer Stephens" about it all (p. 151). This section of the story is concluded by the isolated paragraph: "So they got up and came as soon as they could" (p. 151), the monosyllabic terseness of which contrasts with the preceding verbosity.

A skeptical reading of Marian's account would question the amassing of so much unnecessary information: why she needs to describe her ailments, name all the tasks her husband undertakes, and provide precise times for irrelevant episodes she relates. The woman's narrative, intended to incriminate Mr. Siddicup, succeeds in drawing suspicion toward the couple, but this is deflected when the narrator privileges access to Maureen's thoughts. She recalls why women in the town are wary of the old man, because of his habit of leaving "women's clothes, underwear" lying around his house, and she wonders if he is a "pervert" (p. 152). This fresh piece of information offers the reader another avenue of inquiry, for "Open Secrets" is a mystery, where Munro consciously undermines narrative certitude, consistently creates and sustains suspense, offering more than one explanation for a young girl's vanishing. There are no explicit or unequivocal solutions; it is a case of discerning a pattern in all the "bits and pieces of information," the clues that permeate the narrative. Munro knows that her reader will take time to consider the "many hypotheses" constructed in her mystery in order to distinguish "the correct one" from "false ones . . . faulty versions."[5]

The hypothesis, that Mr. Siddicup is a dangerous pervert who has committed a crime against Heather Bell, is a misleading one, a temporary diversion, and in the scene that follows the Slater's departure from Lawyer Stephens's house, Munro clears the way for a "queer bright moment" that exposes a more plausible suspect. The pace of the narrative is slowed, as attention is drawn to the telling statement in the main clause: "When Maureen shut the door on the pair of them and saw their shapes wobble away through the pebbled glass, she was not quite satisfied" (pp. 152–53). She ascends to the stair landing and watches the couple, asking herself, "Why should they feel a need to sit down after sitting in the dining room for what must have been at least an hour?" The couple do not talk, but sit as though resting "in the midst of hard shared labours" (p. 153), a pose that, in Carrington's apt phrase, suggests "a collusive intensity."[6]

Maureen sees Marian take off her hat and lay it on her lap, and then she witnesses an action that is startling and sinister. Theo Slater reaches over and takes the hat, then, "He settled it in his lap. He bent over and started to stroke it, in a comforting way. He stroked that hat made of horrible brown feathers as if he were pacifying a little scared hen" (p. 153). This description constitutes for me the "queer bright moment" in a narrative that contains more than a few enigmas. In common with most of Munro's fiction, the story was published first in the *New Yorker*, and some readers thought it too cryptic. Douglas Gibson, Munro's editor at McClelland and Stewart, told the writer, "some of our readers had found . . . 'Open Secrets' a little too opaque for their tastes."[7] Responding to this criticism, Munro adds a paragraph to the version included in the collection. She informs Val Ross, in an interview conducted soon after the publication of *Open Secrets*, "I meant to indicate that Theo is probably the murderer," and the new paragraph removes any doubt.[8] In it, the narrator tells how Marian put a stop to her husband's stroking: "She said something to him, she clamped a hand down on his," as though she were chiding a "simpleminded child—with a burst of abhorrence" (p. 154).

The image of the ugly brown hat on Theo Slater's lap is sufficient for me. It is the crucial one, and it is how the object is animated that enables the reader to infer horrifying meaning. Rather than being placed or laid, it is "settled," as though it were moving in agitation, like a frightened creature, while the action of bending over and repeatedly stroking implies the man's obsessive purposefulness. The new paragraph certainly makes it clear that Marian is in control, and that she is in the habit of recognizing and discouraging her husband's obsession, but the epiphany occurs when Maureen witnesses Theo's stroking of the feathered hat. As the subject of the focalization, the protagonist's insight is shared with the reader, and so are her reactions, conveyed in two stark assertions: "Maureen felt a shock. She felt a shrinking in her bones" (p. 155). The form and position of these two statements are unchanged in the revised version.

Now Munro sets about consolidating the connections between the two women—her protagonist and the "husky woman" (p. 143) whom she has steadily observed from the landing. There follows a description of Maureen's sexual degradation at the hands of her husband, the lawyer revered in the community as "too honorable . . . a man in a million" (p. 138). His sexual appetite has become unsavory, and instead of "the formal fondness, of their early times together," he now treats his partner in a brutal, menacing way, bullying and "pounding her" at the moment of "his extremity" (p. 155). It is while Maureen endures this painful assault that she recalls the scene she witnessed minutes before, "the fingers moving on the feathers, the wife's hand laid on top of the husband's, pressing down." She holds this image in her mind "right through her husband's rampage" (p. 156), before she can finally escape to the bathroom to "cleanup" and compose herself. The image is retrieved once more, its significance further enhanced, when Maureen stands at her stove, in the peace of her kitchen at last, and imagines "one of those thick-fingered hands . . . that had worked among the feathers" being "pressed down" on the burner by a dark glove (p. 158). These disturbing signs of sexual fetishes accompany her manhandling, and they thus connect the two women, each of whom colludes in her partner's deviance.

Neither woman will disclose her secret. The narrator explains, "Heather Bell will not be found [and] Mr. Siddicup will not be of any help" (p. 159) and, in a proleptic final paragraph, reports that Maureen will remain in her "lucky marriage" (p. 134) until her husband's death, before she embarks on "another marriage, new places and houses." Then she may feel her memory "twitch" (p. 160). The choice of verb is notable, for it is often used for conscience. There is an indication that Maureen will reflect again on the "open secret" she harbors, but does not know how to tell, because she is constrained by a guilty complicity.

The concluding clauses illustrate the opaqueness that characterizes this puzzling narrative. The narrator reports that although Maureen's memory will twitch, "it will not quite reveal to her this moment when she seems to be looking into an open secret, something not startling until you think of trying to tell it" (p. 160). Anything that would betoken explicitness, certainty, and stability is qualified: the memory will not *quite* reveal the moment; the protagonist will only *seem* to contemplate a secret, not *really* do so; the secret is one that becomes startling *only* when you try to tell it— but you are not *trying* to tell it, you are only *thinking* of the attempt. The queer bright moment—the protagonist's flash of intuition—does remain with the reader, and serves to illuminate some, but not all, of the secrecy.

The opaque and disconcerting stories in *Open Secrets* prepare the reader for *The Love of a Good Woman*, from which "Save the Reaper" and "Cortes Island" are selected for scrutiny in this chapter.[9] In some respects these two narratives do not appear to have much in common: the former, set in familiar Munro territory by Lake Huron, is delivered by a hetero-diegetic narrator and features a protagonist who is a grandmother, in her sixties, while the latter, set in Vancouver, is a first-person narrative told by a newly married young woman; in addition, "Cortes Island," unlike "Save the Reaper," is a linear narrative, containing few textual disruptions. Both these pieces are aptly designated "mystery" stories, for, like "Open Secrets," each has at its heart at least one sinister secret, possibly murderous, certainly unsavory, lodged in a forbidding setting, where hostile characters lurk. The encounter with danger has an impact on both protagonist and narrator. Each of the two stories illustrates, in varying degrees, Munro's continuing desire for narrative adventure. The telescoping of time in "Save the Reaper" is striking—in one scene alone the protagonist's past, present, and future are compressed—while in "Cortes Island" the queer bright moment is relegated to the margins, a brief allusion in an anachronous newspaper report.

"Save the Reaper" appeared in the *New Yorker* a few months before its publication in *The Love of a Good Woman*. It was later included in *The Best American Short Stories 1999*, edited by Amy Tan, where Munro, in the Contributors' Notes, explains that when she wrote this story she was keenly aware of the many changes, in the last quarter of a century, affecting the landscape and society of the southwestern Ontario that was her birthplace and is her home. These have resulted in a "lot more luxury and style . . . as well as a lot more outright deterioration" in a setting where "country people aren't country people any more," but now live with "shaky new patterns and untrustworthy nostalgia for old patterns."[10] The narrator in "Save the Reaper" presents an aging female protagonist, Eve, returning to land near Lake Huron, where she enjoyed summer holidays as a child, and shows she is now out of her time, out of kilter in her personal life. Her mistaken recollections, and whimsical bouts of wistfulness, expose her to danger, but in the exposure she faces up to truths about her irresponsible, self-centered past.

Eve is portrayed as a woman in pursuit of the ideal, and the imaginary. In the opening scene she is driving on country roads near Lake Huron with her two grandchildren, Daisy and Philip, whom she entertains by pretending they are trailing cars occupied by aliens. Eve is looking after the children while their mother, her daughter Sophie, travels to Toronto to meet her husband Ian, who is arriving from California. After Sophie brings Ian back to the summer cottage her mother rented, hoping to enjoy a full month's holiday with her daughter and the children, the family will leave for the north, and Eve is not invited on the hastily arranged trip. The entertainment Eve provides for her grandchildren is almost a replica of the game she once played with Sophie when she was a little girl: urged on by precocious Philip, whose wish to control the game is obsessive, she pursues "newly arrived space travellers on their way to the secret headquarters, the invaders' lair." The chief difference between the two make-believe chases is succinctly encapsulated in the sentence: "Then it was spies—now it was aliens" (p. 146).

This metonymic contrast is the first of many allusions to the passage of time, and its unwelcome consequences for Eve. The summer rental she secured for the holiday is neither picturesque nor reasonably priced, for "things had changed—the cottages were all as substantial as suburban houses, and the rents were out of sight" (p. 149). The village store Eve visits for provisions is "actually a classy supermarket these days" (p. 157), selling exclusive produce, while several other features she remembers fondly have disappeared. The cement square on which her father played checkers; the "hotel with its verandas [and] the railway station with its flower beds spelling out the name of the village"; even the railway tracks: these have made way for "a fake old-fashioned mall with the satisfactory new supermarket and wine shop and boutiques for leisure wear and country crafts" (p. 161). Munro makes clear Eve's antipathy to these signs of modernity: the compound "fake old-fashioned" expresses the tawdry quality of something incongruous and fraudulent; the use of syndetic coordination conveys the sense of retail excess; the shop names convey a suburban rather than a rural setting.

That Eve tends to idealize parts of her past is demonstrated in her present relationship with her daughter, whom she had raised alone, struggling on her earnings as an actress. She had become pregnant during a romp with a visiting Indian academic, on the train journey from Vancouver to Toronto. The reader suspects that Sophie's childhood was more unorthodox than she would have wished; the narrator reveals that she accuses her mother of imposing on her an education in "an ungraded alternative school" where she learned nothing but merely "survived." Sophie does not share her mother's fondness for reminiscence, her face taking on "a look of gravity and concealment" when "the past that she and Eve had shared was mentioned" (p. 154). With Eve as the subject of the focalization, the reader learns of how vulnerable she is to her daughter's rejection—how she desperately wishes to be included in the rearranged expedition, hoping Sophie will invite her along so that they "can ride together as they used to in the summer, travelling to some town they had never seen before" (p. 158). Her desperation is confirmed when the narrator describes how Eve, when she learns the Lake Huron holiday will end prematurely, restrains herself from "bleat[ing] out a question about whether Sophie still thought of coming next summer" (p. 159). There is a suggestion that Sophie may have engineered the holiday's curtailment— did she urge her husband to take her away, or were the new plans genuine? Eve is unsure, and her uncertainty confirms the impression of an uneasy mother-daughter relationship.

It seems, too, that Eve is mistaken about the extent of her childhood happiness, for the narrator describes how she grew tired of "drives in the country with her mother," that she later hated "being identified as her mother's daughter." She recalls how, as a young adult, she and her friends had played a game, naming what they hated most about their mothers. The narrator explains that "Eve had forgotten all about this game until recently" and remembering it now "was like touching a bad tooth" (p. 162). This disclosure immediately precedes the narration of the principal event in the story, the account of the visit to a house Eve thinks she marveled at when little. In the alien-chasing game she plays with her grandchildren, she impulsively follows a white truck down a lane, thinking it will lead to this house. By her narrative configuration, Munro makes a connection between two games: the game of make-believe chases and the mother-hating game of Eve's young adulthood. The timing of this memory, unwelcome and unpleasant, suggests that the protagonist's pursuit of a nostalgic whim may be unwise.

The reader senses that following the truck to its destination will be a kernel event in the narrative, as its importance is signaled in various ways. There is substantial detail in the delineation of features that belong to an alien world far removed from the Ontario countryside Eve drives through. The gateposts at the top of the lane are "shaped like crude minarets," so crooked that they "had lost all reality as gateposts and looked instead like lost stage props from some gaudy operetta" (p. 162). The repetition of "lost" in the span of two clauses draws attention to the eccentric simile used for objects not normally considered conspicuous. They trigger for Eve images of scenes set in colored glass on the whitewashed wall of a house she and her mother visited. These scenes contained outlandish, exaggerated figures and images, like the "fat horse with dinky legs and burning red eyes . . . drunken stars and fat sunflowers nodding over the roofs of houses" (p. 163).

The unsophisticated, emotive vocabulary and anthropomorphic tropes read like the choices of an awestruck, imaginative child. By her use of focalized perspective, Munro lets the reader view these eidetic images magnified and vivified through the eyes of Eve as a little girl. But the older Eve may be mistaken about the precise location of these scenes, for it has been established that her retrospective gaze is wayward. Her recall of a younger self makes her aware of her granddaughter Daisy, and how she will remember this trip in the country. Time is telescoped as Eve, aware of the children's present excitement, imagines how they will act toward each other in the future; perhaps they will be "estranged" (p. 164), as she is from her brother, to whom she has not spoken for three years. Eve's recollection of something negative and unwanted, an estrangement, is ominous.

Danger signals abound in the account of the approach to the house: "heavy old Scotch pines, probably dangerous" line the narrow track; rising up through the trees is "the skeleton of a barn"; "a high wild hedge" guards a house whose windows are stuffed with "dirty foam rubber," one window shining "with aluminium foil." In this unpropitious setting, with its portents of concealment and menace, Eve finds herself and her charges, having unwisely followed the dictates of a capricious, untrustworthy nostalgia. In the midst of her grandson's repeated pleading, "Don't get out," two statements are salient: "She should never have let that game get so far out of control. A child of Philip's age could get too carried away" (p. 165).

These sentences I regard as expressive of the queer bright moment in the narrative, but their full impact did not emerge on my first reading. I grew curious about why Munro chooses the distal demonstrative "that," instead of the definite article, or even the proximal "this" which would be precise in the context, since the game of pursuing aliens is immediately relevant. The determiner "that" might justifiably be applied to the mother-hating game Eve recalls, with some discomfort, just before she drives after the truck; by its use here, Munro makes the anaphoric reference ambiguous. Also, why does she specify "a child of Philip's age" and not merely "Philip"? It is worth noting that, in the *New Yorker* version of the story, collected in *The Best American Short Stories*, Munro *does* use the definite article before "game," and, in addition, she writes that "Philip was too excitable."[11] The selection of a less-specific noun phrase is intriguing; perhaps Munro, in her revision, is encouraging the reader to recall Eve's memory of the pictures set in the whitewashed wall, and how her imagination soared, impelling her to turn the car back down the driveway, even although she "didn't remember the gateposts at all" (p. 163). Does she want the reader to think that it is not only Philip who is too "carried away" by the game, but also the protagonist? I think she does.

At any rate, she heightens the expectation of dramatic incidents awaiting Eve and her grandchildren as they prepare to enter the house, invited by the truck driver. What awaits them is dramatically expressed in the sentence: "Massive disorder was what they had to make their way through—the kind that takes years to accumulate" (p. 167). By employing elaborate grammatical devices, Munro gives exceptional weight to "massive disorder": the cleft clausal structure moves part of an adverbial phrase into an initial position it would not customarily occupy, while the appositive clause after the dash makes the extent of the disorder much more particular. Compounding the untidy chaos are smells of filth and decay, augmented by other smells, of alcohol and semen, that fill the air in the room Eve enters with the children. The scene here is worse than one of disorder: it is bristling with all kinds of malevolence and perversion—a man so heavily tattooed his skin looks blue, one who kicks and curses a small dog, another man described as fat, sweaty, and "entirely naked." Eve's search for her mosaic pictures has come to a squalid end: her elaborate "spiel" about her childhood drive, the images on the wall, the gateposts, and "her obvious mistake, her apologies" yields nothing from her "hostile audience" (p. 169).

Eve is fortunate to escape from this perilous place with the children, all unharmed, but in the hasty flight she still seeks vestiges of her childhood visit, scouring the wall for pieces of whitewash. The narrator reports that "She thought she could see pieces of glass embedded there, glinting" (p. 171), and it is important to note that the accuracy of her perception is doubly qualified, by the modal "could" and by the stative verb "think," denoting "a private state which can only be subjectively verified."[12] It is not only Eve's memory which is fallible, but her powers of observation: one of the frightening men in the house turns out to be a young woman, who slips into the car as Eve drives off, asking for a lift. The interlude with the woman, revealed to be a prostitute, is puzzling, its function in Munro's design not easy to fathom, mainly because Eve's reactions are presented as so ambivalent. She assesses the young woman first as an unfortunate drunk, disheveled and sickly after a "mighty bingeing" (p. 173). She then sees her in sexual terms, after the woman has trailed a hand along Eve's thigh, in a gesture described as a "tired whore's courtesy." The fact that this action "could be effective" dismays Eve, for it revives memories of the "rowdy and impulsive . . . couplings of her life" (p. 174). Her next thoughts are of danger—that the girl will harm her and the children, rob or even kill them. Finally, she treats her with compassion, for she leaves her near the highway south, gives her money, and tells her that she is welcome at her house, if she gets "stranded" (p. 176).

Carrington, in an erudite, allusive essay that explores Munro's treatment of the "mother-daughter theme" in "Save the Reaper," reads Eve's kindness as "very similar to maternal love for the surrogate daughter whom she is rescuing."[13] The fact that Eve provides directions to the cottage, and a detailed description of its appearance, lends weight to this interpretation. It is true that the protagonist appears to undergo a change of heart toward someone she has regarded as a cheap drunk, a promiscuous teaser, a potential thief and murderer. However, her kindness may be attributable merely to guilt, the "relief turning to shame" (p. 176) when she thinks of the woman's plight; it may also be motivated by the desire for any companionship at all, faced as she is with the prospect of solitude at the end of a curtailed holiday. Why does she tell the woman that the family "should be gone by evening, if that bothers you" (p. 177)? It may simply be the case that "still, and always, [Eve] hankered after love" (p. 174), though not necessarily of a sexual kind.

When Eve returns to the cottage with the children, she is anxious not to disclose anything that would alarm Sophie and her husband Ian. Her account of the eventful day is as selective, and as misleading, as her memory: she refers disingenuously to the owner of the house "there playing cards with his friends," knowing she could never speak of "what she was afraid of" (p. 179). To do so would be an affront to the "decency and optimism" of people like her son-in-law, and would expose the extent to which she feels "stranded," her whole life "some sort of unseemly thrashing around, a radical mistake" (p. 179). By her choice of "stranded," Munro effects a connection between Eve and the prostitute, one sustained in the sexual connotations of an "unseemly thrashing around." The word "mistake" could apply to some of Eve's past and present decisions: the brief affair resulting in her pregnancy; the choice of her daughter's education; her fallible childhood memories; the reckless, endangering impulse of the chase. The happy family reunion, possibly the last for a long time, is marred for Eve by the nagging fear that the prostitute will come looking for shelter, with the family still in the house, and then her "carefulness would go for nothing" (p. 180). If this happens, the game will be up. The story is concluded by a paragraph of prolepsis, in which the narrator explains: "tomorrow night Eve would lie down in this hollowed-out house, willing herself to grow light, relieved of consequence, with nothing in her head but the rustle of the deep tall corn" (p. 180). The relevance of the story's title is made a little clearer with the reference to the field of corn. "Save the Reaper" constitutes an allusion to Tennyson's "Lady of Shalott," and recalls Eve's attempt to recite the poem as she drives past barley fields on the way back to the cottage. She believes that her incorrect

version, "Save the reapers, reaping early," sounds better than Tennyson's
line, "Only reapers, reaping early," and in this belief she confirms a continuing self-deception. By choosing the singular noun, Munro moves the
allusion some lines further on in the stanza, to the "reaper weary" listening
"by the moon" to the mournful song. The protagonist in her narrative is
similarly weary, and solitary, the sound she hears only the corn's rustling.

"Save the Reaper" is a narrative in which there are several unsolved
and troubling mysteries. Judith Miller interprets the "reaper" as suggestive of death, and wonders why she is so sure that the house harbors
"someone or something incriminating." I share her unease about the
house.[14] Why is the phrase "massive disorder" so potent? Who created
the mosaic walls? But I also puzzle over what kind of daughter would still
play mother-hating games when she is an adult. Several of the questions
I have about this story remain unanswered, but some of its opaqueness is
cleared if I focus on Eve's unreliable, whimsical nostalgia and consider its
consequences for her.

"Cortes Island," the shortest story in *The Love of a Good Woman*, is a
relatively transparent narrative. With regard to constituents of narrative
structure, it is one of the least complicated in Munro's *oeuvre*. For example,
the narration is wholly in the past tense, usually the simple past; there are
no anachronies, and the span of time covered is short; textual fragmentation is not substantial; and the action is mainly confined to an apartment
block in Arbutus Street, Vancouver. "Cortes Island" is so neatly compact,
so artlessly linear, that the import of its alarming characters, and their disturbing secret, is not fully grasped until the concluding paragraphs.

The unnamed narrator recounts the early months of her marriage,
when she and her husband Chess are living in a rented basement flat in
Vancouver. Much of the story is concerned with her relationship with the
elderly couple, Mr. and Mrs. Gorrie, living upstairs, and with the extreme
reactions she provokes in them. Mrs. Gorrie is portrayed as an intrusive,
malicious woman, obsessed with the vapid rituals of domesticity and eti-
quette, appalled by the narrator's ignorance of them. She is "scandalized"
when she discovers her young neighbor washes "whites and coloreds in
together," a mistake that, she accusingly tells her, shows a lack of "care of
your man" (p. 129). She reproves her young neighbor for what she regards
as slovenliness, and a lack of pride, treating her as someone in need of
general remediation. Mrs. Gorrie has to look after her invalid husband, a
stroke victim, and she pays the narrator to read to him in the afternoon.
It is when the narrator is reading from one of the old man's scrapbooks
that she learns of a troubling event in the couple's past.

That the story is told from a retrospective vantage point is indicated by the number of times the narrator refers to differences between now and then: for example, she observes that "television was still almost a novelty at that time" (p. 130), and uses the same distal time adverbial when she notes how sexual matters in newspapers were delicately mentioned "in the careful manner of that time" (p. 131). Reflections on how she reacted to her circumstances make the culture of the 1950s seem peculiarly distant from the contemporaneous level the narrator writes from. She describes, almost with incredulity, how she and Chess took great pleasure in their sexual freedom, both coming from homes where sex would be sanctioned only in marriage, and even then would be considered unmentionable. In the observation that they "were right at the end of the time of looking at things that way, though we didn't know it" (p. 123), Munro makes her narrator sound like a historian, marking the passing of an era. This kind of distancing strategy works to render Mrs. Gorrie as extraordinary, almost alien, with her freakish pink eyebrows matching "the pinkish red of her hair . . . face thin, rouged, vivacious, her teeth large and glistening" (p. 119); when introducing herself to the young couple, soon after their arrival, she wore "this wolfish smile" (p. 120).

Mr. Gorrie is portrayed as formidable, even monstrous, in his appearance and demeanor, "a large man—large head, wide shoulders, heavy bones" (p. 122). When reading to him, the narrator has time to study his face in detail, noticing "his bad eye like a stone under dark water, and . . . his original wicked teeth . . . with their dark fillings glowering through the damp enamel" (p. 131). As she becomes accustomed to him, she sees him as "an old warrior from barbarous times" (p. 132), used to exercising old privileges. His wordlessness communicates a peremptory power, when his "grunts, snorts, hawkings, barks, mumbles" (p. 133) dictate what and how the narrator should read. The character of Mr. Gorrie is developed and steadily substantiated, from a hulking, clumsy, baleful presence, to something lordly, capable of commands and obedience. His orders are not verbal, since he cannot speak, and Munro renders them first as statements and questions, enclosed in parenthesis, that her narrator imagines Mr. Gorrie would utter. These are then presented in a series of italicized imperatives, and responses, the effectiveness of which as a narrative device merits discussion.

Graphic effects can be richly exploited in literary fiction, when, for example, a writer changes fonts to "distinguish narrative strands and times, narrators or focalizers."[15] Munro often makes use of graphic expressivity, being especially fond of italics, which serve various functions in her work. Sometimes they mark off the wishful speaking or thinking of a character or narrator, as they do in "Privilege" (*The Beggar Maid*), when Rose, in her dreamy schoolgirl crush on the older Cora, imagines being rescued and nursed by her heroine, who will console her with indulgences— *"That's a pretty name. Come on up, honey"* (*The Beggar Maid*, p. 35). These words are actually spoken by the same character in a wholly different, unromantic context shortly before they are reproduced in italics, in Rose's fantasy. Italics are also used when Munro clarifies that her narrator or protagonist is inventing another character's words, in effect putting words into another mouth. At the end of "Save the Reaper," Eve thinks cynically of how the young prostitute might find the cottage, assuring a "homeless, heartless wastrel of her own age" with the words, *"I know where there's a place we can stay"* (p. 180).

In "Cortes Island" the italicized text, consisting of all the narrator thinks Mr. Gorrie is saying to her, is prominent and extensive. The man cannot speak, but his ability to communicate is not in question: the narrator infers meaning from noises and gestures, and duly obeys his wishes. When he indicates that she read to him from his scrapbooks, she has to work hard in order to interpret him, finally settling on a newspaper report from 1923. In this report she reads of the death, in a fire that destroyed his home, of an orchard owner, Anson James Wild, whose body "was found amongst the charred remains burnt almost beyond recognition" (p. 135). The report makes mention of his being a "solitary man," with a wife who was absent at the time of the tragedy, out on a boat with a friend, her return home delayed by engine trouble. The couple's young son was found unharmed near the scene of the fire.

There is one paragraph in this report that stands out from the text. Not only is it visibly the briefest, but its separation in a paragraph of its own is, according to conventions in discourse structure, stylistically marked. It reads: "A blackened tin thought to have contained kerosene was discovered within the ruins" (p. 135), and it succeeds a paragraph consisting of two expository sentences, the first relating to the destruction of the house, the second relating to the discovery of Mr. Wild's body. All these statements conveying information about the burnt house are thematically consonant, and together in one paragraph would constitute an internally coherent unit of text.[16] By disrupting the thematic consistency in this way, Munro makes the reader consider the relative importance of the detail, and wonder if the fire were started deliberately. If so, was it suicide or arson? A later news report in the *Vancouver Sun* is concerned with the subsequent inquest, recording accidental death, and it contains further information about the whereabouts of Mr. Wild's wife. She was, at the time of her husband's death, "on a boat belonging to James Thompson Gorrie of Union Bay" (p. 136).

This disclosure and the information about the kerosene coalesce with startling effect. The reader justifiably suspects wrongdoing—at the very least infidelity, possibly murder. This sense of unease is enhanced by what follows, in several lines of commands and questions, italicized to indicate their status as imagined discourse. The narrator senses that Mr. Gorrie now wants the scrapbook closed and put away carefully, before his wife returns; she interprets self-satisfaction and gleeful spite in his manner, thinking he asks:

> *There you are, what do you think of that?*
> *I don't care. I don't care what you think of it.*
> *Did you ever think that people's lives could be like that and end up like this?*
> *Well, they can.* (p. 137)

The narrator's reaction to what she reads in the reports, and what she infers from Mr. Gorrie's paralanguage, is surprisingly bland, almost indifferent. The offhand admission, "I did not tell Chess about this" (p. 137), is bathetic in its effect, and mirrors the fatalistic acceptance she thinks Mr. Gorrie expresses. Soon, his relevance to the narrator's life fades: she secures a permanent job in the Kitsilano Library, and she and Chess find a new apartment. Mr. and Mrs. Gorrie become material for anecdotes exchanged with "other young couples who had started out as we did, living in cheap spaces in other people's houses" (p. 142).

However, the old man's impact on the narrator's life lasted for a long time, for she used to have "explosive . . . erotic dreams" about him, in which he acted with lustful relish, yet looked the same as he did when she had read to him. He bore all the marks of his "ugliness" with his "pungent smell, his jelly eye, his dog's teeth" (p. 143). The narrator closes with a chastening reminder, to herself and to the reader, of what I regard as the queer bright moment in the story: the mysterious, unsolved, putatively accidental death on Cortes Island, where "the charred beams of the house [had] fallen down on the body of the husband . . . and the forest had grown up all around it" (p.145). Her conclusion retrieves the tragic death, and its concealment.

The mystery in "Cortes Island" is well hidden, in a location that is temporally and textually outside the narrative. The grisly archive has been hoarded for nearly thirty years, in the safe keeping of a rebarbative custodian, whose motives for exposing the secret are, at the very least, disquieting. Perhaps the old man wants the narrator to know of his agency, before he became a helpless invalid, "half-wrecked" and aphasic (p. 132); perhaps he wishes to exact a feeble revenge on her, resenting her youth and potential. Exactly how the narrator reacts to the revelation is not reported: it seems that, at the time, she is neither fazed nor especially intrigued. Like Maureen and Eve, the narrator withholds what she witnesses from those close to her, yet she feels its weight for a long time afterwards.

CHAPTER 5

"THE LOVE OF A GOOD WOMAN"

THE TITLE STORY OF MUNRO'S EIGHTH COLLECTION is long, dense, and intricately structured. The story's complexities are multiply caused and situated: for example, some segments of the narrative are disarranged and anachronous; instances of irony and ambiguity are numerous; omniscient and focalized perspectives are significantly, and at times disconcertingly, juxtaposed; tropes of metonymy and metaphor test the reader's cognitive and interpretative capacities. John Gerlach begins his essay on "The Love of a Good Woman" with the assertion that the story "poses problems for the reader at its conclusion—which is virtually no conclusion at all."[1] I believe that the problems are posed in other places besides the ending: to negotiate one's way through fiction that Catherine Sheldrick Ross calls "a garden of forking paths" is an exhilarating but also demanding experience, where the reader is on constant alert for diversions and ambushes.[2]

"The Love of a Good Woman" exceeds in length any other of Munro's published short stories. It is unusual, too, in having four numbered, headed sections, but, like the title itself, each of the headings is not a straightforward description. The "Heart Failure" of the second section purports to indicate the imminent death of the patient, Mrs. Quinn, who is tended by nurse Enid, the supposed "good woman"; however, the failure of the heart can be regarded as metaphorical, applicable to other characters, while the epithet "good woman" may be ironic, or may not necessarily mean the protagonist.

The protagonist does not make an entrance until well into the narrative. The story begins on the contemporaneous level, with a short prologue in which the omniscient narrator explains that the Walley museum has in its keeping an optometrist's box, which had "belonged to a Mr. D. M. Willens, who drowned in the Peregrine River, 1951" (*The Love of a Good Woman*, p. 3). The description of the optometrist's instruments is elaborate, oddly hybrid in style, with precise technical detail combining with fanciful imagery. The narrator suggests that the "ophthalmoscope could make you think of a snowman," the forehead clamp of the retinoscope "like an elf's head," with its pointed metal cap "tilted at a forty-five degree angle to a slim column" (pp. 3–4). The mixture of exactitude and imaginative analogy with objects that melt away or are unreal is remarkable, foreshadowing the narrative's indeterminacy and cryptic ambiguities.

After this contemporaneous prologue, the narration becomes analeptic. The first section consists of an account of how three local boys come upon the body of Mr. Willens, in his car in Jutland Pond, and how each, for differing reasons, finds it difficult to tell adults of the discovery. The second section is principally concerned with circumstances in the Quinn household, where the young mother is dying from an incurable disease and is being cared for by the nurse, Enid, sometimes the subject of the focalization. It is in this section that the narrator conveys information about Enid's background, stressing her dedication to a nursing career. She has in her new position renewed an acquaintance with Mrs. Quinn's husband, Rupert, a former classmate, and has grown fond of his company, hopeful of a future with him. The possibility of such a future is endangered, however, after she hears the lurid, shocking confidences that his wife delivers shortly before her death. These revelations constitute the third section. According to Mrs. Quinn, the optometrist Mr. Willens did not drown in Jutland Pond, but died in the Quinns' front room, murdered by her husband in a jealous rage when he suspected Willens of making sexual advances on his wife. The last part of this story deals with Mrs. Quinn's dying, and the consequences of that death. Does Enid dismiss the woman's tales as grotesque invention? Does she confront Rupert with her knowledge, thereby inviting danger from a putative murderer, or does she just keep quiet, in the hope that her "collaboration in a silence" (p. 76) will ensure her future happiness? The narrative's ending does not offer an unequivocal answer; indeed, the entire narrative is characterized by equivocation.

Munro's customary manipulation of time is evident at the outset when, after a brief prologue, the omniscient narrator takes the reader back to 1951, to the Peregrine River, where the optometrist's body was discovered. The time difference is inferred from aspect and tense: the present perfect in "For the last couple of decades, there has been a museum in Walley" conveys contemporaneousness, while the verb phrase in "This place was called Jutland" lets the reader know events happened in the past (pp. 3–4). What is unusual about the entire first section is that the characters so substantially drawn in it play no further part in the action, making what

Dennis Duffy calls "an abrupt exit" from the story.³ The narrator provides an expansive account of exactly where and how the boys came upon the body, how they reacted, and why they prolonged their reticence about what they saw. The section devoted to these elements is the longest of the four parts, amounting to more than a third of the text. In terms of plot, setting, and characterization, it fulfills important functions: the finding of the body is a kernel event, the man's death being the heart of the mystery; the portrayal of public and private lives in Walley, by Lake Huron (Walley is Goderich in Munro's fiction), augments and enriches one's knowledge of southwestern Ontario in the 1950s; the boys' individual traits add to the authenticity that is a hallmark of Munro's fiction. But it is in relation to narrative structure and theme that the first section of "The Love of a Good Woman" is crucial. In this respect, it is demonstrative of the writer's consummate narrative aesthetic.

The confident, authoritative narrator leads the reader from the township road out to Jutland, letting it be known, twice, that, although the car tracks by the water's edge are "easy to spot," they are not noticed by the boys, so intent are they on entering the water, in order to later boast of "swimming [there] before the snow was off the ground" (p. 5). In Munro's work, a recurrent allusion to inadvertence points to an important clue, or is a prelude to a startling revelation (as it is, for example, in "Fits"). Here, the boys' failure to notice prolongs the discovery, whetting the reader's expectations. But it has another important purpose, for it crucially alters the perspective from which the "pale-blue shine to the water" and the vehicle's cargo are viewed: oblivious to anything amiss, the boys are close to the pond's edge before they see the car, and have to squat at first, then lie on their stomachs "like turtles, trying to see" (p. 6). The details relayed by the omniscient narrator are thus vividly eccentric, childlike: the man's hand rides in the water "like a feather," the fingernails "like neat little faces." Such is the impact of the spectacle that the boys utter exclamations in tones of "deepening respect, even of gratitude" (p. 7). If the discovery were not viewed from this horizontal vantage point, and through the eyes of young boys, the scene would lose some of its potency.

How Munro continues her narrative after this memorable scene is testimony to her love of disarrangement. The drama is swiftly curtailed, the consequences of the boys' shocking encounter postponed by an unexpected anachrony that suspends answers to the questions, what do the boys do now? whom will they tell first? The narrator takes the reader back to the period before the discovery, with the casually anecdotal, "It was their first time out this year" (p. 7). The account following this introduction works as a retardatory device, frequent in Munro's anachronous and fragmented narratives, and it requires "that the reader engage in temporal re-ordering and make inferences" about what links the disrupted narrative segments.[4] Here, its function pertains not only to narrative dynamics, but also to setting and character: the narrator fleshes out a picture of the turbulent Peregrine River, rushing into Lake Huron, and conveys a sense of the boys' excited pleasure in their environment, and in their own company, familiar as they were with "each other's looks, habits, family and personal history" (p. 10). The emphasis in the account is on consuetude, and on the ordinariness of the boys' activities, once they are on the river flats, and are free, "out of range of the chimes of the courthouse clock" (p. 11).

When the boys are back within the confines of the town, after the discovery, their carefree demeanor has changed, and "jumping, dallying, splashing, were all abandoned" as they "made their way as adults would do" (p. 11). Following the return to the adult world are reports on each boy's peculiar domestic circumstances, which explain their reluctance to tell of what lies in Jutland Pond. Cece Ferns is scared of his violent, alcoholic father, from whose unpredictable rages he has built a hiding place; Bud Salter has to contend with two self-centered, vacuous sisters who would sneeringly diminish their brother's tale, were he allowed to tell it; Jimmy Box's household is so cramped and impoverished that there is little space for any member of the extended family to hold court. The narrator methodically explains each boy's handicap, the reasons that might account for why "they all kept their mouths shut, all three of them" (p. 21). They meet after their dinner to confirm their silence, before, ironically, fastening on the most inappropriate of audiences for their disclosure—a deaf, somnolent special constable, who does not fix his hearing aid in time to understand them, and they run off. The suspense ends tamely, when Bud eventually tells his mother, who contacts the police.

In her decision to devote so much space to the discovery of the body, and its aftermath, Munro takes a risk, but it is rewarding. The "Jutland" section works as a slice of social documentary, depicting "working class lives in the north end of town" (p. 11); it offers the reader the chance to view events through sharp young lenses; the nonlinear presentation creates narrative suspense, and serves as a means of marking off the territory of childhood, where the three boys act like "free—almost free—agents" from the adult world of responsibility they must enter with "the weight on them of where they had to go and what had to be done" (pp. 10–11). Moreover, and most importantly, the first section firmly establishes the themes of keeping quiet, not telling, opting for an expedient silence, themes that are made prominent in the remainder of the narrative.

Enid does not tell Rupert about what she has learned from his wife; she does not record the whole truth about the manner of her patient's dying; she does not, it would appear, inform authorities of what Mrs. Quinn told her about how Willens died. One anachronous segment, near the conclusion, allows the reader greater insight into why Enid prefers reticence and silence. After Mrs. Quinn's death and funeral, she returns to the house, dressed in her finery, armed with her plans: she will ask Rupert to take her out in his boat, and on the river she will confront him with what she knows, urging him to confess. She is sure her "gamble" will pay off, and that he will agree, his "first step in a long, dreadful journey" (p. 73). But she panics when her plan gathers momentum, and she makes an excuse to enter the sickroom. It is here that she has her inspiration, not to tell, not to go ahead with her scheme. In the now bare and empty room, Enid recalls Mrs. Quinn's mocking verdict on confidences Enid claimed her patients shared with her, "Lies . . . *Lies. I bet it's all lies*" (p. 74). She now applies this judgment to Mrs. Quinn's confession, and to her own question, "Could a person make up something so detailed and diabolical?" she decides the answer is yes, if they were the product of "a dying person's mind" (p. 74).

This readjustment is made easier by the memory of her father's infidelity, which she witnessed as a child when she burst into his office. Her mother had dismissed her daughter's account as a dream, an explanation Enid later accepted. The episode, occupying little textual space, is inserted after Enid's recollection of her patient's outbursts, and before the story's final scene, the walk to the water with Rupert, which she undertakes knowing that "she hadn't asked him yet, she hadn't spoken. Nothing yet committed her to asking" (p. 75). Enid's memory conveniently provides her with what Ross describes as the "recognition of the benefits of secrecy."[5] The brief flashback is ended with the word "*Lies*" repeated once more, made salient by italics, and its isolation in a paragraph. Munro uses all these different devices—lexical reiteration, graphic expressivity, temporal disruption, and narrative configuration—in order to accord importance to this pivotal memory.

The fourth section of "The Love of a Good Woman" is entitled "Lies," but its specific referent is ambiguous. It is, finally, how Enid designates Mrs. Quinn's accounts of Willens's death. She can then justify her decision not to confront Rupert with his wife's accusations, but instead do nothing, and collude in secrecy. Throughout the narrative Enid is shown to be guilty of deceits and evasions; she had broken a promise to her father when she continued in her nursing career; she lies to Rupert about her real motives for returning to the house after her patient's death; when she starts weeping in the sickroom, her tears are not out of grief, as her companion would think, but "with an onslaught of relief" (p. 76) that she can now look forward to the benefits accruing to her. When she chooses to categorize what she has heard as "lies," Enid, ironically, reacts just as her patient had predicted when she said, "I could tell you something you wouldn't believe" (p. 56), before beginning her shocking account.

Several instances of irony in "The Love of a Good Woman" relate to the protagonist, since what Enid says to and about her patient is often the opposite of what she thinks. She thus weakens the claim that her "hope was to be good, and do good, and not necessarily in the orderly, customary, wifely way" (p. 42). When Olive Green, Rupert's sister, gives her the scant information she has about Mrs. Quinn's background—she had been a chambermaid, and was raised in a Montreal orphanage—Enid condescendingly deems it "an interesting life" (p. 33), when she thinks otherwise. In an emotive passage where she is the subject of the focalization, she exposes her snobbery, likening Mrs. Quinn to "girls she had known in high school—cheaply dressed, sickly looking girls with dreary futures." Although Enid is a practiced and competent nurse, she finds her present duties difficult, for "she could not conquer her dislike of this doomed, miserable young woman" (p. 38), and is revolted by her physical decay, her coarseness. She even attributes the symptoms of Mrs. Quinn's disease to "a willed corruption," this attitude jarring with the ethos of her profession, as well as with "her nature—to be compassionate" (p. 38). Ross points out that "Enid is the strongest candidate for the role of "good woman," but there is evidence that this appellation is not always merited, and may even be ironic.[6]

Just as the "Lies" in the title is ambiguous, so is the heading of the second section, "Heart Failure." For a start, the specific phrase is located in Enid's medical report, contained in the fourth, and final, section. Mrs. Quinn's death is not recorded in the place prefigured by the heading, and this dislocation suggests the heart failure may have a broader application. Underneath the heading is the medical term *glomerulonephritis*, which Enid has written in her notebook. The narrator explains that "Mrs. Quinn's kidneys were failing, and nothing could be done about it" and goes on to list the unpleasant symptoms of the disease—the "acrid and ominous [breath], spasms of sudden pain [and] violent itching" that caused "torment" (p. 31). The clinical cataloging of this young mother's terminal condition would surely provoke compassion in any context, certainly in a caregiver. Later disclosures of the nurse's revulsion and dislike of her patient, then, are surprising, especially in light of her saintly reputation in the community (p. 44). She betrays a lack of warmth toward

Mrs. Quinn, and the evidence encourages me to regard "heart failure" as signifying, yes, the cause of death, but also indicating coldheartedness.

It is in this section, too, that the narrator recounts the sexually disturbing "ugly dreams" Enid has, when she sleeps on the couch in Mrs. Quinn's room. In them she is "slick with lust," driven by a "coldness of heart" that, when she awakens, makes her feel disgusted and humiliated (p. 51). She prefers to dismiss these dreams as "just the mind's garbage," embarking on a nocturnal cleaning regime as the "best way to be penitent" (p. 52). One could interpret these dreams as symbolic of Enid's sexual repression, a reading Ross considers in her essay,[7] or one could see them as emanating from a discomfort with her present duties—caring for someone who disgusts her, and whom she despises. As a nurse, she is repressing the emotions she *should* feel. It is significant, I would argue, that the narrator reports how Enid, when she lies awake trying to recover her equilibrium, hears the "sick woman's breath grating and *scolding*" (p. 51, italics added). Perhaps Enid imagines that she is being scolded for her "coldness of heart."

Mrs. Quinn is negatively portrayed, but she is usually perceived through the hostile eyes of her nurse. She would not, in Enid's estimation, merit the epithet "a good woman," for she is a poor housekeeper who has allowed her two girls to become "as wild as little barn cats" (p. 34) and who seems indifferent to her husband's company. She is bitterly self-mocking, insisting that the household will greet her death with expressions of relief: "That's what you'll all say. Good riddance to bad rubbish" (p. 36). The idiom is later retrieved, when the narrator reports that Enid senses Mrs. Quinn's intuiting of her dislike; Munro draws attention to the phrase by italicizing it, and by placing it in a separate paragraph just before an ellipsis, encouraging the reader to interpret it as Enid's wishful thinking. The nursing care she administers is dutiful and accomplished, but it comes over, somehow, as reflexive, lacking in spontaneous sympathy. When she asks her patient if she wants a minister to visit her, Enid tries to sound solicitous, but she is conscious that "the spirit in which she ask[s] [is] cold and faintly malicious," and she has to concentrate on "making herself speak compassionately and encouragingly" to her patient (p. 54).

Her treatment of Mrs. Quinn in her last day of life could be considered quite callous, hardly befitting a reputation as an "angel of mercy" in the Walley community (p. 52). On the morning after she has heard her patient's revelations, Enid is in a quandary about what to do with the new information. She is sure the "wicked, outpouring talk" is the woman's "last spurt of energy" (p. 64), yet she neglects to stay by her bedside, walking out into the meadow by the farmhouse, when "she knew that she should go back, instead, and check on Mrs. Quinn" (p. 63). She summons "bountiful good spirits" as she prepares treats for the woman's daughters, with the result that they sense "holiday possibilities" from her "unusual mix of languor and excitement." In the description of the day's events, the omniscient narrator manages to present Enid's actions and thoughts in an unfavorable light, for example, "She wanted to make the day a special one for them, special aside from the fact—which she was already certain of—that it would be the day of their mother's death" (p. 64). In the previous example, the rhetorical scheme of anadiplosis focuses attention on the word "special," and invites the reader to consider its incongruity in the context. Because the ensuing relative clause is enclosed in parenthesis, the imminence of the woman's death is relegated, in Enid's value system, to the status of an afterthought. Explaining that Enid wishes the children to remember something pleasant, something that would "throw a redeeming light on whatever came later," the narrator wryly adds, "On herself, that is, and whatever way she would affect their lives later" (p. 64). This explicit appositive clarifies the nurse's true motives.

Enid neglects her nursing duties: she does not bother to take her patient's blood pressure or temperature; she does not immediately call the doctor; she neither speaks to the dying woman nor touches her hand, but finds the time to relax on the steps of the house, "stretch[ing] out her legs in the sun" (p. 65). The disclosure that Mrs. Quinn dies with her "head hanging over the side of the bed," the "sheet pulled out," constitutes a poignant image, and provides further evidence of Enid's withdrawal of care. Once again, the narrator adds a telling piece of information—that Enid "did not record or mention to anybody" (p. 67) this detail in her concluding notes. These laconic notes compose a short segment of text separated from the narrative by two ellipses. Munro's configuration serves to mark off and highlight the section, the content of which is surprisingly heterogeneous, a mixture of clinical record and personal diary, as in, "July 6. Hot day, vy close. Try fan but no. Sponge often. RQ in evening. Start to cut wheat tomorrow. Everything 1 or 2 wks ahead due to heat, rain" (p. 67). Especially noteworthy is the number of times Enid mentions Rupert Quinn (RQ). There are four allusions, four in six days' entries, to his activities and concerns; the references to her dying patient are all negative, documenting her complaints, her resistance, her "terrible talk"; significant, too, is how Enid chooses to record the death, referring to her patient patronymically as "Mrs. Rupert (Jeanette) Quinn" (p. 67). This is the only time in the entire narrative that the woman's forename appears, as a bracketed afterthought.

Coral Ann Howells wonders, as I do, why Enid dislikes Mrs. Quinn so much, and "why there is such a strong sense of mutual hostility between the two women."[8] It is easier to understand the peevish antipathy of a terminally ill woman who, in her husband's judgment, "wasn't lucky in her life" (p. 76): less explicable are the nurse's feelings of disdain, and the deliberate withholding of pity. In her essay on Munro's story, Judith McCombs argues that "Enid feels her goodness and vocation fail" when it is opposed by "Mrs. Quinn's vulgar sexuality, her bitter mockery, her repudiations of conventional comfort."[9] McCombs believes that the nurse's hostility toward her patient derives not only from her "righteousness and prudery, but also sexual rivalry with Mrs. Quinn."[10] I am not so generous in my evaluation of Enid: the goodness McCombs sees in her character I interpret as merely a reflexive sense of duty, professional competence devoid of empathy or tenderness. Other readers and other Munro scholars might regard the character of Enid less critically, the character of Jeanette Quinn more harshly. Dennis Duffy, for example, describes the latter as "bitter, vicious, indifferent to her husband and children" and he notes that "there is a hint that her fatal illness originated in a reaction" to an abortifacient drug."[11] It should be remembered, however, that this "hint" derives from Olive Green's uninformed speculation. Munro provides no definite answer as to how the woman fell victim to the disease that would kill her: Rupert Quinn's assessment, that his wife has had little luck in her life, seems accurate. Much in this narrative remains ambiguous and cryptic.

No doubt readers and scholars will disagree on the meanings of certain images in "The Love of a Good Woman," which Munro makes salient by, for example, her syntax, or by the use of cohesive devices like reiteration, or by some disruption in the text's continuity. For a start, what symbolic significance is to be made of the museum's red box, which appears in the prologue? That Munro accords elaborate and vivid detail to the description indicates its weight. Of course, it prefigures the discovery of the instruments' owner, Mr. Willens, apparently drowned in the Peregrine River, and thus serves as a catalyst for the flashback. More specifically, the alleged murder of the optometrist is cleverly foreshadowed in the reference to paint, since the "ugly brown paint" (p. 53) applied to the Quinns' front room floor to cover bloodstains emerges as a crucial clue. After rereading and studying "The Love of a Good Woman," I return to the red box to view its constituent parts less literally: the hole in the ophthalmoscope through which "various lenses" are moved makes me think of how the perspective shifts in Munro's narrative, as the omniscient narrator gives way to the subject of the focalization, the character Enid; the fact that the retinoscope has a "flat face [that] is a dark sort of mirror" (p. 4) strikes me as an understated nod toward the story's opaqueness. Ordinary, harmless objects are transformed in the search for deeper meaning. On my first encounter with this story, I wondered why Munro presents the minor character, Mrs. Willens, so fully, and why she highlights her skill as a gardener, making much of the "only thing in bloom . . . a forsythia bush at the corner of the house" (p. 22). This shrub assumes a life of its own, "spray[ing] yellow into the air the way a fountain shoots water," its branches shaking with the movement of "a stooped brown figure . . . a lumpy little woman" who emerges from its cover (p. 23). I infer from the cameo portrait the character's cheerful eccentricity, but it is the forsythia bush that interests me most. First of all, it is, as Ross observes, a "seasonal marker,"[12] and the information that it flowers early in spring enables me to make the temporal reordering in order to trace the precise sequence of events after Mr. Willens's death, and before the onset of Mrs. Quinn's fatal illness, in the sweltering summer heat. Second, the forsythia bush obscures Mrs. Willens from view: she is hidden by it as the three boys approach her house, and the branches she cuts off for them to take home are described as a "screen of flowers" in front of her (p. 23). It is tempting to treat the shrub as one of several images in the narrative that sustain the idea of protective cover, of concealment. Munro may be suggesting that Mrs. Willens is a deceptively flat character who is not to be categorized as merely the optometrist's widow: the narrator reports that she has grown accustomed to her husband's irregular hours, perhaps turning a blind eye to the reasons. At any rate, when Mrs. Willens comes forward to the three boys with the present of her forsythia, she, like them, is withholding, for she has not told anyone of her partner's absence.

There is something hushed and secretive, too, about the way that Enid cultivates Rupert's company, and interest in her, while she is his wife's nurse. He returns home "later and later in the evenings" (p. 45), after working in the fields, and would often sit with Enid, having brought her the newspaper. One night he finds the house in darkness, as she has allowed the children to sleep downstairs. The front room is candlelit; Enid rushes to quiet him and explain the circumstances; the couple exchange "whispered conversation" (p. 46). She pours tea for him; then they share the newspaper, Enid coyly and self-deprecatingly inviting his help with the crossword clues. The scene is cozily domestic but also rather clandestine when one considers that Rupert's wife lies in her sickbed, unaware. How Enid prepares for the expected demise of Mrs. Quinn, and her hoped for ensconcement in her place, yields further evidence of the nurse's sly purposefulness.

The weeks she spends nursing Mrs. Quinn are especially hot and wet, with the result that there is tremendous fertility in the land. "Everything was ahead of itself, as people said": the trees and grass are drenched, "bushes all bound up with wild grapevines and Virginia creeper," and "hay ready to cut in June . . . before the rain spoiled it" (p. 45). Growth is quickened, as are Enid's affections for Rupert and her plans for a future with him. Images of bloated growth and excess recur when the narrator describes how Enid indulges the children on the day of their mother's death. Dishes of jelly are "crammed with fruit" (p. 64), glasses of milk sweetened with chocolate syrup; Enid shows the children how to blow bubbles, "blowing steadily and carefully until as large a shining bladder as possible trembled on the wire" (p. 65). Enid is depicted in expansive mood, her good spirits bountiful at the prospect of what might accrue to her.

The final scene by the river presents Enid seemingly poised on the threshold of romance. The season's fecundity is illustrated in "the big fleshy thistles" Rupert cuts down, and in "the roof of summer leaves" the couple walk under, toward a path overhung by vines, where "roots [have] swelled up" (p. 78). In Munro's work, luxuriant growth in the landscape is sometimes associated with sensual pleasure for the female narrator or protagonist: reference was made previously to the opening of "Five Points," where lovers Brenda and Neil, desperate for each other, meet on a side road thick with rampant vegetation. But features in this riverbank setting can be interpreted as harbingers of danger—the protruding roots that "you had to watch that you didn't trip over," the overhanging vines that might "hit your head," the fading light itself (p. 78). (Several Munro scholars note, moreover, that Rupert is carrying a little hatchet.) The signs are not assuredly propitious.

The boat predominates. It was featured earlier, at the start of the fourth section, after Enid has heard Mrs. Quinn's outpourings and seeks the riverbank to think. Attracted by the boat's movement on the water, she imagines that its gentle rocking tells her, "*You know. You know*" (p. 64), a reminder of the onerous information she possesses. At first Enid thinks of the boat as a kind of nemesis, where she will confront Rupert, or meet her fate, but she is saved from that dilemma by her timely reappraisal of Mrs. Quinn's stories as lies. Rowing out in the river under the willow trees is now associated with "an entirely different possibility" (p. 76). The image of the boat works metonymically, but the associations change: first of all, it betokens for Enid the burden of responsibility, maybe even conscience, then it represents possible fulfillment, but a conditional one. By isolating the figure of the boat in a single paragraph, "And the boat waiting, riding in the shadows, just the same" (p. 78), Munro makes it prominent. The narrator explains, "if [Enid] concentrated on the boat's slight and secretive motion, she could feel as if everything for a long way around had gone quiet" (p. 78). The little conjunction "if" plays a crucial part here. The clause it initiates expresses a condition, namely that the "situation in the matrix clause is directly contingent on that of the conditional."[13] By its use, Munro reminds the reader that the benefits Enid anticipates come at a price: the retention of a secret, a secret represented by the boat's gently rocking motion.

The ending is indeterminate. As Gerlach explains, "we wait with Enid at the termination of the final page [for] we've reached the limits of what we can know."[14] The reader can only speculate, reinforcing the speculation with textual evidence. Whereas Duffy sees Enid as "the clueless Gothic heroine" about to embrace "a demon lover,"[15] I regard her as far from hapless or vulnerable, but rather, single minded and determined, someone who grasps the opportunity presented to her. It makes sense to imagine that she will marry Rupert Quinn and take over a house "where all order [is] as she ha[s] decreed" (p. 77), for she has demonstrated considerable aplomb in the pursuit of her objectives. She is likely to be the anonymous donor who sends the red box to the Walley museum, finding it perhaps in the woodshed bin she had never looked into (p. 76). There is no revelatory prolepsis explaining how Enid will enjoy the benefits of the chance she would not balk at: Munro instead concludes her narrative with allusions to muted sound and obscured vision.

"The Love of a Good Woman" has attracted a great deal of critical attention, which is not surprising when one considers the story's length, density, and figurative richness. Ross calls it "an encyclopedic reservoir of . . . previous Munro stories" from which loyal readers will hear particular echoes affecting one's interpretation.[16] For instance, one might find in the character of Enid similarities to the intrusive and manipulative nurse, Audrey Atkinson, from "Friend of My Youth." Elements in the story are distinctively Munrovian—the landscape by the Peregrine River, the working-class lives of small town Ontario.

It is because of the story's challenging complexity that I devote a chapter to discussing it. It is ambitious in terms of its structure: on first reading, one wonders why substantially drawn characters in the first and longest section disappear from the scene so abruptly. The shifts in narrative perspective are so subtle that it is sometimes not immediately clear whether events are being viewed through the lenses of the heterodiegetic narrator or through those of the subject of the focalization, the character Enid. The potent image from the prologue instantly comes to mind—of the hole one looks through, "as the various lenses are moved," sometimes blurring and distorting, but also clarifying. The piece illustrates Munro's customary manipulation of time: it begins on the contemporaneous level, with a brief framing prologue, while the ensuing narrative is analeptic, focusing on events in 1951. In "The Love of a Good Woman," however, Munro makes greater use of brief snatches of anachrony within the anachronous account, and these serve mainly as retardatory devices, affording the narrator the opportunity for exposition, or for ironic comment. What is contained in one such pocket of retrospection, Enid's childhood memory, is immensely important for an understanding of her character, the facility with which she can justify inaction and silence.

The workings of memory continue to exercise Munro. In the stories I discuss next, from *Hateship, Friendship, Courtship, Loveship, Marriage* and *Runaway*, I argue that there are subtle changes apparent in how she presents the interplay between characters' past and present lives. Memory is not always seen as a source of guilt or a reminder of disappointment, it can sometimes be a means of escape, even a shelter. Many of these later stories are shaped by the effects of memory on the protagonist, as when, for example, in "The Bear Came over the Mountain," an abruptly introduced, incongruous textual fragment suggests the associative quality of Grant's tender nostalgia.

CHAPTER 6

WHAT IS REMEMBERED

IN ITS STRUCTURAL SOPHISTICATION, RICHNESS OF THEME, and moral complexity, "The Love of a Good Woman" is one of the most thought-provoking stories in Munro's *oeuvre*, arguably her most ambitious achievement. In the two collections published in the first half of the 2000s, namely *Hateship, Friendship, Courtship, Loveship, Marriage* and *Runaway*, the writer continues to surprise and challenge readers, and scholars. Much in the fictive territory is familiar—the southwest Ontario settings; one narrator's impulsive infidelity, another's long-practiced aloofness—but the reader will notice some changes in the landscape.

A few are superficial. For example, the titles of the stories in *Runaway* differ from previous ones in that they are all single words, and mostly abstract nouns. A cursory sweep over past collections shows that the rarely occurring single-word titles, for example, "Marrakesh," "Dulse," and "Lichen," tend to be either proper or concrete nouns. This later preference for abstraction might signify nothing at all, but it does constitute a change in her convention. Moreover, as in *The Beggar Maid* and, to a lesser extent, in two of the so-called Helen stories in *The Moons of Jupiter*, the writer has created linked stories that chronicle stages in a female character's life.

Aspects of narrative aesthetic that are by now familiar in Munro's work, for example, temporal disordering and alternations in perspective, also distinguish these two collections. There are noteworthy differences, however, for most of the stories in *Hateship*, and all but one in *Runaway*, are told entirely by a heterodiegetic narrator, and when the protagonist becomes the center of consciousness, the external voice is rarely muted for long. Moreover, the temporal location of a particular narrative episode is, in most cases, overtly signaled, with transitions from one time to another not so frequently executed, and boundaries firmly demarcated. The overwhelming impression gleaned from many of the stories is cinematic. Scenes are captured in their discrete lucidity and brilliance, held and "snapped shut" in the memory, "gathered in like treasure and finished with, set aside."[1] Memory is of immense importance, shaping the direction a narrative takes. Meriel, in "What Is Remembered" (*Hateship*), returns wistfully to an event in her young adulthood that might have radically altered the direction her present life has taken; Grace, the protagonist of "Passion," revisits a place she knew well in her youth, hoping she might see it perfectly preserved, but instead finds it "diminished, still existing but made irrelevant."[2]

I have chosen two stories—"Nettles" from *Hateship*, and "Tricks" from *Runaway*—for my particular scrutiny, believing they clearly illustrate fresh emphases and strategies in the writer's narrative craft. Before discussing them, I would like to make some general comments about the fiction Munro publishes in the late twentieth and early twenty-first century, believing it constitutes an identifiable period in Munro's *oeuvre*—a time when her characters are noticeably older, older than middle age, and when nearly all go through periods when they are out of kilter, displaced. One reviewer asserts, "Her characters are . . . separated from their home not by distance but by their own changes. They travel from country to city, from poverty to wealth, from ignorance to sophistication, but they are always looking backward, at what they have left behind."[3] In her depiction of Eve, the protagonist of "Save the Reaper," Munro conveys an older woman's sense of familial estrangement. In *Hateship* and *Runaway* she is exploring in great depth themes of exile and alienation, most poignantly in the triptych of "Chance," "Soon," and "Silence," from *Runaway*; she is also examining other ways whereby one can be estranged—by the fugacity of memory, and by its loss.

It is a not surprising fact that Munro's female characters have grown older with their creator. Most of the narrators and protagonists in her later work are women who are no longer middle age; usually they have, like Pauline in "The Children Stay," gone away, and stayed away for decades, from the lives they once led (*The Love of a Good Woman*, p. 213). When the writer takes her reader back to transformative episodes in her characters' pasts—at what they have left behind—she tunnels far. The story "Jakarta" begins anachronously, at a time when one of the main characters, Kent Mayberry, is a young father, married to Kath; in the present, he has been through at least two marriages, is likely in his sixties, and cannot travel long car journeys without his pills, without feeling tired out (p. 86). In the opening paragraphs of "Jakarta," the *exact* time of the action is not given. It soon becomes clear that the narration is retrospective, although the tense and aspect provide no immediate clues: "Kath and Sonje have a place of their own on the beach, behind some large logs. They have chosen this not only for shelter from the occasional wind—they've got Kath's baby with them—but because they want to be out of sight of women who use the beach every day" (p. 80). The impression conveyed is of habituation and routine: the location is specific, and invariably chosen, while the perfective aspect conveys the sense of prior time preceding the present, past actions with current relevance. Munro's strategies heighten the narrated experience, stressing its peculiar, static quality. At the end of this scene the narration becomes contemporaneous, and the relationships between the young women on the beach and the older man journeying across North America, visiting relatives from several families, are established. Much has changed in the intervening years: the characters in this opening scene will not remain long in the roles they occupy when introduced.

Munro's care with her fictional chronology is legendary. In her later work she has become more precise with her dating. It is true that in one or two earlier stories specific years are mentioned, as in "Oranges and Apples," where the opening dialogue is spoken "in the spring of 1955" (*Friend of My Youth*, p. 107). However, such examples are not numerous. Certain stories in *The Love of a Good Woman* begin at clearly marked points in time (e.g., "Rich as Stink," where the character Karin is presented waiting at the airport "on a summer evening in 1974" [p. 215]). In both *Hateship* and *Runaway*, specific indicators of time are likewise evident early on. The first-person narrative "Nettles" is initiated by the temporal adverbial "In the summer of 1979" (*Hateship*, p. 154); "Chance," from *Runaway*, begins, "Halfway through June, in 1965" (p. 48); and Nancy's first diary entry in "Powers" is dated "March 13, 1927" (p. 270). The narrator might not mention the actual year, but a cultural or historical allusion will suffice, as it does in "Family Furnishings," from *Hateship*. Because the opening scene presents the narrator's father and his cousin as children, playing in a stubble field, where they "stomped on the ice and enjoyed its crackle underfoot," the reader recognizes a flashback that is soon confirmed by the elegiac, "It was the end of the First World War" (p. 84).

The reader of Munro's fiction is usually able to determine, quickly, whether the initial action is concurrent or retrospective. Tense markers are not always the means of knowing. Monika Fludernik points to the increasing frequency of present-tense narration in current literary fiction, and notes that often "tense has little to do with time, or even with temporal categories *per se*."[4] She discusses various instances of grammatical idiosyncrasy in modern narrative fiction, arguing that the purpose "must be sought in literary effect and the artificial shaping of language as deliberate literary strategy."[5] Most of her illustrative examples come from Michael

Ondaatje's novel *The English Patient* (1992), but Fludernik might well have chosen Munro's work to corroborate her thesis. Few writers are as dexterous or as purposeful in their use of tense and aspect as Munro, as I consistently argue: in shifts between narrative past and present, her "subtle modulations of tense" are a huge part of her aesthetic.[6] In her later work she employs these nuances of tense and aspect just as often and as successfully. But it is Munro's use of deixis, rather than tense, that is often the more accurate means of temporal signposting. There are signs of a heavier reliance on temporal deictics, terms or expressions like "here" and "yesterday," that anchor utterances to their contexts much more firmly than tenses, the usage of which has become, in literary fiction, increasingly arbitrary.

Time in fiction is, of course, different from real or empirical time, which is conceived of as a continuum where a point of reference offers a view back into the past and forward into the future. As Fludernik observes, "what complicates matters in fictional narrative is the determining of that focal point of reference."[7] In Munro's work, and particularly in these later stories of *Hateship* and *Runaway*, the importance of deixis in the identification of focal points is crucial, because customary expressions of duration, sequence, and chronology—namely tense and aspect—are not assumed to be reliable, as in the beginning of "What Is Remembered," from *Hateship*: "In a hotel room in Vancouver, Meriel as a young woman is putting on her short white summer gloves. She wears a beige linen dress and a flimsy white scarf over her hair. Dark hair, at that time" (p. 217). Although the verb phrases are the simple present and the present progressive, the appositive "as a young woman" strongly suggests a looking back, which the distal deictic determiner in "at that time" confirms. Indicated as an afterthought, this tiny physical detail encourages the reader to imagine Meriel now as an older woman with graying or dyed hair.

The opening sentences of "Passion," from *Runaway*, offer fascinating material for the grammarian and the narratologist. In this short passage there are instances of deixis other than temporal. Different periods in fictive time are inferred from tense and aspect, and the markers of temporal deixis provide the nuances, while those of discourse and emotional deixis express the solid presence of the narrator: "Not too long ago, Grace went looking for the Traverses' summer house in the Ottawa Valley. She had not been in that part of the country for many years, and of course there had been changes. Highway 7 now avoided towns that it used to go right through . . . And this part of the Canadian Shield has many small lakes, which the usual sort of map has no room to identify" (p. 159). "Passion" begins with Grace's return to Bailey's Falls, where she made a life-altering decision, not to marry the younger son in the Travers family, Maury, who was expecting her to be his bride. What influenced her decision was her brief elopement with Neil, the unhappily married older brother, an adventure that convinced her that staying with and marrying Maury would be a "treachery to herself" (p. 190). The adverbial at the start of the quoted passage is vague, implying an indefinite moment in the recent past. Why "not too long ago" is preferred to merely *not long ago* is, perhaps, because the expression comes over as informal, like the gambit of oral anecdote. The narrator establishes a comfortable authority further strengthened by the mention of the new directions Highway 7 has taken, and by the subsequent observation about the landscape and its topography. The present tenses refer to the "here and now" of a heterodiegetic narrator familiar with "this part of the Canadian Shield." The proximal "this" is an instance of discourse deixis, because it relates not to time, but to an immediately preceding piece of text, namely Highway 7. By specifying "this" the narrator narrows the field of reference, for "that part" relates to a much wider area, the Ottawa Valley, and, in addition, is grammatically compatible with the past-perfective aspect.

One could argue that the kind of deixis illustrated in the sentence beginning "And this part of" is empathetic or emotional deixis, a little theorized phenomenon, common in colloquial style, which is intended to achieve closeness, as a spatiotemporal *this* does. The pioneering linguist Robin Lakoff argues that the variety is used "to give greater vividness to the narrative, to involve the addressee . . . more fully," and she considers the device appropriate only in informal contexts.[8] Whether this instance of deixis in "Passion" exemplifies the discourse or emotional type may seem a matter of tedious sophistry to some, but to me it represents one of many interpretative challenges encountered in studying Munro's fiction. By opting for "this part" rather than "that part" of the Canadian Shield the narrator sounds less distant, in manner, and in terms of an understanding of the locale.

In a short space of text, the reader travels through three time zones—a period shortly before the present, a time far back in the past, maybe several decades ago, and what is understood as now, in real or empirical time. What is also achieved in the introduction is the firm placing of the deictic center, the linguistic term for the anchorage points in discourse.[9] These comprise, principally, the central speaker (or narrator), the central time and place at which the utterance is produced, and the point the speaker (or narrator) has reached in the production of the utterance. The deictic center is *now*, in *this part* of the Shield dense in unidentifiable lakes, a place the protagonist, Grace, returns to after many years, finding it greatly changed. "Now there was a village," reports the narrator (p. 160). Such idiosyncrasy, call it grammatical incompatibility, namely "the past-tense verb in collocation with a deictic like *now*," is common in modern literary fiction; it illustrates what Fludernik calls the "presentifying" function of the past tense,[10] and here it transfers the deictic center into the consciousness of the character, Grace, who is the subject of the focalization in the ensuing narrative.

In Munro's later work, and particularly in stories narrated in the third person, indicators of the deictic center are, sometimes, not immediately apparent, nor are they firm points of anchorage. Tense and aspect alone cannot be relied upon to tell whether the action narrated is roughly contemporaneous, recently or long since past, or imagined in the future. The initial sentences of "Post and Beam," in *Hateship*, read "Lionel told them how his mother had died. She had asked for her make-up. Lionel held the mirror" (p. 186). The past tense of narration is no indicator of how recent Lionel's telling is, nor is it immediately clear in which character's consciousness the deictic center will be located: it could be Lionel, or one of "them." The use of the less common, stylistically marked cataphoric pronoun reference, where the pronoun precedes its coreferential noun phrase, alerts the reader's curiosity as to the identities of Lionel's interlocutors, Lorna and Brendan. These are not revealed until some paragraphs later, where the centrality of Lorna is gradually established, as the narrator reports on her feelings and attitudes toward Lionel, and his mother, who, surprisingly, turns out to be a minor character. It is not until the very end that the entire narrative is confirmed as retrospective, concerned with events in an unsettled period in Lorna's marriage to the much older Brendan, a mathematics professor who once taught Lionel. "It was a long time ago that this happened," the narrator finally informs the reader, as though partly justifying, partly excusing how Lorna, "when she was twenty-four years old," had come to accept a reduced happiness, which was "nothing now but what she or anybody could sensibly foresee" (p. 216) in the days ahead.

That one slice of a life has been suddenly separated from its body of accumulated years is a recurrent sensation when reading these later stories. In "The Bear Came Over the Mountain," from *Hateship*, the protagonist, Grant, makes his regular visit to the nursing home where his wife, Fiona, has been recently admitted. Anguished by the sound of Fiona's "soft talk and laughter" as she sits with her new companion Aubrey in the conservatory, their "bower," Grant stares forlornly into the fountain's pool and reminisces. He thinks of when he and Fiona were students, watching a baseball game, and recalls "the skittering of their hands, the shift of haunches, eyes never lifted from the field" (pp. 294–95). The pleasure of this vivid reminiscence, sectioned off by two ellipses, contrasts with the painful agitation he now endures, "stalking and prowling" through the corridors, "trailing around after Fiona and Aubrey" (p. 295).

"Silence" is the concluding one of three stories in *Runaway* chronicling stages in Juliet's eventful life. Its opening scene presents the character aboard a ferryboat, making the short trip to Denman Island to visit her daughter Penelope, who has been staying in a spiritual retreat and has not been allowed visitors. The narrator, in consistent present tenses, describes a "striking-looking woman" (p. 126) often recognized by strangers because of her successful television career. A fellow passenger strikes up a conversation with Juliet, much of it relayed verbatim. Such a carefully detailed segment of dialogue in fiction constitutes a scene, regarded as slow in terms of narrative speed, and intended to convey essential character indices. What Juliet reveals in the conversation is how much she has missed Penelope—how, according to the narrator, "one day without some contact with her daughter is hard to bear, let alone six months" (p. 127). This scene on the ferry crossing contains a singular episode in the protagonist's life, when she is presented as a woman in her professional prime, a devoted mother excited at the prospect of being reunited with her beloved daughter. By the end of the story the reader knows that the reunion never takes place, for Penelope, for reasons undetermined, decides to cut off all communication with her mother. Near the end of "Silence" the narrator asserts, "the Penelope Juliet sought was gone" (p. 157), the laconic finality in such brutal contrast to the expansive, joyous optimism captured earlier.

What the narrator identifies is a stark truth that Juliet must accept: she no longer knows her daughter, and her daughter does not wish to know about her, any more. She has become a wholly different person, the kind of character the adolescent Rose in "Wild Swans" admires, who "can manage a transformation like that [and] enter on preposterous adventures in your own, newly named skin" (*The Beggar Maid*, p. 67). In these later stories, where the female protagonist is in contemporary time an older woman, at least in her sixties, the memory works harder with the imagination to re-create something that is perhaps "diminished, still existing but made irrelevant." What is remembered may not be entirely accurate, for she feels justified in returning "to her memory, editing it and revising it to suit her."[11]

In "Passion," for instance, the narrator, having recounted events that led to Grace's life-altering decision, explains that Grace cannot be sure if she recalls accurately Neil's final words to her, or, indeed, if he spoke at all when they parted: "she does not know to this day if those words were spoken, or if he only caught her [and] wound his arms around her" (*Runaway*, p. 195). The aptly entitled "What Is Remembered" is concerned with the treachery and selectivity of memory. Meriel, as a young woman, boldly embarks on a sexual adventure with a man she meets at the funeral of a friend of her husband's; he is usually referred to as "the doctor," as though he were a stereotype from a Harlequin romance. To add to his exotic appeal, he is a flying doctor, with his own plane. He offers Meriel a lift to the nursing home where she visits an old woman she calls her aunt, and after whom she was named. After the visit, the inevitable happens: knee-trembling kisses on the sidewalk precede an "erotic slide" in a sparse, functional Kitsilano apartment. In the present, in her "reliving of this moment," she prefers, instead of the real location, "another scene, and that was the one she substituted, in her memory." Her chosen memory installs her in a faded, once fashionable hotel, where "private woes and sins" have long been accommodated, and there she pictures herself crossing the lobby, "her whole body permeated by exquisite shame" (*Hateship*, p. 234). When she thinks that she will be able to store the experience away neatly in her mind, setting it in order, and in favored circumstances, she finds she cannot, for "wave after wave of intense recollection" always throws up something new, or missed, that she has to make adjustments for. No matter that she returns to the memory "at gradually lengthening intervals," it always remains for her "a secret poultice" (pp. 237–38).

In an interview with Peter Gzowski, Munro explains that "What Is Remembered" is about "how our imaginations, how our fantasies can play such an important role in our lives,"[12] even when these fantasies are misrepresented, like the relived and rearranged memory, the comforting poultice of Meriel's infidelity with the doctor, one summer in Kitsilano, when she was a young married woman. By the time that Meriel begins her "erotic slide," the reader senses that it may be a single occurrence, mainly because the doctor is presented in such shadowy terms, the barest description of his appearance and character provided. In the journey toward the nursing home, he hardly speaks; indeed, his spoken words take up little narrative space, considering his impact on the protagonist. When the brief passionate encounter is over, and Meriel "was carried back again, driven through the park and across the bridge" to the ferry, as though she has no agency, it becomes clear that she will have no claim on her doctor (p. 235). Indeed, the narrator candidly explains that Meriel "held on to two predictions . . . Her marriage with Pierre would continue, it would last. She would never see Asher again. Both of these turned out to be right" (p. 236).

A few of Munro's later stories contain predictions, or instances of prolepsis. Earlier in "What Is Remembered," when Meriel and the doctor are at the nursing home, the narrator describes how Meriel leaves the old woman, explaining, "She would never see Aunt Muriel again, and she never did" (p. 231). This segment of prolepsis, referring to a future beyond the temporal frame of the narrative, is properly termed an "external" type. The other kind of prolepsis is known as "internal," where events alluded to come within the span of the primary narrative level.[13] An interesting instance of prolepsis occurs in "Chance," the first of the three linked stories in *Runaway*. Juliet, the protagonist, is a young teacher making her impetuous, risky journey to be with a man she met once on the Vancouver train. This journey was marred by a suicide, the gruesome detail of which Juliet had vowed never to tell anyone. The narrator observes in an aside, "(Actually, she did tell it, a few years later, to a woman named Christa, a woman whose name she did not yet know.)" (p. 64). "Chance" ends with a further allusion to Christa, who "will become Juliet's great friend and mainstay during the years ahead" (p. 86). This reference to an apparently extratextual future would indicate that the prolepsis is external. However, "Chance" is one of three *linked* stories, and in the third of these the character Christa will play an important role, as Juliet's friend and mentor; strictly speaking, then, the prediction does cover events within the narrative frame, and constitutes an internal prolepsis.

What functions do these prolepses serve? Although they reduce suspense, since they reveal future circumstances, they whet the reader's curiosity as to exactly how these have been shaped. In the Juliet triptych, and in Munro's later work, in general, the prolepses convey the panchronic authority of the narrator, moving freely along the axes of characters' lives. Munro has stated a fondness in her work for "looking at people's lives over a number of years, without continuity [like] catching them in snapshots";[14] in looking at them now, as they were, and as they will be, her omniscient narrator is photographer, archivist, and clairvoyant.

There is, in *Hateship* and *Runaway*, a strong sense of the discreteness of remembered incident, a kind of compartmentalization of experience, and of its context. When Grace, in "Passion," decides to drive off with Neil, she pays no heed to the consequences of her actions, either for Neil's wife, or for the younger brother she is expected to marry. The narrator explains that the protagonist acts almost involuntarily, "as if a gate had clanged shut behind her," and the separate brilliance of her actions "remained clear and detailed" for her (*Runaway*, p. 182). This image of an intense experience isolated, shut off, and untainted so that it retains its distinct intensity is not new in Munro's fiction, but is especially prevalent in her later work, when her older characters are wont to reflect on their days of youth.

The story "Nettles," from *Hateship*, features an older narrator who recalls a summer weekend in her middle age when she had hoped to enjoy a passionate reunion with a childhood sweetheart, but is once more disappointed because the love turns out to be "not usable" (p. 184). I have chosen to examine "Nettles" in some depth, as it illustrates many of the features discussed previously, and can be regarded as broadly representative of Munro's later fiction, specifically that narrated in the first person. The narrator is, in the present, much older than the woman who announces herself in the opening sentence, "In the summer of 1979, I walked into the kitchen of my friend Sunny's house near Uxbridge, Ontario, and saw a man standing at the counter, making himself a ketchup sandwich" (p. 154). The precision of the deixis fixes time and place, and although the man is not identified, the reader senses his importance, because the context is so firmly established. The instances of present-perfective aspect in the next two paragraphs signal the switch to contemporaneous narration, as the narrator explains, "I have driven around in the hills . . . and I have looked for the house," adding that the husband who accompanies her in her "idly persistent" search is her "second husband, not the one [she] left behind that summer" (p. 154). The distal determiner in "that summer" hints at the passage of some years since 1979. After this brief anchorage in the present, the narrator returns to the past, but goes much further back, to her childhood. Although chronology is considerably disrupted in the first page of text, with three different time zones presented, it is easy to determine which is concurrent or long past or more recently past. The boundaries are firmly demarcated, mainly by specific deictic references, working in conjunction with perfective aspect and also by the textual configuration.

A substantial part of the narrative is devoted to the narrator's reminiscences of her childhood friendship with Mike McCallum, the well driller's son. At the time of their friendship, the narrator was eight, the boy a year older. In an evocation of the idyllic Ontario summer holidays they spent together, the narrator makes it clear that he was no ordinary playmate, but someone for whom she felt a tender, worshipful affection. She is adamant that there was nothing sexual in the friendship, none of "that bothered search for hiding places . . . and immediate raw shame," but instead a "tingling contentment" (pp. 162–63) in his company. This idyll came to an abrupt end when the well driller and his son moved on, to another part of the country, leaving the narrator bewildered and stricken. To simulate the abrupt and unexpected severance of this childhood friendship, Munro cuts swiftly to the summer of 1979, when the narrator visits her friend Sunny. At this stage in her life, the narrator is far from feeling any kind of contentment: she has left "husband and house and all the things acquired during marriage (except the children, who were to be parcelled about)" (p. 166) and she is trying to make a career out of her writing. Despondent and lonely, she accepts an invitation to her friend's country cottage. The narrator's walking into the kitchen, to be confronted with Mike McCallum standing there, is an event narrated twice, and a seemingly trivial detail—that he is in the act of spreading ketchup on a sandwich—is included in both depictions of the scene. Munro here is playing with a temporal component in narrative known as frequency, which refers to the relation between how often an event appears in a story and how often it is mentioned or narrated. Rimmon-Kenan explains, "Strictly speaking, no event is repeated in all respects, nor is a repeated segment of the text quite the same, since its new location puts it in a different context which necessarily changes its meaning."[15] In this example of repetition, the two segments of text are not the same, and the differences say much about Munro's narrative craft. The anonymous man in the story's opening is named the second time, by which point the reader knows who he is and what he represents to the narrator. By not identifying him immediately, Munro whets the reader's curiosity about who he is and why the narrator would include precise information about what he eats. (The ketchup sandwich seems a peculiarly childlike taste.) The "new location" of the repeated event does signify a change, and the reader knows there will be developments in the relationship between the narrator and Mike McCallum.

Now that this spark of good fortune has reunited the couple, after a gap spanning decades, the narrator becomes suffused with energy and bonhomie. Reminiscences are shared, family news exchanged, and a mood of congeniality and homeliness prevails. In the midst of this homely domesticity, the narrator acknowledges it would be improper and "sleazy" to pursue her sexual desire for McCallum, and so, sleeping alone in the guest room, she has to suffer "monotonously lustful" dreams (p. 174). Her restraint prepares her well for her role, on the next day, "riding beside him, in the wife's seat" to the golf course, where she has agreed to caddy for him (p. 176). She finds comfort in this subordinate, supportive role, following him around, watching him, as though she were providing "a reassuring sense of human padding around his solitude." The extent to which the narrator has reduced her sexual drive, and modified her ambitions, is captured by Munro in a remarkable image: "Lust . . .

was all chastened and trimmed back now into a tidy pilot flame, attentive, wifely" (p. 178).

Equally striking and memorable is the imagery used to describe the storm that curtails the game of golf. Taking shelter from the heavy rain, the pair head for the bushes at the end of the course, from where they watch "this rush of weather" approach. As she often does when presenting an episode that is usually the precursor to sexual passion, Munro draws attention to the luxuriance of natural growth: the narrator looks out at "a meadow of weeds . . . in bloom" with "goldenrod, jewel-weed with its red and yellow bells, . . . flowering nettles with pinkish-purple clusters" while, at a distance from where they stand, they "could see trees tossing around like bouquets" (p. 179). The latter simile is especially noteworthy, for it would seem to connote wedding celebrations, suggested, too, by the words "golden," "jewel," and "bells." Such a reading may appear fanciful unless one takes into account the earlier image of the chastened, wifely flame.

Less favorable are the associations of "something coming" from the thickening "midnight clouds," an ominous "something" that is magnificently animated "as if a large portion of the sky had detached itself and was bearing down, bustling and resolute" toward them (p. 179). The drenching rain and buffeting wind it brings force the narrator and her companion to crouch down in the grass, he placing his hands on her shoulders in a gesture "of restraint, more than comfort." That the narrator perceives the gesture as restraining suggests that she is at the mercy of the elements. When the storm passes, the two of them rise "shakily" to their feet and, with barely the strength to smile, kiss briefly in "recognition of [their] survival" (p. 180) before walking out into the open and the emerging sun. The narrator senses the survival will be marked in some way, now that they are "safe and confronted with radiance" (p. 181), but what she surely anticipates—a fervent embrace, perhaps, followed by some kind of declaration—does not happen. Instead, Mike McCallum tells her of the tragedy of his youngest son's death, a revelation that renders the narrator dumb with shock, as well as despair. When she can speak, she says simply, "It isn't fair," acknowledging to herself the ambiguity of her judgment (p. 182).

In her interview with Gzowski, Munro speaks of the importance of this scene when she explains, "The . . . story is really about how . . . passionate, romantic attachment . . . comes up against what you might call real life, though goodness knows it's real enough too, but some terrible facts of life, like the facts about the child in the story. And then it simply can't go any further."[16] The narrator cannot go further with her fantasy of romance with Mike McCallum, not in the face of such unspeakable tragedy. Instead of a romantic attachment, what connects the narrator now with the man she obviously desires is the intimacy of a secret they will share, and this will have to suffice. She acknowledges that to hope for anything more would be futile, choosing the apposite metaphor of a "sweet trickle, an underground resource" to describe her affection for the well driller's son.

The anachronous part of the narrative, recounting the events in the summer of 1979, closes firmly, with the narrator's admission that she neither asked for, nor received news of McCallum "during all the years of [her] dwindling friendship" with Sunny. This would be too final, too neat a conclusion. In a brief paragraph that reads like a postscript, Munro returns the story to the present, with the wiser, calmer narrator reflecting on the "nettles" she and McCallum had crouched amongst when they sheltered from the storm. These were the cause of the rashes, the harmless "evidence on their bodies" of the adventure they had come through together (p. 184). But she was mistaken, she tells us, about her identification of "the flowering nettles with pinkish-purple flowers," for they were not nettles at all, but another kind of weed. What is the significance of the self-correction? The fact that the narrator, in the present, has researched the "joe-pye weed" is further evidence that she revisits the memory, and its location, correcting any misperceptions she had. Her observation that the nettles are, like the uncommon weed, "present, too, in all the flourishing of the waste meadow" (p. 185) leaves an impression of the memory's lasting, like a steady companion.

The indelibility of memory is one of the themes explored in "Tricks," the penultimate story of *Runaway*. It is a tightly structured narrative consisting of two clearly separate sections, the first part concerning events in Robin's, the female protagonist's, youth, in the early sixties, when she is age twenty-six, and the second part set in the present time, forty years later. As a young woman, Robin is in the habit of going on her own every summer to Stratford, to watch a matinee performance of a Shakespeare play. She enjoys this temporary escape from a "makeshift and unsatisfactory" existence, working as a nurse (p. 239), and looking after an invalid older sister, portrayed as embittered and scornful. On one of these regular excursions to the theater, Robin loses her handbag, with all her money, but fortunately a stranger, out walking his dog in the park, comes to her aid. He invites her for tea at his house, really part of his clockmaker's shop, before buying her a rail ticket home. The evening ends with the couple's kissing on the railway platform and agreeing to meet the following year, at the same time in summer, with Robin accepting certain conditions—that she will look as she does on their first meeting. But the reunion never happens, for when she approaches the shop, around the appointed date, she looks in at someone who appears decidedly unwelcoming, and she has the door shut in her face. In the second, shorter part of the narrative, we see Robin as a stylish professional woman in her sixties, a specialist in psychiatric nursing. One of the patients recently admitted to her ward is, she discovers, the twin brother of the man she had once hoped for romance with. He has been in care since his brother's death some years before. She realizes it was the twin brother, a deaf mute, whom she had seen in the shop on her return visit. She has been tricked by twists of fate she could not have bargained for.

Munro's narratives are notoriously difficult to summarize and to paraphrase. The reason I attempt this précis is to satisfy my contention that a plot summary of "Tricks" resembles that of a Shakespearean play, or something from the genre of folk literature, a fairy tale, except the heroine does not achieve what she desires. Components of the narrative have an exaggerated quality akin to melodrama: the annual, ritual journey; the lost handbag and ticket; rescue by an exotic stranger; a lovers' tryst; mistaken identity. The characters are marked by misfortunes: a naïve, gauche young nurse burdened with a caretaker's responsibilities; the ailing older sister, Joanne, cynical and discouraging; the next-door neighbor, Willard, a shy bachelor encamped "in the middle of his dead parents' furniture" (p. 245); the silver-haired Montenegrin looking after his dependent, disabled brother.

There are several allusions to how out of the ordinary the protagonist is. In the opening scene, Willard calls Robin "a wonder" (p. 237) because she can follow Shakespeare's plays; her fondness for them is not shared by anyone she knows, and the fact that she feels at ease going to the theater on her own, "surrounded by strangers," makes "Robin realize how different she herself must be from most people" (p. 239). She has never been in a romantic relationship, even although she has had plenty of opportunity; the narrator suggests that a "certain kind of seriousness" about her might deter suitors, but adds that Robin cannot "think of anybody she wished she had married" (p. 249). The picture that emerges is of an unsophisticated, immature young woman, and it is interesting that Munro chooses to clothe her protagonist in a green dress, and equip her with a "seldom-used little paisley-cloth bag," making her seem quite girlish (p. 239). The first words she utters, "I'll die . . . I'll die if they don't have that dress ready," sound childishly hyperbolic, and the fact that the piece of dialogue is twice repeated in the story conveys its importance, one that can be evaluated in terms of characterization, theme, and narrative structure.

Its repetition in the first instance emphasizes Robin's "defiant" assertiveness in the face of her sister's customary scorn (p. 236). At the third appearance of the utterance, the reader knows that the narrator is about to tell us whether or not Robin will be reunited with the imperious Montenegrin. The repetition this time reveals more about the character, suggesting a desperate resolve; it is noted that Robin gazes at her companions, Joanne and Willard, thinking how "far they were from the tension and defiance, the risk of her life" (p. 256). The replay of this one utterance not only deepens the reader's understanding of Robin's motivation, but also sustains the idea of replication, for Robin is required to make the same journey, to the same place, looking the same as before. Munro's creative use of frequency displays her consistent concern with narrative design and purpose. "Tricks" is replete with features that one associates with reflexive fiction, that is, fiction that draws attention to itself as a fictive construct.

The story contains several allusions to what is written, and to naming: there are references to dramatic works, to Serbian history and poetry, to the Cyrillic alphabet, to the "real name of Montenegro . . . *Crna Gora*," to obscure towns, rivers, and mountains on a Montenegrin map that Robin studies "with a magnifying glass" (p. 254). Just before she boards the train home, Danilo hands her a piece of paper on which the words "*Danilo Adzic . . . Bjelojevici. My village*" are written, as though by inscribing his identity he confirms and proclaims it (p. 252). It is, too, on a piece of paper, a printout from the hospital records, that Robin reads the truth about the Adzic twins, and realizes "the trick that has been played" on her (p. 268). That which is written or named in this narrative is associated with or confers great authority—like Shakespeare's plays in the literary canon. In the manner of the drama Robin admires, there is considerable dramatic irony in the story. The first play she sees at Stratford is *King Lear*, whose tragic hero suffers, of course, from foolish pride, and it is as a result "of vanity, of silly gratification" (p. 240) that Robin loses her handbag in the first place, for she had left it in the theater washroom where she spent time titivating herself. The loss of the handbag is the kernel event in the narrative, initiating an adventure that profoundly affects the main character. The play she attends a year later is *As You like It*, involving usurpation by brothers, and the changing of identities. As the narrator explains, "Shakespeare should have prepared her [Robin]. Twins are often the reason for the mix-ups and disasters . . . A means to an end, those tricks are supposed to be" (p. 268). There are other elements in the narrative that would not be out of place in the theater: for example, where Danilo lives and works is described as an "odd little house, held in place by . . . buildings on either side" (p. 259); he has a Doberman named after a goddess, a dog that mysteriously bumps into people, and is possessed of extraordinary perception; on the day of Robin's hoped-for reunion with Danilo, the portents are inauspicious, as many are in Shakespearean dramas (p. 257).

The narrator draws attention to the extravagance of settings and events. While Danilo cooks stroganoff for supper, Robin looks at magazines written in an unfamiliar language, and thinks "that she [has] entered a foreign world" (p. 246). After having returned to the routines of her own life, she becomes obsessed with Montenegro, with its history, geography, and culture, believing herself "chosen to be connected to that strange part of the world." It seems to her full of "dark schemes, cinematic plots and dangers" (p. 255), a description that could reasonably apply to events in "Tricks." That such instances are meant as ambiguous, reflexive comments upon the text is an impression strengthened by the narrator's concluding assessment of what the protagonist has been through: "That was another world they had been in, surely. As much as any world concocted on the stage. Their flimsy arrangement, their ceremony of kisses, the foolhardy faith enveloping them that everything would sail ahead as planned" (p. 269). This kind of reflexivity, a hallmark of literariness, is made manifest elsewhere in "Tricks," a story I would argue consistently displays its artifice. Apart from the reminders of what is written, read, and studied, there are several occasions when the premeditated, constructed nature of the narrative is clearly evident, and the control of the narrator is made overt.

On the night Robin meets Danilo, and goes back to his house in Downie Street, the narrator notes that she accepts the invitation without hesitation, for "She was not worried. *Afterwards* she wondered about that" (p. 243, italics added). Then there follow reasons for this lack of concern, one being the man's courteous manner, akin to that of a kindly schoolteacher. Again, the narrator reports a consequent revision of an earlier impression, adding, "*Later*, indoors, she was able to see that the grey hair was mixed with a rusty red" (p. 243, italics added). These two expressions of deixis show the protagonist reappraises what she sees; they also demonstrate the authority of the heterodiegetic narrator, possessed of rare "optical and cognitive powers."[17] The powers associated with this kind of narration are further displayed in a paragraph that stands out because of its brevity: "She had trusted him for faulty reasons. But she had not been mistaken to do so" (p. 244).

The use of the past-perfective aspect, as opposed to the simple past tense, and the choice of the substitute pro-form "so" together impart a degree of formality, as well as a smug certitude. These two statements again convey narrative authority, and they also reassure the reader that nothing amiss will happen to the main character. For in her conviction that some kind of future with Danilo is assured, that her destiny has been decided, Robin betrays a sentimental ingenuousness the reader suspects is misplaced. The zeal with which she undertakes her research on Montenegro, the delight she derives from thinking of one she dares to call her lover, how she is aware of the "shine on herself, on her body, on her voice" (p. 255), all point to her abdication. The pathos of surrender is captured when the narrator reproduces a short piece of dialogue first uttered on the railway platform. Two lines of text are italicized for effect, and exposed by an ellipsis: *"It is important that we have met. Yes. Yes"* (p. 256). In this exchange, the man's solemn, pompous justification and the young woman's eager acquiescence are highlighted.

Munro regularly uses italicized text for particular heightening effects in her stories. In Chapter 4, I discuss the functions of the graphic device in "Cortes Island" and "Save the Reaper." In this example from "Tricks," a tiny piece of a dramatic scene is retrieved, its significance further enhanced by unorthodox presentation and textual arrangement. The two short scenes that follow do not sustain the drama, rather, they are anticlimactic, for they tell of the problem threatening the anniversary of Robin's return to Stratford: she is deprived of the green dress, and must make an alteration to "the day's pattern" (p. 256).

A skillful piece of structural patterning links the period of Robin's enthrallment, when she is a naïve romantic, and the time, forty years later, when she learns of the existence of Danilo's twin. The narrator describes how, in her year of waiting, Robin becomes so absorbed with Montenegro that it is constantly in her imagination: "the cold weather and the ice far out into the lake made her think of winter in the mountains" of that country (p. 254). The first sentence of part II, as the action moves to contemporaneous time, reads: "Now the real winter has set in and the lake is frozen over almost all the way to the breakwater" (p. 261). The commonality in the two statements is too marked to be coincidental and, for me, it illustrates the remarkable cohesion and careful symmetry in Munro's fiction. However, these statements do more than confirm an aesthetically pleasing pattern in textual arrangement: in connecting the two winters, one imagined and in the past, the other real and in the present, the narrator reminds the reader of the contrast between Robin's fantasized romance and the bitter reality of her disappointment.

Part II continues with a brief résumé of the principal changes in Robin's circumstances, and in the town where she still lives. The narrator reports that her social life is fulfilling, for she enjoys the company of new friends, as well as the comfort of "sporadic and secret" lovers. The impression of contentment and acceptance of one's lot are conveyed in the portrayal of a protagonist who claims "that there's very little now that she regrets" (p. 266). Had "Tricks" ended on this note, the reader might have felt satisfied that the character deserved such comforts, after raising her youthful hopes of romance high, to have them swiftly dashed. But another trick is to be played, when Robin learns that one of the patients admitted to her ward is Danilo's twin, in care since his brother's death some years before. Her reaction to the printout containing this information is presented in an unorthodox way:

> Outrageous.
> Brothers.
> Twins.
> Robin wants to set this piece of paper in front of someone, some authority.
> This is ridiculous. This I do not accept.
> Nevertheless. (p. 267)

The presentation illustrates defamiliarization, a property associated with literariness. The appearance is unusual, as the statements are arranged in a list, constituted by mainly holophrastic sentences. The three grammatically regular ones display signs of stylistic marking, in, for example, the scheme of anadiplosis and the transposition of subject and object in the penultimate line. The effect is to simulate the rapid, instantaneous quality of Robin's reflexes, and to make clear the sense of incredulity that is mitigated by the concessive "nevertheless." This conjunct prepares deftly for the passage of sustained free indirect discourse, where the narrator lets the reader see how Robin tries to understand exactly how events, forty years ago, must have led to "the trick that has been played" on her (p. 268).

The process of rationalization begins with an attempt to visualize the clockmaker's shop that summer evening in her young adulthood. She considers how crucial the exact time of her arrival might have been, how easily she had retreated, then, more pragmatically, she speculates on the problems she and Danilo would have had, "he with Alexander, she with Joanne" (p. 268). She accepts she will eventually be grateful for discovering the mistaken identity, as she can now blame fate for the loss of love. The story ends with Robin convinced she has been cheated, but consoled by the thought of her adventure, and what might have been; luckily for her, nothing faded, for "her memories, and the embroidery on her memories just kept wearing a deeper groove" (p. 255), like it wore for Meriel in "What Is Remembered" and the unnamed narrator in "Nettles."

Lester E. Barber, writing on the stories in *Runaway*, reckons that "Tricks" is "somewhat different from the others in the collection for its directness and simplicity."[18] It is true that the dramatic events in the story, which would be at home in a Shakespearean play, propel the action at a rate that seems quicker, less digressive than is usual in Munro's short fiction. The last short paragraph, where the narrator delivers Robin's terse, unequivocal verdict on her misfortune—"She wished she could tell somebody. Him"—is a model of directness (p. 269). In terms of narrative devices and techniques, however, the work displays quite a few tricks, notably in the instances of patterning and replication, in the clever use of irony, and in the many signs of its constructedness.

The noun "tricks" features prominently in Munro's earlier work. Readers will recall the narrator of "Material," who grudgingly acknowledges the "lovely tricks, honest tricks" her husband uses in his story of Dotty, who "has passed into Art" as a result of his skill (*Something*, p. 48). The unreliable narrator of "Tell Me Yes or No," from the same collection, boasts of "tricks" and "trapdoors" in her creative imagination but admits "she does not understand their workings" (p. 124). Narrators in Munro's later work do not so readily display this kind of self-consciousness, associated with the genre of metafiction.

The first version of "Home" belongs to the vein of metafictional writing Munro produced in the 1970s. It first appeared in 1974, in *New Canadian Stories*, reemerged in 2002, in the *New Statesman*, a British journal, before being anthologized in *The View from Castle Rock* (2006). Munro's radical revision of this story, also of "Working for a Living" and "Hired Girl," makes for rewarding research and analysis, and forms the bulk of my subsequent chapters.

CHAPTER 7

"A CONSTANT REWORKING OF CLOSE PERSONAL MATERIAL"

I BEGAN THIS BOOK BY PRAISING ALICE Munro's well-documented attention to narrative coherence: to the integrity of voice, the strength of a story's architecture, the connections between spaces in a structure she likens to a house, whose enclosed spaces may be "ample and easy, or full of crooked turns, or sparsely or opulently furnished."[1] In her essay on the "Rose and Janet" manuscript, Helen Hoy examines the extraordinary lengths Munro will go to before she is satisfied with the "final shape" of a collection;[2] the first biography of the writer, by Catherine Sheldrick Ross, contains further evidence of discipline, and concern for accuracy, in the holographic sketch of Jubilee, the copy of a heavily edited manuscript page, and the reference to repeated drafts of one small textual segment.[3]

In this chapter, the heading of which is taken from the writer's 1994 interview with Chris Gittings,[4] I look at some of the redrafting Munro undertakes for the versions of "Working for a Living," "Home," and "Hired Girl," collected in *The View from Castle Rock*.[5] I argue that these revisions illustrate a great deal not only about her narrative aesthetic, which is the focus of this book, but also about values she espouses with regard to social class and cultural identity. In her reworking of the memoir "Working for a Living," the writer expresses increased reverence for and pride in her upbringing and background. The revised "Home" produces a narrator better able to articulate the complex connections with her past, while the "Hired Girl" in the 2006 collection is more determinedly critical than her predecessor of the social strata and "wider class differences" at home, which is the land east of Lake Huron.[6] I propose to discuss each of these pieces in turn, spending longer on Munro's revision of "Hired Girl," which I compare with an early story, "Sunday Afternoon" from *Dance of the Happy Shades.* The changes Munro implements in "Hired Girl" are both linguistically and stylistically marked; furthermore, because the story makes me keenly aware of my own social and cultural displacement, it is particularly edifying to work on.

Few Munro scholars would dispute Val Ross's claim, in the *Globe and Mail,* that "*Castle Rock* [is] as close as Munro has come to turning her family's life into stories."[7] The writer disclosed in 1994 that she was amassing "a lot of material . . . family history" she intended to use later, in some form, and she fulfils her intention in *Castle Rock,* where, as she explains in the book's foreword, "family history has expanded into fiction," notably in the title story.[8] The second part of this collection consists mainly of stories Munro wrote over a number of years prior to 2006 but did not anthologize because she felt "they didn't belong" (*The View from Castle Rock,* p. x). She tells Aida Edemariam, "Before I had heart surgery [in 2001], I rewrote everything that hadn't been published, so that it would be around in a better version."[9]

In the memoir "Working for a Living," Munro pays homage to her father, and to the pride he took in his work, as a trapper, a fox farmer during the Depression, a foundry caretaker, and in his later years, a writer. The story is also a tribute to her mother, to her enterprise and self-belief as a saleswoman. The "better version" of "Working for a Living," from the first part of *Castle Rock,* is not radically different from the piece published in the arts magazine *Grand Street* in 1981, but several changes are worthy of discussion. These I have grouped into categories: textual reconfiguration, changes at the level of lexis and syntax, and additions and omissions.

By configuring the text differently, Munro can accord greater salience to a particular segment, or topic, as she does at the outset of the 2006 piece. The original memoir starts with a preamble concerning the differences "between people [in Huron County] who lived on the farms and people who lived in country towns and villages" (*Grand Street,* p. 9); this is left until later in the second version, which begins with a summary of Munro's father's education. She recounts his success in entrance exams, his progress to "Continuation School" with its "strange language or logic" (*Castle Rock,* pp. 128–29), stressing her father's singular experience of an education he regarded with gravity and pride. The reordering means that the father is introduced immediately, his presence asserted before any other. Another shift in emphasis gained by altering the shape of the text occurs when Munro is describing her father's love of trapping and hunting in the bush. She strives to capture the sense of how bold and adventurous he was, turning his back on a future as a young farmer, the future his parents expected for him. From the account of her father's "Fenimore Cooper-cultivated hunger" for wilderness, she wrests the interrogative sentence, "A life in the bush, away from the town, on the edge of farms—how could it be managed?" (p. 132), isolating it in its own paragraph. This relocation makes the question seem importunate, as though it were being urgently articulated by the father himself, or by his parents. The fact that he did succeed is seen as an incredible accomplishment, against the odds.

In the careful revisions of "Working for a Living," changes at the level of lexis and syntax are more numerous than any structural adjustments. Those I have chosen demonstrate how the writer hones her craft; in addition, they reflect how she may have changed how she perceives her subject matter. In honoring her father's working life, and delineating his character, Munro's lexical choices would always be scrupulously apposite: readers may know that a "furious" Munro tried to sue "an academic at a Canadian university" who, interpreting some of Munro's fiction as autobiography, opined that the writer had "a feckless father."[10] Nobody would infer "fecklessness" from the representation in "Working for a Living." In the first version of the memoir she describes her father, living with his parents in Blyth Creek, "as an odd and lonely character, though not somebody that anyone feared or disliked" (*Grand Street*, p. 13). A similar statement is made in the later piece, but with subtle and important amendments: he is "a solitary and slightly odd young man, though not a person who was in any way feared or disliked" (*Castle Rock*, p. 132). Before, Munro deems her father "odd"; now she presents him as only "slightly" so, the difference being one of degree. Unlike "lonely," the adjective "solitary" connotes an elective solitude, even contentment in one's own company, while the epithet "character" is discarded, tainted as it might be by an impression of eccentricity and a disregard for decorum. These revisions are not radical, but they guard against the construal of anything negative.

One example of change at the level of syntax in conjunction with lexis occurs when Munro recounts how the land was cleared in the Huron Tract, in the middle of the nineteenth century, and notes the farmers' antipathy to forest: in both versions this observation is made, but vehemently so in 2006. The two comparable statements are as follows: "The early farmers had no liking for trees . . . They *must have loved* the look of the open land" (*Grand Street*, p. 111, italics added); "The early farmers hated the very sight of a tree and admired the look of open land" (*Castle Rock*, p. 130). My attention is drawn to the modal verb phrase (italicized), the preference for which conveys speculation absent from the 2006 quotation, which comes over as robustly unequivocal. The "must-have" construction, according to Dorrit Cohn, is a marker of "conjectural and inferential syntax," commonly found in the genre of "biographical psycho-narration," where the biographer or life historian tries to convey how the subject feels "without transforming him or her into an imaginary being."[11] The "must-have" construction is removed from the passage in Munro's 2006 memoir, with the result that her authority to write confidently without conjecture on the early settlement of the Huron Tract is strengthened. This authority is built on sound knowledge, as well as the substantial research into her forebears that Munro has undertaken. The substitution of emphatic, emotive verb forms ("hated the very sight of" and "admired") for ones that convey less conviction and certainty ("had no liking for" and "must have loved") does have a bearing on how the reader imagines the settlers regarded their new land.

The choice of a particular pronoun determiner is no superficial matter, either. The 1981 narrative of Munro's mother's sales triumph with the rich American tourists contains the following: "In the summer, then, the summer of 1941, she went off to Muskoka with a trunkload of furs" (*Grand Street*, p. 22), whereas in the revision the mother leaves "with *her* trunkload of furs" (*Castle Rock*, p. 146, italics added). The sentence is impressive anyway, with its mellifluous, measured repetition, the jaunty rhythm of the adverbials, and the neatly placed conjunct embracing all that precedes it—the account of the precarious nature of silver fox farming, anxiety about money, and her mother's audacious plan for possible profit. By writing that it is not just *any* trunkload of precious furs, but that it belongs to her mother and is her precious responsibility, Munro makes the expedition seem more of a risky adventure, embarked on by a woman of independent nature.

A significant addition of five words in the new version of Munro's memoir confirms the writer's sense of admiration for what her mother achieved in Muskoka. The scene of her triumph, of "how she had saved the day" (*Castle Rock*, p. 154) with her salesmanship, is poignantly evoked in a series of memorable images—the display cabinet with the sign *Silver Fox, the Canadian Luxury* resting on top; the mother, "brisk and elegant" in unfamiliar attire, her hair in a "neat coronet of braids" (p. 150); father and daughter standing awkwardly, incongruous as "tramps or scarecrows" (p. 151) in the opulent surroundings of the Pine Tree Hotel. One short sentence in each account is especially eloquent. The verdict on the mother's triumph is, in 1981, "Vindication; salvation" (*Grand Street*, p. 26), but is rendered in 2006 as "Vindication for her, salvation for us all" (*Castle Rock*, p. 152). With the addition of these five small words, Munro differentiates one outcome from the other, and the mother's individual feat is recognized for it was—a rescue mission for her family.

The admiration the daughter expresses for her mother, for "saving the day," is however, in both versions, diluted by feelings of unease. Munro recalls how much she disliked the venality of the enterprise, "the whole idea of putting yourself to use" for profit, having to flatter and ingratiate yourself with others for their approval (p. 153). But she has reappraised the episode, as she acknowledges in an interview. With reference to "Working for a Living," she tells Val Ross "she is appalled that she was not grateful for her mother's attempts [to] improve the family income," admitting, "My mother had all the instincts that would have made us prosper. But my feelings were so intensely private and protective of dignity. Ha!"[12]

Later additions to the memoir make clearer the daughter's gratitude, and they also amplify the worth of the mother's achievement. After recounting how the fox fur sales did not "develop into a year-round business" as her mother had hoped, she justifies this optimism. She explains that her mother could not "have foreseen" how circumstances would prevail against such an enterprise, with America entering the war, tourists staying at home, and resorts closing. Munro alludes to something more devastating that her mother could not have predicted: "She couldn't foresee the attack on her own body, the destruction gathering within" (*Castle Rock*, p. 152).[13] As a younger writer, closer to when her mother "was recalling this summer, and insisting on the gifts she had," Munro declares, "I was not sympathetic" (*Grand Street*, p. 27). Three decades later, Munro omits this denial; the pity she feels now is surely evident in the rewritten passage.

The latter part of the memoir is concerned with the father's work as a night watchman in the foundry, a job he had taken after the fox farm lost too much money. Munro recalls one evening, during her last year in Wingham, when she had to deliver a message to her father, and learned about what foundry work entailed. She makes several additions to the final segment in her revised version, but one that especially interests me occurs in her commentary on the workplace, and on the laborious tasks her father and his workmates take pride in. In the first version, she writes, "Much that I saw that night was soon to disappear: the cupola, the hand-lifted ladles, the killing dust" (*Grand Street*, p. 34), providing, in her revision, stark evidence of the effects of this "truly killing" dust. She tells of how, "on the porches of small, neat houses, there were always a few yellow-faced, stoical men [who were] dying of *the foundry disease*, the dust in their lungs" (*Castle Rock*, p. 162, italics in original). This sobering image suggests Munro does not look back wistfully on industrial traditions and practices that involved "skills and dangers" and gave men "much foolhardy pride" (p. 162); she applauds the men's endurance, but points out the heavy price paid for it.

The revised memoir does not end in the way that the first version does, with reference to what each parent held dear in his or her work. The newer version concludes with an extract from Robert Laidlaw's novel about pioneer life, *The McGregors* (1979), and Munro's brief, affectionate comment on a chosen scene. She explains that her father took up writing after he left the foundry, and that he derived immense pleasure from it. By choosing to incorporate her father's work into her own, to blend his writing with hers, Munro does indeed proclaim the connection between their two working lives, proudly displaying, in Thacker's succinct phrasing, "the communion between writer-daughter and writer-father."[14]

A writer-daughter narrates the short story "Home," Munro's powerful evocation of the country east of Lake Huron. The narrator describes one of her regular visits back to the house where she grew up, to see her father and his second wife, Irlma. The house is much changed from how it was in the narrator's time there: she describes the changes, not all of them welcome, and is amazed at how a place so dear and familiar to her "can be dissolved, in a way, and lost" inside its new shell (*Castle Rock*, p. 289). The narrator recognizes the cultural and familial connections with her "home," but it is the personal that is dearest, as she affirms when she lyrically re-creates "the scene of the first clear memory of my life" (p. 314). The earliest version of "Home" appeared in 1974, in an anthology of *New Canadian Stories*, and was rewritten by Munro in 2001, before being published in 2002 by the *New Statesman*. The version in *The View from Castle Rock* is quite similar to the one published in the British magazine, with minor amendments.

I examine some of the revisions "Home" has undergone, identifying major differences between the 1974 version and that of 2006. I consider, for example, what the deletion of the metafictional elements in the original might signify, and discuss the narrator's relationship with home, arguing that Munro lessens some of its complexity in her revision. The narrator in 2006, describing how the house that was her home is being gradually "dissolved," seems surer of her belief, "I do not lament this loss as I would once have done" (p. 289), because she can compensate for the loss in her memory and imagination. Robert Thacker observes that the work "is most often seen as a story but is much more a memoir."[15] I prefer, however, to treat "Home" as a work of fiction, noting that in her revisions the writer has removed references to her hometown Wingham, replacing real street names with fictitious ones (p. 300); in addition, she has effected substantial changes in the physical descriptions of the characters Irlma and Connie (formerly Marge), presumably to discourage autobiographical readings that might have been tempting before. With its revisions, "Home" moves away from the genre of memoir and firmly inclines toward fiction.

The self-conscious narrator commenting on her own narration is a phenomenon of Munro's work in the 1970s, in stories from *Something I've Been Meaning to Tell You*, and less so in *The Beggar Maid*. Helen Hoy explores this aspect of Munro's style in "'Rose and Janet': Alice Munro's Metafiction," an essay cited more than once in this book; Carrington describes "Home" as a story that "incorporates . . . self-consciousness into a full-blown metafictional structure."[16] The writer's experimentation with reflexivity, a hallmark of metafiction, does not last long, as Hoy explains, revealing that "she [Munro] would like to rewrite it ['Home'] deleting the self-reflexive commentary, which was a great relief at the time but now strikes her as a tired device."[17]

The four separate segments of commentary in the 1974 version of "Home" are presented in italics, and are thus distinguished from the narrative in regular font. Some of the reflexivity is deleted from the revision. Removed entirely are the narrator's various expressions of unease about her style and representation: she complains of how ponderously she writes about the journey home (*New Canadian Stories*, p. 137); she berates herself for her handling of "*the voices, the way people talk*" (p. 142); she fears she will be accused of "*vengeful reporting, in spite of accuracy*" (p. 149) about Irlma, and launches defensively into a character sketch of her sterling qualities. In the original conclusion she flaunts her presence, confessing, "*I don't know how to end this*" (p. 151), asking for her reader's affective engagement in questions like, "*You can see this scene, can't you,*" finally congratulating herself on "*the effects*" she has created (p. 153). At the ending of the revised version there is no reader address, no such allusion to the work as a fictive construct.

Although some pieces of the metacommentary are retained in the revised version, they do not look the same. The account of the narrator's dream of her dead mother, as a ghost returning to her house, appears virtually unchanged, but is integrated into the narrative in regular font. Enclosed by two ellipses, the singular, dramatic impact of the account is now heightened. Similarly enclosed by blank spaces, like bookends, is the narrator's painful confession concerning her behavior toward Irlma. She has had more of the stepmother's company during this visit, as her father is unwell and has been admitted to the hospital. She guiltily recalls the "cool, judicious tone—that educated tone" (*Castle Rock*, p. 310) with which she shows her disapproval of Irlma's candid remarks about her parents, and admits to feeling "ashamed" for her reproof: "I did not think it had been tactful of her to tell me. *Tactful*, yes. That was the word I used" (p. 310). The whole incident is narrated in disjointed prose, broken up by asides, instances of repetition, and reformulations in parenthesis; the narrator sounds tentative, keenly aware of the sensitivity of the subject matter, and treading warily. In the original version, this part is detached from the narrative, in italics, its controversy acknowledged by the statement, "*And something happened which I did not put in the story*" (*New Canadian Stories*, p. 152). In the revised version, the narrator is able to bring this scene *into* the story, to deal with it directly, instead of obliquely, with the result that the episode can be seen as integral to the process of her renegotiation with "home" in all its transformations.

When she was far away from her home, she says she "was greatly moved by the memory of it" (*Castle Rock*, p. 288) and would imagine walking through its rooms; now, she claims that it does not mean so much to her, that the place belongs to "some self I have finished with and none too soon" (p. 290). On previous visits home she sought out mementoes from her childhood, just to reassure herself they remained. In the early version of "Home" Munro employs the modal verb "would" and the marginal modal "used to" when describing her narrator's habitual actions, as in, "I used to go into the front rooms . . . I would go through the bookcase" (*New Canadian Stories*, p. 136). In the comparable passage in 2006, it is made clearer that she has dispensed with these nostalgic rituals. The negation in contiguous sentences is emphatic: "I don't go into the front room now . . . I don't go looking for my old high-school texts . . . I don't open the 'classics'" (*Castle Rock*, p. 290). The different choice of verb phrase makes Munro's narrator seem less sentimental about her former home.

Coming home for the narrator means realizing and accepting that she is now ill suited for the country life she was born into. Substantial passages in both original and revised versions of the story deal with the explanation of how incongruous and hemmed in she feels, carrying out farmyard chores "like one of those misfits, captives . . . who should have left but didn't, couldn't, and are now unfit for any place" (*Castle Rock*, p. 312). The sentence "It is enough to make me scream and run" (*New Canadian Stories*, p. 151) concludes the 1974 narrative, and what follows is the last and longest section of metacommentary. In the new "Home" the narrator makes no such declaration of defeat; she recovers from the mood of dejection she entered, spreading hay for sheep in the stable, and connects with the outside world, greeting her stepmother's niece Connie as she drives into the yard. Instead of digressing into a series of self-conscious writerly musings, the narrator carries on narrating.

The ending of the 2006 version of "Home" is more affirmative than the ending of the 1974 story. One of the reasons is the encounter with Connie comes across as heartening, for she brings good news from the hospital concerning the narrator's father, and she urges her cousin to return to her own life as a writer, appearing to understand she has a right to it. In this respect she is unlike the earlier "Marge" character, from the same scene, for whom the writer's life is "*incomprehensible*" and who unwittingly reminds the narrator of the "*hard voice of [her] upbringing*," condemning her for her pretension (*New Canadian Stories*, p. 152). There is in the new work no self-conscious, guilt-ridden reflection on the value of a writing life: the scene in the barnyard is narrated as a fluent movement outward from the "very corner of the stable" where "the beginning of the panic" came on the narrator, and made her feel so displaced (*Castle Rock*, p. 314).

The vividly evoked scene in the stable, the narrator's "first clear memory of life," is a memorable conclusion to "Home." This descriptive passage appears in the original as a postscript the narrator casually offers as "*something else I could have worked into an ending.*" When it is integrated into the body of the narrative, it is the story's climax. The expressions of time used to introduce the closing scene are altered in the course of Munro's revising, and these changes intrigue me. In the earliest version, the image is recalled in the past, "*I recognized later*" (*New Canadian Stories*, p. 152). For the *New Statesman*, Munro prefers the present tense—"When I think about all this later, I recognise that" (*New Statesman*, p. 93)—before she finally settles on a present tense verb and a modal expressing future time: "When I think about all this later, I will recognize" (*Castle Rock*, p. 314). What might the changes signify? The image that closes the story is for the narrator eidetic, permanent and precious, so indelible that she recalls tiny details in the composition—the clothes she wears, the lantern hanging on the stable wall, the cobwebbed windows, the sound of the milk streaming into the pail. She feels able to date the picture she re-creates, "late fall or early winter. Maybe it was still 1934" (*Castle Rock*, p. 315). This image is of the home she remembers, and will always remember. Munro's substitution of the modal verb phrase "will recognize" for former past and present choices conveys a sense of continuity, longevity, and it suggests that the narrator will view the scene again and again.

The various revisions examined previously do more than illustrate and confirm the writer's dedication to her narrative craft and design. The reworkings reveal much about her values—her deepening respect for the material she uses, her attachments to family and place in land east of Lake Huron, and a discernible pride in those roots.

In an interview with Munro, published more than twenty years ago, Geoff Hancock suggests to her that her stories "contain a veiled social commentary," adding that there is a "kind of class system at work" in which "we go down the ladder in Hanratty to the other side of the tracks."[18] In reply, Munro explains that when she returned to her home territory, having spent a long time away from it in British Columbia, she became instantly aware of and very interested in class differences. That class distinctions matter to some of her readers is richly illustrated in the anecdote Munro tells Hancock about the student who, during a seminar on *Lives of Girls and Women*, taught by a friend of Munro, declares that "the class should know that Alice Munro came from the wrong side of the tracks."[19]

The arrogance and petty-minded snobbery displayed by this attitude are recurring traits in the less attractive Munro characters, from her earliest fiction to her most recent. There are several instances of what Hancock refers to as "social commentary" in *The Beggar Maid*, for example, in the title story, where Patrick dismisses Rose's home town as a "dump" (p. 91) and does not disguise his contempt for it, and for Rose's family. In "Chaddeleys and Flemings: Connection," from *The Moons of Jupiter*, Richard, a character similar to Patrick, wants his wife, the narrator, to be "amputated from [a past] which seemed to him such shabby baggage" (p. 13); he derogates her accent, her native town, and the relatives who come to visit her, referring to her aunt as "a pathetic old tart" (p. 17). Munro's continuing concern with social class is evident in later fiction, most notably in "Family Furnishings," from *Hateship*, a story whose female narrator chronicles events in "a ramshackle background" her fiancé disapproves of, regarding all "failures in life . . . as lapses" (p. 87).

The writer's humble upbringing is well chronicled in "Working for a Living," while further insights are gleaned from biographies, interviews, and from her eldest daughter's memoir, published in 2001. From these sources we learn that, before leaving for university, the young Alice Laidlaw worked as a maid for a family in Rosedale, an affluent neighborhood in Toronto. This family also owned a summer cottage on an island in Georgian Bay, near Pointe au Baril.[20] Munro explains to Catherine Sheldrick Ross that when working for her rich employers, she "felt set apart from the people around [her], and the experience sharpened [her] sense of class differences."[21] The writer also confides to Eleanor Wachtel: "It was probably a very important experience that way, because I saw all sorts of class things . . . Being a servant in a household . . . you see things about you and them—the barrier—which totally surprised me."[22]

The "barrier" between wealthy employer and poor servant is explored in "Hired Girl," a story anthologized in *The View from Castle Rock*, and first published twelve years previously in *The New Yorker*. Munro's revisions of this story are worthy of detailed analysis, for they reveal not only her sedulous craft, but her purposeful desire to make social class and its concomitant inequities a more salient theme in the later work. In its depiction of the narrator's fierce resentment of her status, and her calculated antagonism toward her employer, the narrative differs from Munro's earlier treatment of the social embarrassment that coming from a poor family causes characters such as Del, Rose, Janet, and the unnamed narrator of "Family Furnishings."

In *Remnants of Nation: On Poverty Narratives by Women*, Roxanne Rimstead argues that while Munro, in her fiction, often "draws attention to poverty and cross-class experiences" she does so with "a distanced gaze"[23] from a position that is intended "to control and survey the scene of poverty for its representational and aesthetic impact."[24] In this respect, Rimstead asserts, her perspective is unlike that of Margaret Laurence, whose fictive portrayals of the poor are more political, and more engaging of the reader's empathy. It seems to Rimstead that Laurence, in, for example, *The Diviners* (1974), invites the reader to share in the sense of outrage at the poverty that is being described and the social injustices exposed as unacceptable. Rimstead's remarks on the "distanciation" of Munro's gaze are more pertinent to Munro's earlier work,[25] particularly *The Beggar Maid*, where the protagonist, Rose, is shown playing "an onlooker's part" (p. 42) in the theatrical presentation of a past variously transformed or disguised, or offered as diversion to a dinner party audience (p. 91). In her acquiescence to the "obedient image" of a less vulgar self, prescribed by rich, snobbish Patrick, Rose does not question why his family needs their ostentatious wealth, their abundant luxury; instead, she awkwardly pretends to be at ease amid such surroundings, even though, as the narrator explains, she "was destroying herself," allowing her accent to "be eliminated, her friends . . . discredited and removed" (pp. 85–88).

In "Hired Girl," there is little evidence of this self-conscious shame about a less privileged background. Indeed, in her revision of the story, for *The View from Castle Rock*, Munro presents a narrator who regales her addressee with "poverty narratives," not delivered for their aesthetic value, but as weapons of instruction and retaliation. In terms of its setting and characterization, the story is reminiscent of "Sunday Afternoon," from *Dance of the Happy Shades*.[26] Although it is sometimes cited briefly as exemplary of her early fiction, "Sunday Afternoon" has not attracted sustained critical attention. George Woodcock, in his essay on realism in Munro's fiction, describes the story as a "little social study, highly class-conscious for a Canadian writer."[27] The class consciousness is immediately discernible in the story's first paragraph, in the presentation of the employer, Mrs. Gannett, as leisured and glamorous, "flashing the polished cotton skirts of a flowered sundress," she enters the kitchen where her maid, Alva, is "washing glasses," and delivers instructions on what and how to serve the guests, "the usual people" who have arrived for lunch (*Dance*, p. 161).

The incongruity of Alva in Mrs. Gannett's world is systematically developed in a series of discrepant juxtapositions and contrasts. Thus the "tones of shrill and happy outrage" Alva hears from the patio, where the guests are drinking freely, make her keenly aware that she is not permitted "to show a little relaxation and excitement." The narrator's wry, bathetic observation that "Of course, she was not drinking, except out of the bottoms of glasses" (p. 163) conjures up the image of an unaccustomed luxury, guiltily snatched. Alva keenly feels her own gaucheness, in her utility uniform, and in the "heavy, purposeful, plebeian sound" her "white Cuban-heeled shoes [make] on the stones of the patio . . . in contrast to the sandals and pumps" (p. 164); the description of the room she occupies, tellingly above the garage, continues the theme of inconsonance, for it is the "only place in the house where you could find things unmatched, unrelated to each other" (p. 167). The stark distinction between the servant's life and that of her employer is encapsulated in two successive sentences: "She could not actually leave the house; Mrs. Gannett might want her for something. And she could not go outside; they were out there" (p. 165). The sentences are similarly constructed, for both consist of coordinate clauses, the first expressing a negation, the second explaining it. By such construction, Munro conveys two antitheses, between freedom and incarceration, and between inside and outside.

The story is told by a heterodiegetic narrator, but there are several occasions when Alva becomes the subject of the focalization, such as when the reader learns of how Mrs. Gannett summons her maid, using her voice like a bell: "It was queer to hear her call this, in the middle of talking to someone, and then begin laughing again; it seemed as if she had a mechanical voice, even a button she pushed, for Alva" (p. 164). The informality of diction, the use of the proximal deictic "this," and the reformulation in the similes characterize free indirect discourse, and they serve to instantiate Alva's perspective on events. It is clear from glimpses of this perspective that Alva feels she is of little consequence, a sort of inanimate labor-saving device, available to order.

Alva is further belittled at the story's conclusion, when she is subjected to sexual advances from Mrs. Gannett's cousin. Close study of Alva's meeting with the amorous young man exposes vestiges of both social and sexual inequality. The nameless cousin is from "Mrs. Gannett's side of the family" which, the narrator points out, is "the right side" (p. 161), and in the space of four lines he is twice referred to as "Mrs. Gannett's cousin," the repeated relational term reinforcing his social credentials. He has his cousin's peremptory authority, one he flirtatiously wields, demanding that Alva "Say thanks" when he passes her a glass to wash. This order is issued shortly before he takes "hold of her lightly, as in a familiar game and [spends] some time kissing her mouth" (p. 170). Carrington reads Alva's experience as further evidence of inequality in the relationship between privileged class and servant, and I would agree.[28] The story ends on the word "humiliation": Alva is described as looking forward to a "tender spot, a new and still mysterious humiliation" and this description surely undermines the confidence she feels after the "stranger's touch." After he has kissed her he returns to the patio, to the outside Alva is excluded from, walking "with the rather graceful, mocking stealth of some slight people" (p. 170). Even in such a brief vignette can be discerned the assured and practiced condescension that Alva is subject to throughout the narrative.

This early story, in its depiction of the barrier between privileged employer and underprivileged servant, foreshadows the fuller exploration of that relationship in "Hired Girl." Its narrator is a more complex and more substantially developed character than Alva. At the very outset she makes it clear that she is not comfortable with the role of maid, that she resents her status, and that she dislikes her affluent employer, Mrs. Montjoy. In the revised version of "Hired Girl," published more than a decade after its first appearance in *The New Yorker*, Munro intensifies the narrator's feelings of discomfort and antipathy; she widens the chasm between employer and maid, holding up to scrutiny and ridicule the mores and social pretensions of Mrs. Montjoy and her summer cottage guests. It is primarily through the commentary of her feisty, sharp-eyed narrator that Munro can more critically examine that chasm.

There are several differences between the version of "Hired Girl" that appeared in 1994 and the one published in *The View from Castle Rock*. These differences are, in the main, illustrated in the presentation of Mrs. Montjoy and her treatment of the narrator, in the narrator's interaction with other characters, her commentary on her status and situation, and the nature of her self-knowledge at the conclusion. In her revision of this narrative, Munro sharpens the narrator's, and the reader's, consciousness of class difference.

The authority of the employer and the passivity of the employee are reflected in the syntax of the initiating sentence, "Mrs. Montjoy was showing me how to put the pots and pans away" (*Castle Rock*, p. 227), in which Mrs. Montjoy is the subject and the narrator is the indirect object. The reader learns that the narrator had been collected from Pointe au Baril station some days before and had been brought to the island by boat. The unflattering description of Mrs. Montjoy is common to both versions, but while in the first the narrator concedes that her employer's "commonest expression [was] one of impatience held *decently* in check" (*New Yorker*, p. 82, italics mine), in the second the judgment is harsher, for the "impatience [is] *barely* held in check" (*Castle Rock*, p. 229, italics added). The difference in adverbial choice suggests that the woman's "impatience" verges on irascibility. It is during the journey from Pointe au Baril that Mrs. Montjoy asks the narrator if she is "Feeling a tad sick?" (p. 229), a question that differs from the earlier version with the addition of "a tad," an adverbial that in speech act theory would be categorized as a *hedge*, a qualification or toning down of an utterance. The *Oxford English Dictionary* determines the status label of this lexical item, that is, when it means "a little" or "slightly," as "*colloq.* (orig. and chiefly *N.Amer.*)," its first recorded usage being in 1940.[29] All the citations given are from American or Canadian sources; most of the later ones exemplify the same facetious understatement discernible in Mrs. Montjoy's question.

In both versions of the story, the narrator notes that this question is accompanied by "the briefest possible smile . . . like the signal for a smile, when the occasion did not warrant the real thing" (*New Yorker*, p. 82, and *Castle Rock*, p. 229). Mrs. Montjoy's behavior is inappropriate because she is flouting one of the four maxims of conversation that, according to the philosopher H. P. Grice, express the general cooperative principle in language.[30] The four maxims in Grice's theory of conversational implicature (the additional levels of meaning beyond the semantic meaning of the words uttered) refer to quantity, quality, relation, and manner; in the context of Mrs. Montjoy's question, quality is the pertinent one, the principles of which are expressed as follows:

The maxim of quality
  Try to make your contribution one that is true, specifically:
  i) do not say what you believe to be false.
  ii) do not say that for which you lack adequate evidence.[31]

The shivering narrator is holding on to the sides of a boat "flung out on the choppy evening waters of Georgian Bay" (*Castle Rock*, p. 229). She is obviously unwell, yet Mrs. Montjoy makes her jocular, pseudosolicitous enquiry, perhaps, the narrator suspects, because she senses fear rather than nausea. In any case, she has flouted the maxim of quality, first, by asking a question whose answer she must know, and, second, by deliberately qualifying and diminishing her concern, to the extent that it is difficult to construe as heartfelt. The fleeting, perfunctory smile seems to undermine the genuineness of "Feeling a tad sick?," a question that is pragmatically anomalous because it "contradicts the standard Quality implicature, that one believes what one asserts and [that] when one asks a question, one may standardly be taken to be asking sincerely."[32] The insertion of the informal, hedging, and often intentionally ironic "a tad" serves to expose this character's insincerity.

There is abundant evidence, in both versions of the narrative, that Mrs. Montjoy regards the narrator as someone of little consequence, merely a maid hired for summer help. In the later version, Munro makes the older woman's attitude toward her maid seem more functionalist; for example, when the narrator overhears Mrs. Montjoy talk to a guest about the problems they share keeping domestic staff happy, she remembers her comment: "So you just make allowances . . . You do the best with them you can" (*Castle Rock*, p. 237). In the same scene in the *New Yorker* story, the statement of resignation reads, "You do the best you can" (p. 84). The third-person pronoun reference reduces the humanity of the subjects, presenting them as an undifferentiated mass. Another remarkable instance of Mrs. Montjoy's tendency to refer to her maid as inconsequential occurs in a scene when she helps her husband find a book that he has mislaid. She advises him, correctly, that he has left it in the living room, where the narrator is working. Because she has picked it up, and is eagerly reading it, Mr. Montjoy thanks her, remarking on the "queer kind of book" that he considers it to be (Isak Dinesen's *Seven Gothic Tales*). At this point, his wife enters the room, declaring, "We'll have to get out of the way here and let her get on with the vacuuming" (*Castle Rock*, p. 242). In *The New Yorker*, Mrs. Montjoy's words are, "We'll have to get out of the way here—Elsa has to get on with the vacuuming" (p. 85). There are two noteworthy points to be made here, and both serve to substantiate my claim that, in her later presentation of Mrs. Montjoy, Munro wishes to accentuate her lack of empathy, her superiority, and her rudeness.

First of all, in the earlier version of the story the narrator has a forename that is not retained in the later one. This subsequent anonymity is, I will argue, of particular importance when the narrator is addressed by one of Mrs. Montjoy's flirtatious male guests. For the moment, it is the use of the third-person pronoun that merits attention. As the writer has decided that her narrator will be nameless, she has to opt for pronominal reference, but its use in this scene is marked. The syntax of the utterance makes it even more so: while in the earlier version, the narrator is the subject of the second clause, in the second she has become the object, a change in syntactic relations that reduces the narrator's agency.

The use of the third-person pronoun in this speech event is revealing. The situation consists of two speakers, with a third party present, who is spoken of by one of the interlocutors. In his discussion of deixis, the general term for the various lexical and grammatical features that relate utterances to contexts, Lyons reminds us of the exact nature of the grammatical category, third person, in relation to first and second: "It is important to note that only the speaker [first person] and the addressee [second person] are participating in the drama. The term 'third person' is negatively defined with respect to 'first person' and 'second person': it does not correlate with any positive participant role."[33] In *Personal Pronouns in Present-day English* (1996), Katie Wales examines third-person forms and speech roles. She notes that there are many kinds of communication, in various contexts, when the role of listener is shared between third party and addressee, and what distinguishes the latter from the former is that the addressee knows she or he is being addressed. Wales explains that "this third party may be referred to exophorically, for some reason, by the speaker."[34] In the social code of politeness, Wales observes, a person's name is preferred to the pronoun when the referent is present; when the speaker breaches this code, she or he may do so out of embarrassment, or perhaps animosity.[35] When Mrs. Montjoy refers to her maid exophorically, excluding her from any "positive participant role," she breaks a fundamental maxim of politeness, but it is not because she is embarrassed, or feeling particularly inimical, but because she regards the young woman as irrelevant, to the company and to the conversation.

Like Mrs. Gannett in "Sunday Afternoon," Mrs. Montjoy is also anxious to establish the boundary between the hired girl's milieu and that of the family and guests. The narrator is quickly made to understand that when she is not working, she cannot occupy the same space as the adults she serves. When she carries her own meal out to the deck from the kitchen, her employer reminds her, with elliptical urgency: "Three plates there? Oh, yes, two out on the deck and yours in here. Right?" (*Castle Rock*, p. 237). The proximal deictic "here" represents, as it did for Alva, the domestic sphere where the maid belongs. This particular episode, added to the new version of "Hired Girl," further illustrates the elaborate demarcation between the territories of servant and employer that seems more sharply defined in Munro's revision.

In her permitted interaction with Mrs. Montjoy's ten-year-old daughter, Mary Anne, the narrator can express her resentment at this delimitation—what Munro remembers, from her own experience, as a "setting apart" from others. When asked by the younger girl about the sports she is best at, the narrator begins, "Everybody I know works too hard to do any sports" (*Castle Rock*, p. 238), and then she launches into a detailed account of the poverty-stricken, work-beleaguered lives of people in her hometown. Her "exaggerations or near lies" (p. 239) allow her to give vent to a sense of injustice at the chasm in wealth and opportunity between her own class and that of the Montjoy family. While in the earlier version the narrator acknowledges her hometown had once boasted a tennis court and a golf course "in the thirties" (*New Yorker*, p. 84), in the revision the period is more precisely named "the Depression" (*Castle Rock*, p. 239), the initial capital indicating its historical importance as a time of industrial and financial decline. The referential term, "the thirties" does not have the same emotive impact.

It is in order to achieve maximum impact on the young and impressionable Mary Anne that the narrator dramatizes and exaggerates the hardships of her own way of life. But she also recognizes that another purpose is to "make clear the differences" (p. 241) between her home circumstances and those of her employer's daughter. It is this urge to differentiate between one way of life, characterized by affluence and privilege, and another, by penury and denial, that I think furnishes evidence of a less objective, more empathetic view of poverty. Rimstead maintains that Munro's "gaze . . . towards the poor" is "so distancing" as to suggest "powerlessness and neutrality"[36] and also suggests that her protagonist's or narrator's recollections of an impoverished upbringing are a source of "primarily personal shame, melancholy or aesthetic enthralment" rather than as "matters of political importance and community alliances."[37] But in "Hired Girl" there is little vestige of the narrator's shame or sadness; on the contrary, she fulminates against her listener's ignorance of how less fortunate people, namely, the self-sufficient people of her community, cope with privation.

She succeeds in stimulating her listener's conscience, as well as her inventiveness: "'That isn't fair,' said Mary Anne. 'That's awful. I didn't know people could eat dandelion leaves.' But then she brightened. 'Why don't they go and catch some fish?'" (p. 240). The equivalent passage in the 1994 story is exactly the same, except for one revealing verb phrase: by substituting "brightened" for "added" in the original, Munro makes Mary Anne's suggestion seem like part of an entertaining parlor game, where the most imaginative ideas are awarded points for ingenuity. Try as she might, the young girl cannot envisage the kind of poverty that the narrator describes, for it is so far removed from her cosseted experience. While the narrator acknowledges that her tales are exaggerated, she is certain that "not one of these statements—even the one about the dandelion leaves—was completely a lie" (p. 239).

The narrator's intention, to widen the gulf between two households, between two classes, is confirmed in the following statement, the climax to her evocative description of the family kitchen at home: "It seemed as if I had to protect it from contempt—as if I had to protect a whole precious and intimate though hardly pleasant way of life from contempt. Contempt was what I imagined to be always waiting, swinging along on live wires, just under the skin and just behind the perceptions of people like the Montjoys" (p. 240). The corresponding section from the 1994 version reads: "It seemed that I had to protect it from contempt—that I had to protect a whole precious and intimate though often unpleasant way of life from contempt, which I supposed to be nourished in the icy hearts of people like the Montjoys" (*New Yorker*, p. 85). Munro has effected important changes in her revision. First, she has made the word "contempt" stand out by using the scheme anadiplosis, the repetition of the last word of a clause at the beginning of one following. Because the normal sequence of clause elements (subject-verb) is subsequently reversed, the word "contempt," the object, is foregrounded, as it is not in the original. Indeed, attention is somewhat deflected in the *New Yorker* version as a result of the reformulation initiated by the dash. Another change worth commenting upon is the greater elaboration of the *source* of the contempt. While Munro originally locates it in the "icy hearts of people like the Montjoys," where it is "nourished," in her revision she presents the contempt as pervasive, a latent, reflexive reaction, always there beneath the surface.

I believe the changes that Munro has wrought in this scene underscore the narrator's angry defensiveness of her own class, and they heighten her antipathy toward wealthy, privileged people she thinks have no understanding of or respect for her class. The hired girl is presented as a more politically motivated spokeswoman for her family, and class, endeavoring to ascribe dignity to their struggles.

In the narrator's interaction with some of Mrs. Montjoy's summer guests, their lack of respect is clearly discernible. Her encounter with the "courtly" Mr. Hammond exposes the same kind of patronizing sexual arrogance displayed by the employer's cousin in "Sunday Afternoon." The changes Munro has made intensify the condescension. In the earlier story, the character, entering the kitchen for more gin, addresses the narrator first as "Minnie," but after being told by his wife that Minnie is not her name, he addresses her, several times thereafter, as "Elsa." In the revised version, as I explain previously, the narrator is purposefully nameless, so the correct forename is not given, although Mr. Hammond is informed that he is mistaken in calling the young girl "Minnie." He continues to do so, however, speaking "in an artificial, dreamy voice" that the narrator recognizes as "deeply skeptical and sophisticated" (pp. 246–47). In his first few addresses to the narrator, he uses what he thinks is her forename, five times; more than twenty percent of his spoken words consist of the vocative. Such a high proportion of these nominal elements is unusual in an exchange between strangers.

In a corpus-based paper on terms of address in present-day English, the grammarian and linguist Geoffrey Leech subdivides vocatives into semantic categories; in his categorization, the address form "Minnie" would be termed a "familiarized first name."[38] Leech explains that "familiarizing vocatives, including first-name address, typically signal acquaintanceship or friendship."[39] In this scene from "Hired Girl," the vocative is linguistically marked, for its repetition is excessive, and it is used by an addresser who is *unknown* to the addressee. Sara Mills points out that while first names are exchanged between interlocutors on equal terms, "those in asymmetrical power relations will use differential naming patterns."[40] Such asymmetry certainly exists in the relationship between the young maid and the much older, sophisticated, wealthy man whose meals she serves. I would argue that Munro, in her revision, portrays the character of Mr. Hammond as more patronizing, and more inappropriately flirtatious, so that the asymmetry is magnified. In the *New Yorker* story, he similarly overuses the vocative, but he addresses the hired girl by her given forename when told, and when he reverts to "Minnie," he appears to do so because he is inebriated. There is not the same sustained, mocking condescension in his manner.

Immediately following the episode in the kitchen, the narrator recounts another belittling experience at the hands of the Montjoys' guests. As she heads to her room in the boathouse, she meets a couple of young guests, girls her own age, who are returning from their swim. By their behavior toward the narrator, they make plain their belief in their social superiority. The *New Yorker* version reads: "They stepped aside when they saw me but did not quite stop laughing. They made way for my body without looking at me" (p. 87). The revised version is as follows: "They stepped aside politely, not to drip water on me, but did not stop laughing. Making way for my body without a glance at my face" (*Castle Rock*, p. 248). The changes are not radical, but they do make more of the guests' dismissive attitude toward the maid. For example, in the earlier version, the adverb "quite," termed a "downtoner" in English grammar, indicates that the laughter does not cease but is diminished; in the latter excerpt, however,

there is no attempt to suppress it. In both versions, the narrator comments on the girls' failure to make eye contact with her, but in the passage
immediately preceding, the rudeness appears more of a slight, for the
supplementive clause on its own separates the ignoring from the stepping
aside, somehow making it more of a consequent and conscious act.

The narrator's commentary on her relationship with Mrs. Montjoy,
her family, and her guests constitutes a remarkably accurate assessment
of her social status in the household. She not only identifies material differences between her own rural background and the affluent world of the
summer cottage in Georgian Bay, but she also becomes aware of attitu-
dinal differences, noting how strange it is that Mrs. Montjoy's daughter
should bemoan her intelligence, when, in the narrator's township, clever
boys are more likely to be looked on with suspicion, even disparaged as
"sissies" (*Castle Rock*, p. 231). Although she acknowledges that she feels
incongruous in the island setting, sensing the ubiquitous presence of "an
indolent reminder. *Not for you,*" she will not admit to feeling "humbled
or lonely, or that [she] was a real servant" (p. 232). One assertion she
makes toward the end of the narrative epitomizes both her pride and her
astute self-awareness; after reflecting on the hypocrisy of her behavior
toward Mrs. Montjoy, the narrator declares, "I did not have the grace or
fortitude to be a servant" (p. 252). In the earlier version, the verb phrase
is contracted, and the negation is thus reduced in force. Furthermore, in
her revision, Munro separates the statement in a paragraph of its own,
according it greater prominence, making it seem a confident, even defiant summation.

The reflective narrator perceives, in this display of assurance, a desire
for "equality, even with a person I did not like" (p. 252). The assurance
derives mostly from the narrator's sense of intellectual superiority over
Mrs. Montjoy, expressed early in the story, when she reveals her understanding of the allusion, in the name of the family boat, to Nausicaa in
Homer's *Odyssey*, a name Mrs. Montjoy mistakenly believes is "for some
character in Shakespeare" (p. 230). The narrator makes further discoveries
that enhance her feeling of power and lessen for her the disparity in status
between servant and employer. First, having learned that Mrs. Montjoy's
senile mother does not recognize her own daughter, she takes perverse
pleasure in telling her so (p. 236). She also feigns ignorance about the
death of her employer's older daughter, delicately eliciting details of the
tragedy from Mrs. Montjoy, all the while knowing she is being hypocritical. The narrator later evaluates her action in the confession: "Cruelty was
a thing I could not recognize in myself. I thought I was blameless here,
and in my dealings with the family" (p. 252). The deictic "here" oddly

jars with the past tense verbs, its incongruity serving to distinguish her present candor from her former deceit.

The conclusion of the story published in *The View from Castle Rock* differs from that published in the *New Yorker*. Both versions end with the scene in the boathouse, on the narrator's last Sunday, when Mr. Montjoy unexpectedly visits her and brings her the gift of his book, *Seven Gothic Tales*. Munro conveys the narrator's awkwardly expressed gratitude, and then her swift appropriation of what she feels is rightfully hers, something that "had always belonged to me" (*Castle Rock*, p. 254). In the earlier version, Munro inserts a flashback, several paragraphs from the end, in which the narrator recalls a conversation with Mary Anne, who, in an attempt at affiliation, had explained to her that her father "used to be poor like you." The attempt fails, however, for the narrator refuses to "give anybody whose father had been a doctor the credit for being poor" (*New Yorker*, p. 88). This flashback is omitted entirely from the revised version, and its omission removes blatant evidence of the narrator's inverted prejudice, snobbery just as unattractive as Mrs. Montjoy's *hauteur*.

In both conclusions the reader might leave with a less favorable impression of the narrator's behavior: in the *New Yorker* story, her resentment of Mr. Montjoy's working-class roots seems extreme, while in the more recent story it is her peevish self-absorption that comes across in her dismissal of "the person who interested me least, whose regard meant the least to me" (*Castle Rock*, p. 254). But in her later version, I believe, Munro somewhat mitigates her narrator's churlishness, for in the instances of reflection can be glimpsed a vestige of humility. Thinking on Mr. Montjoy's reasons for giving her the book, the narrator observes: "Drunk or not, I see him now as pure of motive, leaning against the boathouse wall. A person who could think me worthy of this gift. Of this book" (p. 254). This self-deprecation comes much later, after the admission of "alarm [and] resentment" at "having a little corner of myself come to light" (p. 254). At the time, the narrator resents the possibility that she might have betrayed any vulnerability, any commonality with a member of the Montjoy family; as an older narrator, she seems able to acknowledge a kindness and think less of the motivation behind it. This measured evaluation serves to deepen the narrator's psychological complexity; more importantly, its reasonableness somehow authenticates the narrator's beliefs about class, which were expressed in the diatribe to Mary Anne and in the incisive commentary on her wealthy, privileged employers and their peers. For in her retrospective wisdom she has not retracted, and does not retract a thing, nor is she afflicted by "a sensation of moral paralysis" that, according to Roxanne

Rimstead, often dissipates "emotions such as anger, shame or resentment" at the conclusions of Munro's poverty narratives.[41]

The changes that Munro effects in the second version of "Hired Girl" produce a narrator who is unlikely to hear, as Alva does in "Sunday Afternoon," the "plebeian sound" her footwear makes, and who freely admits that she is unsuited to the role of serving others she considers rude and uninformed, people who hold sway over her by virtue of their social category. In her revision, Munro intensifies and makes salient the class distinctions evident in the earlier *New Yorker* version, presenting them "as matters of political importance and community alliances."[42] The resulting narrative is a much more incisive, more critical social commentary that could not be described as "veiled."

In *Too Much Happiness*, Munro explores material far bleaker than nuances of social class, as several reviews of the work attest. In the *Toronto Star*, for example, Geoff Pevere's piece is entitled "Munro Explores the Darker Side";[43] in the *National Post*, Philip Marchand's review of Munro's collection is headed with the warning, "She'll curl your hair."[44] There is a discernible darkening of the writer's vision in the new collection, and in the final chapter I discuss some of the narrative strategies and different kinds of disarrangement that Munro uses as vehicles for disquieting themes—murder, terminal illness, calculated cruelty, sexual perversion.

CHAPTER 8

"MAROONED ON ISLANDS OF THEIR OWN CHOOSING"

FAITHFUL READERS OF MUNRO'S FICTION WILL ENCOUNTER familiar material in *Too Much Happiness*. For a start, the reader might recognize a few images and collocations from previous stories: the narrator's memory, in "Some Women," of a summer so hot "the streets of the town . . . were sprinkled with water to lay the dust"[1] recalls the scene Louisa, from "Carried Away," captures in a letter to soldier Jack Agnew, in the summer of 1917, when she tells of the watering tank dousing the *"streets every day, trying to lay the dust"* (*Open Secrets*, p. 8). The startling image for blood loss Munro uses in "The Love of a Good Woman," in Jeanette Quinn's dramatic account of Mr. Willens's death is retrieved in "Dimensions," at the scene of the accident involving Doree's bus. Mrs. Quinn tells Enid, with relish, of how the blood from Willens's head looked like "pink stuff . . . like when the froth comes up when you're boiling strawberries to make jam" (*The Love of a Good Woman*, p. 58). In the later story, the narrator describes the young truck driver lying at the side of the road, bleeding, the "trickle of pink" oozing from under his head "like the stuff you skim off from strawberries when you're making jam" (*Too Much Happiness*, p. 30). The graphic image is in keeping with the idiolect of both narrator and focalizer, for it is an ordinary, domestic analogy that working-class women like Doree and Jeanette Quinn would readily use.

All but one of the stories are set in Canada, with names of real locations in Ontario sprinkled throughout—Mildmay, London, Kincardine, Bayfield, Guelph, Toronto, Wallenstein. The narrator of "Face" looks back on a time when he "lived on the cliffs above Lake Huron" (p. 139) with a view like Stella, in "Lichen," whose summer cottage also sits "on the clay bluffs overlooking Lake Huron" (*The Progress of Love*, p. 32). The narrator of "Wenlock Edge," an arts student at university in London, Ontario, introduces us to a bachelor cousin who regularly takes her out to the restaurant "Old Chelsea . . . upstairs, looking down on Dundas Street" (*Too Much Happiness*, p. 62). The university to which the narrator of "Family Furnishings" (*Hateship*) has won her scholarship is also in London, Ontario, but unlike her predecessor, she has "hardly ever been south of Dundas Street or east of Adelaide" (p. 100).

In several other respects, *Too Much Happiness* illustrates qualities characteristic of Munro's fiction. The stories are unsettling. One first-person female narrator writes of her sexual humiliation;, another documents an extreme, deadly loathing; a third-person narrator reveals one man's lunatic jealousy, another recounts a son's inscrutable withdrawal from familial love.[2] There is a substantial amount of textual fragmentation, especially in the ambitious title story, where narrative speed is often accelerated to keep pace with Sophia Kovalensky's restless mind and peripatetic life. Ellipses proliferate, again most noticeably in the novella, the conclusion of which consists of a series of small explosions of information, arranged in block paragraphs, the last looking like an epigraph: "Sophia's name has been given to a crater on the moon" (*Too Much Happiness*, p. 303).

There are in most of the stories several instances of anachrony, accompanied by necessary modulations and shifts in tense and aspect: "Wood" is an exception in this regard, for it sustains, generally, a linear momentum appropriate for the actions of a single-minded, "covetous and nearly obsessive" central character (p. 231). This story first appeared in 1980, in the *New Yorker*, and is similar in some ways to work that Munro wrote at that time and included in her fourth collection, *The Moons of Jupiter* (1982). The omniscient third-person narrator introduces the male protagonist of "Wood" as though he were the subject of a realist television documentary: "Roy is an upholsterer and refinisher of furniture. He will also take on the job of rebuilding tables and chairs that have lost some rungs or a leg, or are otherwise in a dilapidated condition" (p. 224). The narrator of "Mrs. Cross and Mrs. Kidd" displays the same assured, panchronic knowledge of her subjects, as the combination of simple present tense and perfective aspect suggests: "Mrs. Cross and Mrs. Kidd have known each other eighty years, ever since Kindergarten . . . Mrs. Cross's first picture of Mrs. Kidd is of her standing at the front of the class" (*The Moons of Jupiter*, p. 160). In the first paragraph of the coterminous "Labor Day Dinner," the third-person narrator, in the manner of a social geographer, explains that the farmhouse of the story's setting is refurbished in a "style [that] is often found in Grey County; perhaps it was a specialty of the early builders" (p. 134). Like both these earlier pieces, "Wood" is narrated in predominantly present tenses, and events do not range over the wide sweeps of time customary in Munro's fiction. Most of the action in all three takes place in a delimited setting: a nursing home called Hilltop; a southern Ontario farmhouse; an area of overgrown bush that provides material for the protagonist's "private but not secret" interest—woodcutting (*Too Much Happiness*, p. 225).

In this narrative, Roy's preoccupation with wood is made abundantly clear in passages of substantial embellishment. The painstaking elaboration of a setting's concrete features is crucial to the unerring authenticity Munro establishes in her work; here, the description of the bush reads less like fiction, more like the referential, subject-specific prose of a science textbook, as when the narrator informs the reader that the "maple's grey bark has an irregular surface, the shadows creating black streaks, which meet sometimes in rough rectangles, sometimes not." That the wood is being perceived through the perspective of a man passionate about his craft becomes clear in the eccentric and subjective references to the "elephant skin" of the "arrogant-looking" beech, the "devilish curling and curving" of the oak tree's branches (p. 229). The purpose of all this accumulated, keenly observed detail is, I believe, to illustrate further how embedded the character is in his habitat, and how entirely absorbed he is in its splendor.

This obsession may, the reader suspects, have become too much, and may have adversely affected Lea, his wife, who has lately become grave and listless. Yet she is able to summon up strength he feared she would never regain, driving her car once more, with the intent to meet and talk to him, but as it turns out, to find and rescue him, after he has stumbled in the snow and broken his ankle. Munro uses a wonderfully apt image that might represent Roy's guarded self-protectiveness, a mental state that is shown to be his blind spot. He looks at the darkening forest in a new light, accepting that his familiarity has grown complacent, has made him as careless and unprepared as "any holidayer gawking around at nature, [or] somebody who thought the bush was a kind of park to stroll in" (p. 238): "But now he pays attention, he notices something about the bush that he thinks he has missed those other times. How tangled up in itself it is, how dense and secret" (p. 245). The bush he thought he knew like the back of his hand has undergone a transformation, without his realizing. Inadvertence, as the reader knows, can have serious consequences for Munro's characters.

Joyce Carol Oates, in a review of *Too Much Happiness*, writes in praise of these resonances, the instances of recurrence and retrieval, and the continued exploration of trusted themes and narrative situations that readers familiar with Munro's stories now recognize: "Of writers who have made the short story their métier, and whose accumulated work constitutes entire fictional worlds . . . Alice Munro is the most consistent in style, manner, content, vision."[3] The vision has become darker, however, and there are adjustments in style—irregular and elliptical sentences abound, as do terse paragraphs and truncated or disrupted utterances. For the first time, too, since "Thanks for the Ride" in *Dance of the Happy Shades*, a male narrator appears, in "Face," looking back on an unresolved incident in childhood he calls "the Great Drama of my life" (*Too Much Happiness*, p. 142). This narrator is a far cry from the callow, awkward youth Munro invented back then: he is the kind of man who relishes dramas, and indeed admits that he may come across as "tiresomely self-dramatizing," having had a career as an actor whose "agreeable, slightly quirky radio personality" (p. 143) won him many admirers. A career in radio suited someone who had grown up conscious of a disfiguring facial birthmark he dramatically describes as the color of "grape juice or paint . . . a big serious splash that does not turn to driblets until it reaches my neck" (p. 139). The birthmark is at the center of the childhood incident referred to as the "Great Drama." It is sparked off by the narrator's playmate Nancy, who lives in his rich family's rented cottage, and whose mother may be his father's lover. One summer afternoon Nancy smears her face with red paint, in order to resemble her friend, but her innocent although misguided gesture is interpreted by him as "an insult, a leering joke" (p. 153) that provokes a series of unfortunate consequences: displays of bitter, resentful anger from both mothers; the trigger for the young girl's later self-mutilation; the end of the narrator's friendship; possibly the beginning of an adult aloofness he refers to more than once.

Certainly his narration suggests someone shy of spontaneous expression. His account is delivered in a mannered, self-conscious style, replete with arresting tropes, instances of artifice, and rhetorical flourishes. In the very first sentence he declares, "I am convinced that my father looked at me, stared at me, saw me, only once" (p. 138). The statement sounds adamantine in its conviction, as a result of the asyndetic coordination of verb phrases that are staccato-like in their insistence. Also, the claim that the father looked only once at his son is exaggerated and unverifiable. The narrator likes to display his linguistic dexterity, placing words in quirky, surprising juxtaposition, as when he describes his student companions as "wits, dedicated time-wasters, savage social critics, newborn atheists" (p. 141). He sometimes addresses his reader not as though he were trying for interaction or engagement, but as if he were an orator practicing his art, preempting reactions to the tale, as when he explains how he became an actor and asks, "Surprising?" (p. 143). He then goes on to answer the imagined question. His most memorable response comes at the conclusion, when he speculates over what might have happened had he and Nancy met each other in later life, "both bearing our recognizable marks." They might have spoken only briefly and awkwardly, exchanging "useless autobiographical facts" (p. 162). He asks, "You think that would have changed things?," before delivering his own ambiguous verdict, "The answer is of course, and for a while, and never" (p. 163). The statement is characteristic of his narration—evasive, clever, and stylistically flamboyant.

The blunt title "Face" is out of keeping with such cryptic ambiguity, for it points with stark directness to the story's core image. Its directness and literalness are unlike most of the titles in *Too Much Happiness*, this noun phrase being a bitterly ironic description, particularly in relation to the main story. The titles are, in the main, harbingers of grim subjects.

Analyzing the appositeness and significance of titles in Alice Munro's *oeuvre* would make fascinating research. The title sometimes refers to a concrete object, or a striking image that assumes immense importance for the story's protagonist, like the "Nettles" the narrator and Mike McCallum crouch among when they shelter from the torrential rain. The title is more often a clamorous word or phrase used by the story's narrator or one of its main characters. "Save the Reaper" is Eve's inaccurate rendition of a line of poetry, one she stubbornly maintains is better than Tennyson's original. At the conclusion of "The Ticket," from *The View from Castle Rock*, the narrator's Aunt Charlie appears anxious about something other than the wedding dress she is making for her great niece. She takes the narrator aside and, as she presses "four fifty-dollar bills" in her hand, she warns her "in a shaky urgent whisper" that marriage "'might not be just the right ticket for you'" (p. 183). In this case, the idiomatic source of the title is homely and familiar.

The titles in *Too Much Happiness* are just as cleverly apt, but the origin or import of each is usually disquieting. "Dimensions" derives its title from the letter the insane Lloyd writes to his wife Doree from the "facility" where he is incarcerated for the murder of their three children. He writes that he has seen the children, has *"seen and talked to them,"* proof for him that they must inhabit other *"Dimensions"* (*Too Much Happiness*, p. 25). The phrase "Too Much Happiness" is reputedly uttered on her deathbed by Sophie Kovalensky, the focus of the title story. These words do not seem to be an accurate reflection of the woman's experience, for she dies "ravaged by pneumonia," her brilliant intellect not fully acclaimed in her life, her love not reciprocated by the haughty, jealous Maxsim, who speaks at her funeral "rather as if she had been a professor of his acquaintance" (p. 303). There could be nothing more shockingly

ironic than the title "Child's Play," a confession of childhood "wickedness" told by a coldhearted and seemingly unrepentant narrator (p. 222).
The story, like many of the stories in *Too Much Happiness*, makes for harrowing reading: only "Wood" and, to a limited extent, "Fiction," could be
described as hopeful. There is some vestige of hope offered at the end of
"Dimensions," but the road toward the ending is unbearably bleak. Here
is the verdict of British reviewer Peter Kemp: "Too much happiness is the
last thing with which people in these pages have to contend . . . Darker
than anything Munro has previously published, this book can make your
skin crawl with its uncoverings of the transitoriness and precariousness
of . . . existence."[4] While this twelfth collection unnerves, with the savage
irony of the titles and the darkness of the content, it also impresses, with
its narrative ingenuity and stylistic élan. In this final chapter, I suggest
that Munro, as she has done consistently in forty years of publishing short
fiction, continues to surprise and disarm, with new strategies and different means of disarrangement.

These are amply displayed in "Child's Play," one of the most chilling
narratives Munro has yet produced. The retrospective, homodiegetic narrator is Marlene, a retired anthropologist, wry, aloof, and observing, who,
with a clinical regard for detail, tells of a time in her childhood when,
at a summer camp, she and her friend Charlene killed Verna, a disabled
girl whom the narrator knew and despised. Yet her account is far from
clear and straightforward, for there is much that remains untold, as the
reader infers from the many instances of omission, ambiguity, hesitation,
and reformulation that permeate her narrative. From a Toronto hospital,
where she is now terminally ill, Charlene has arranged for a letter to be
given to the narrator, in which she asks her to visit on her behalf a priest
she has already contacted, who has promised to help her, presumably as
she seeks forgiveness. The two former childhood friends have not met
since the time of Verna's death, many decades before, although Charlene tried to renew the friendship. The meeting with the chosen priest
does not happen, and whether or not Marlene fulfils her friend's wishes
is unknown, and seems unlikely. The narrative turns out to be a form of
confession, although there is little sign of remorse, any wish for "tricky
forgiveness" (p. 220).

"Child's Play" is an uncomfortable story to read and study. One of the
reasons, for me, is the quality of the narrative voice, a voice Munro has
rarely imbued with such cynicism. This is discernible at the outset:

I suppose there was talk in our house, afterwards.
How sad, how *awful*. (My mother.)

There should have been supervision. Where were the counsellors? (My father.) (*Too Much Happiness*, p. 188)

The context for the utterances is not stated, only implied; some "awful" misfortune seems to have happened, the consequence of neglect or care-lessness, and it has provoked strong reactions, yet the narrator can only grudgingly "suppose" there was "talk." The adverbial "afterwards," nor-mally postmodifying or complementing, to denote a specific temporal location or duration, remains unrelated to any other syntactic entity in the contest; so the reader cannot know what preceded the "talk." One wonders why the mother's expression of sympathy is mocked, and why both parents' spoken words are presented like lines of dialogue in a play, as though inauthentic. The impression of a withholding narrator is fur-ther enhanced by the salience of ellipsis—three instances in the space of just over half a page.

Regarded as "one of the fundamental narrative speeds" in fiction,[5] ellipsis is a distinctive and pervasive feature of Munro's narrative art, as I have argued throughout this work. The ellipses at the start of "Child's Play" are unusual, however, unlike other instances discussed; indeed, the singular arrangement is rare in her fiction. The gaps are clustered at the story's beginning, before the narrator has established the fictive world where they might signify time passed in it. Rather than accelerating nar-rative speed, the ellipses here seem to put a brake on the tale, as though the teller has trouble with momentum, needing three attempts before she hits her stride with the retrospective account. The phenomenon more precisely illustrates paralipsis, a term used by Gérard Genette to describe a narrative omission, a lateral ellipsis where the narrative does not pass *over* a moment in time, but sidesteps it, so that details of an event are deliberately withheld from the reader.[6] In three separate attempts to begin her story, the narrator leaves in her trail meager scraps of information the reader will need help in following.

In the rest of this chapter I examine how Munro develops this disturb-ing narration, arguing that in "Child's Play" she "offers something slightly different . . . especially in her use of an almost melodramatic violence."[7] The act of extreme violence at the heart of the story is the killing of Verna, an act of "wickedness" Munro explores in the context of injurious preju-dices in the narrator's cultural heritage.

In the review from which I quote, Michael Gorra points to a "jagged or bitten-off" quality in the endings of Munro's recent stories, where "edges are sharp, never rounded into smoothness."[8] I think that "Child's Play" illustrates this jagged quality in abundance, and not just in the shock-ing ending: the narration is characterized by textual fragmentation and disruption, with sudden changes of subject and shifts in time; sentences are fractured midway, many reduced to phrases; one-line paragraphs isolate the narrator's clipped, dogmatic statements; words are removed from their habitual moorings, placed in incongruous contexts or discrepant juxtapositions. These phenomena are always present in Munro's fiction, in varying degrees, but not concentrated with such intensity as they are in "Child's Play."

One remarkable feature of the narrative is the frequency of parenthetical structures that disrupt its fluency. These are indicated by correlative punctuation marks—pairs of brackets or dashes. There is a sprinkling of brackets, performing an orthodox function around additional information or explanation, as in the introduction of "Child's Play" discussed previously. Far more common in Marlene's narrative are dashes, which proliferate to such a degree they can be regarded as stylistically marked, and thus worthy of attention. Dashes "tend to give a . . . dramatic and informal expression, suggesting an impromptu aside, rather than a planned inclusion."[9] In "Child's Play" the dashes most often surround pieces of appositive commentary and reformulation in the middle of sentences, where the narrator breaks off a statement to elaborate on, refine, or qualify what she writes. Recounting, at summer camp, the "differences" between herself and Charlene, the narrator notes, "Both of us had our tonsils out—a usual precaution in those days—and both of us had measles." One of the camp counselors, she informs us, "lost her fiancé in the war and wore his watch—we believed it was his watch—pinned to her blouse" (p. 191). When, years later, she reads in the newspaper of Charlene's marriage, she notes, "She—the bride, it said—had graduated from St Hilda's College in Toronto" (p. 208). In each case, the dashes enclose a needless intrusion of the teller's presence, adding little substance but conveying something of her punctilious nature, her desire to be in control. Moreover, there are moments in the narrative when her excessive regard for detail, developed in a career as an anthropologist, makes her added comments appear insensitively clinical, as when on her hospital visit she notes the "frizz of hair—still brown—about a quarter of an inch long on [Charlene's] scalp"; she recalls and records this minute feature, but expresses no pity for the dying woman, a former friend, no emotion save that she "was not surprised" at her appearance (p. 213).

Her insensitivity is starkly revealed in her choice of title, *Idiots and Idols*, for the book she had published on her research into what she describes as the "attitude of people in various cultures—one does not dare say the word 'primitive to describe such cultures—the attitude toward people who are mentally or physically unique" (p. 210). Here, the interruption shows her self-censoring to be hypocritical, founded on academic affecta-tion, not linguistic respect, for she cites the offensive word to clarify her meaning, thereby negating the political correctness she claims to observe.

Elsewhere, bracketed pieces of commentary expose the narrator's wish to withhold or diminish rather than amplify: "I cannot—this is true—I cannot be bothered getting that straight now," she says, of the number of lovers she might have had (p. 211). The reformulation, indicated by the dashes and the repeated "I cannot," conveys her impatience with discom-fiting personal information. Indeed, details about her emotional or sexual life tend to be kept vague and equivocal. When she touches on the sub-ject of past relationships, she refers obliquely to three "important" men, whose importance she attempts to qualify in tortuous, fragmented prose:

> What I mean by "important" is that with those three—no, only two, the third meaning a great deal more to me than I to him—with those three, then, the time would come when you want to split open, surrender far more than your own body, dump your whole life safely into one basket with his.
>
> I kept myself from doing this, but just barely. (p. 211)

In her switch from first- to second-person pronoun, she avoids the risk of confessing to the moment of her own possible surrender, instead keep-ing to safer generalized ground. The narrative "you" when it suddenly emerges, briefly and singly in a first-person account, is, according to nar-ratologist Brian Richardson, a device "admirably suited to indicate a sup-pressed subjectivity . . . and is peculiarly appropriate for describing the mind of a conflicted individual."[10] Marlene is reluctant to abdicate control of her narrative, and of emotions that would weaken her independence.

Another singular feature in the passage quoted previously is the high proportion of function words to lexical or content ones: of the fifty-seven words in the first sentence, more than forty are parts of speech such as pro-nouns, determiners, prepositions, and numerals, that is, words essential for syntactic cohesion, but contributing less in content than, for example, nouns and full verbs. When function words greatly outnumber content words, one consequence is that utterances are loosened from their deictic contexts, making meaning vague and generalized. In Marlene's attempt to clarify, she provides no information about the "lovers," who are referred to merely by number in spite of their stated importance; she also succeeds in obfuscating exactly when and why "you" (meaning herself) would want to commit to another. The image of the basket, into which somebody would "dump" his or her future, is disquieting, because it is suggestive of a shopping transaction rather than a profound relationship. The narrator struggles to find the appropriate vocabulary for articulating intimacy.

She is far more comfortable and unequivocal when judging other people, noting their flaws. Her narration teems with examples of tendentious views and harsh judgments, delivered without reflection: a "sharp-voiced and bossy" camp counselor "even has an unpleasant name. Arva" (p. 191); another has "custard flesh wobbling on her thick arms and legs" (p. 223); only a "roughly brought up sort of girl" would have her camp stay paid for by charity (p. 191); Charlene in her hospital bed is described pitilessly as "a bloated body [with] a sharp ruined face" (p. 213). The account of her treatment of Verna is a testimony to irrational, violent loathing. The girl's "small head" makes her "think of a snake," and the skin on her face looks like "the flap of our old canvas tent" (p. 195). She says she hated her "as some people hate snakes or caterpillars or slugs. For no decent reason" (p. 201). The laconic phrase or the reduced clause, broken off from the construction it is part of, is one of the narrator's verbal tics, and makes her verdicts and prejudices seem immutable and final.

At times the prose is almost telegraphic in its brevity and reduction, making the narrator sound paranoid in her urgency: "No. Better not a note" is how she dismisses the idea of replying to Charlene's husband, after he has written to tell her of his wife's illness (p. 212). Her actual dialogue is remarkable for briskness, its lack of adornment: she prefers one-word responses and questions, and falters when she has to elaborate, reveal too much, as in the cathedral when she mentions Charlene's letter, saying, "'She asks me—I have a note from her here—She wants to see Father Hofstrader'" (p. 218). When she wonders about her former friend's religious faith, thinking, "She might have converted secretly. Since" (p. 216), she leaves the utterance incomplete, with no reference to what might have encouraged the conversion. The reader may ask, perhaps it was the actual drowning of Verna, or maybe the time when it happened? At any rate, the omission is thought-provoking, and is made salient by Munro's isolation of the six words in a one-line paragraph. The expected syntactic arrangement has an important piece missing, and what is not named hovers at the end of the oddly truncated line.

It is not only irregular syntax that creates textual gaps. Anachronies disrupt linearity, enabling Munro to postpone or withhold vital pieces of information that may confirm suspicions fuelled earlier. The first great temporal leap occurs after only a few paragraphs, when the narrator breaks off from cryptic musings about childhood, and the past, how scenes from it come "sprouting up fresh, wanting attention . . . though it's plain there is not a thing on this earth to be done." This teasing prospect

of a confession is swiftly snatched away with the analepsis that begins
beguilingly, "Marlene and Charlene. People thought we must be twins.
There was a fashion in those days for naming twins in rhyme" (p. 189).
Whatever has sprouted up fresh is thus postponed, but the expectation
of a nostalgic account of female friendship would be misplaced, in view
of earlier, unpropitious signs.

The most telling temporal shift occurs when the narrator recounts the
last day at summer camp, when she and Charlene are in the lake with
the other girls, and Verna "is making her way towards us, wearing her
pale blue rubber cap." The narrative sharply veers away from that time
to return to the present, with the deadpan, banal admission, "I have not
kept up with Charlene" (p. 207). A gap of fourteen pages, nearly a third
of the text, has lapsed before the retrospective account resumes in all its
shocking detail, and the lengthy postponement certainly contributes to
the impact of the final scene.

Most of the distinctive and unattractive qualities of the narrative voice
are illustrated in this scene. The narrator's liking for mocking parody is
in evidence, as she simulates in her elliptical way how adults might have
reacted, forgiving the girls had they confessed: "Yes, yes. Hardly knew
what they were doing" (p. 222). But the manner in which Munro presents Marlene's account of the drowning confirms it was a deed done
"consciously" and recalled clinically. Words lose the neutrality of their
ordinary denotation and acquire hideous meaning. In Verna's struggle
to break the surface, her head "rise[s], like a dumpling in a stew"; the
ridges on her bathing cap make it "less slippery" for the girls to grip,
obligingly pushing upward "into [the narrator's] palms" (p. 222). In this
scene, frightening in its clarity and unsparing detail, the narrator depicts
Verna as nonhuman before she loses her life—she is a "jellyfish in the
water," a rubber object, a pattern on a bathing cap (p. 221). In the imagined aftermath of the drowning, she is "One of the Specials," a nameless
girl, "something out there in the water" (p. 223). The narrator did not
witness the "unease starting" by the lakeside because she and Charlene
had already left with their parents, without any parting ceremony. The
story ends in a single-sentence paragraph, occupying one line like several
stark statements before it: "But I believe we were gone by then" (p. 223).
On one level, it sounds like a casual remark, explaining the hasty departure from camp, but on another it is the recognition they have finished
with childhood, and it seems to rule out any hope the narrator would
try for forgiveness.

But try she does, as the ending in the contemporaneous level hints at,
albeit faintly. Munro offers us two endings, really: one signals the text's

completion, ending the retrospective account at summer camp, where the perpetrators escape; the other occurs three pages previously, and transfixes the narrator in her car, outside a Guelph church, after she has spoken to the priest and dealt with what she dubs "all this palaver." Now rigid with indecision, she admits, "I knew what was necessary and possible but it was beyond my strength, for the moment, to do it" (p. 220). The deceptively bland adverbial, brought to our attention by its enclosure, decidedly qualifies the certainty of her denial. What if the story had ended here, on the primary level, with the tenuous possibility of redemption for the narrator? The fact is that it does not. Munro's decision to return the narrative to the scene of the drowning makes for a bleaker ending, because it heightens the tragedy of one childhood ended, and young lives spoiled, wasted.

I find it hard to read anything affirmative from this grim but nevertheless immensely moral narrative. Its morality lies in the writer's insistence that we ask, how did the narrator get like that, and how much is a child to blame? The case against the culture she grew up in is convincingly presented, especially if we look closely at some of the language circulating in that culture. Munro hastens to provide us with examples of linguistic disrespect in the early 1940s, when her narrator explains that, besides their rhyming names, she and Charlene were considered twins at camp because both wore "coolie" hats, at a time when "it was possible . . . to say *coolie* without a thought of offence [or] *darkie*, or to talk about *jewing* a place down" (p. 189).

But it is the epithet "Specials" that catches the eye, running through the narrative as pejorative shorthand for children, like Verna, with learning difficulties. The word appears first of all in the singular, with the reference to the "Special Classes" (p. 199) Verna attends. The adjective quickly becomes a noun in the plural, to recur with marked frequency in the remainder of the narrative—sixteen times, always capitalized. The process of conversion, by which a word moves from one word class to another, produces here a label that *reifies* the prejudice, turning it into a convenient vehicle for opprobrium. The narrator can only imagine the lakeside scene after Verna's drowning, but is specific about how the camp counselor would speak impatiently of the missing girl as "One of the Specials."

Seldom has Munro portrayed a Canadian provincial setting so negatively. She carefully demonstrates that her narrator's "aversion" was not so out of "tune with an unspoken verdict of the time and place" she lived in (p. 196), where children like Verna were educated in buildings not designed as schools, and where, at summer camp, they were "deliberately separated and distributed amongst the rest" as though their presence had to be diluted. The passive voice predominates in the description of how Verna and her classmates behave at camp: they are "yelled at and fetched back" when they wander off, "herded by" the other campers, and they are "marched in" (p. 201) at supper, to join the other girls, who sing, oblivious of the irony in the verse that Munro makes prominent:

> *The more we get together, together, together*
> *The more we get together,*
> *The happier we'll be.* (p. 202)

By these numerous and prominent references to the social and educational segregation prevalent at the time, Munro holds up for scrutiny the cultural heritage that creates children who, in their drowning of Verna, did not feel they were "wicked," but thought their actions were somehow "the culmination, in our lives, of our being ourselves." Munro encourages the reader to question why the narrator and her companion should have felt so impelled, driven to such extremity that they had no choice, and had "gone too far to turn back, you might say" (p. 222).

Extremity is a theme running through *Too Much Happiness*: the husband's controlling jealousy in "Dimensions," Edie's fanatical sanctimony in "Fiction," Nina's tranquil passivity in "Wenlock Edge," the father's balefulness toward his disfigured son in "Face"—these are all extreme reactions. In "Child's Play" Munro examines in greater depth the *consequences* of an extreme act in childhood, on a narrator who identifies her phobic hatred of Verna as "a starting point" in a journey toward adulthood where she has become an unfeeling, bitter old woman (p. 210). The narrator grows up in a neighborhood marked by social and religious division, where intolerance and a "taken-for-granted superiority" could thrive (p. 196). There are repeated allusions to the social and historical context, when certain conventions and fashions prevailed. The clause, "This was at a time when" (p. 208), in which a marker of the present ushers in a past-tense verb, is distinctively Munrovian. Such a signpost occurs in numerous Munro narratives, signifying that what happened long ago has resurfaced, and will not go away.

Charlene belatedly seeks absolution for what she has done, but the narrator is not "tempted," and the possibility that she might carry out her dying friend's wishes is remote indeed, given the manner of the story's conclusion. For what is narrated here confirms the extent to which she incriminates and condemns herself, ruling out even a "tricky forgiveness" (p. 220). The glacial observation—"But I believe we were gone by then"—is delivered by a new kind of first-person narrator in Munro's fiction, possessed of a despairing nihilism that is expressed in her unswerving, clipped assertions, in captious judgments, and her cruel, sardonic parodies. In the narrator of "Child's Play," Munro unveils another addition to her cast of troubled and troubling characters that have transgressed: this narrator outdoes the others, however, in the violence of her actions, and the disjunction of her tale.

I have argued throughout this book that in the substantial body of the writer's accumulated work there is remarkable consistency. There are elaborate evocations of Canadian small-town settings, containing details as homely and specific as tongue-in-groove paneling, chesterfields, and thimbleberries in wild Ontario orchards. The fact that locations and institutions peculiar to the Canadian setting are often named (Goderich, Hastings County, Blyth, Owen Sound, Canadian Tire, CGIT, Union Station, Highway 401) consolidates the authenticity of the fiction, as does the plausible dialogue, sometimes rich in idioms like "took a notion to" or "carrying the lard." Stories begin without much preamble, plunging the reader into fictional worlds where characters appear to live humble, ordinary lives that are transformed by "elegant caprice," by "streaks of loss and luck" (*The Beggar Maid*, p. 154). Because Munro likes to explore themes of guilt, duplicity, and the surrender of control, her narratives often feature infidelity or sexual jealousy, creating the kind of "drama in people's lives . . . a writer is naturally attracted to."[11] Munro explains that in her fiction, "The reality is you don't always get the man you want," so a female character, like Louisa in "Carried Away," will look for "alternate realities . . . several potential realities available to her in her future."[12] There has always been an awareness of alternative worlds in Munro's fiction, notably in work published after 1990.

Time and memory play immensely important roles in her stories: what is remembered may be consoling, fickle, or fugacious, and what cannot be remembered is replaced by images more bountiful. Munro captures her images in an abundance of rich tropes and schemes, with a liking for contradiction and dissonant associations that oxymoron and metonymy express. In her most recent stories, some of the images are shockingly graphic and violent, like the "chunk of chopped liver" a father likens his son's birthmark to (*Too Much Happiness*, p. 139) or the "expressions blown away" in a murderer's photograph of his slain family (p. 130).

Munro's work contains frequent instances of anachrony that convey relations between past and present, or point to futures imagined by a homodiegetic narrator, or confidently predicted by an omniscient one; in third-person narratives, the perspective may change several times, so that events can be seen from different angles. With each new publication, the "shifting time frames and multiple viewpoints" characteristic of her fiction have increased in number and complexity, often occurring in longer, densely layered stories that can be termed novellas.[13] Amid such complexity and diffuseness of viewpoint, it is sometimes difficult to align oneself with a reliable witness and get a hold on "scaffolding helpful in making sense of these latest works," as the reader encounters so much ambiguity and ambivalence, especially in the endings.[14] These tend toward the indeterminate, although, as more than one reviewer has remarked, some of the endings in the latest collection seem abrupt and final. Munro's stories cannot be read cursorily; they require careful perusal, mainly because the narration proceeds in a digressive and meandering way, rarely linear. The direction is always purposeful, however, for there are few writers so attentive to the architecture of their fiction. Several scholars cite her clever, apposite analogy of the house that has to have a "sturdy sense of itself [and is] durable and freestanding," a structure she will study time and time again to make sure there are no cracks, or obscured vistas.[15]

One of my chapters borrows for its title Munro's wonderful phrase "the queer bright moment" for the "central incident . . . the scene that seems to hold the most essential key to the story."[16] I have extended Munro's definition to make this phrase apply to a nugget in the text, which may be an image, a glimpse of a character trait, a fleeting impression captured by the narrator, that is somehow made prominent on the page. And it sheds light on a mystery, it is a clue to a greater understanding of the story—like the feathered hat on Marion Slater's lap, or the axe wound on Simon Herron, or even, perhaps, the yellow lilies in the snow that seem to be associated with Fiona's love in "The Bear Came Over the Mountain." These are, to quote from Judith Maclean Miller's marvelous essay on "Deconstructing Silence," the "tellings and the not-tellings [that] eddy around and around" in her stories.[17]

Most of the previous hallmarks of Alice Munro's fiction distinguish her latest collection, and will her next. In *Too Much Happiness*, and "Child's Play" in particular, there is evidence of further additions to her ample repertoire of characters, ideas, themes, and narrative strategies. In the concluding paragraph of his review of *Hateship, Friendship, Courtship, Loveship, Marriage*, Michael Ravitch makes some general remarks about Munro's fiction: "There is no despair, and little anger. She keeps such intense emotions at a distance. Awful tragedies occur, but always off-stage."[18] I do not think these statements apply so accurately to the twelfth collection, and certainly not to "Child's Play." Marlene's childhood aversion is documented in all its angry ferocity, and it culminates in an unspeakable tragedy narrated unsparingly. The consequences of her actions are illustrated in the quality of her narrative voice—sardonic, skeptical, mistrustful—surely the most unappealing Munro has so far produced.

She has created this voice using a number of devices, like the disjunctive syntax, the telegraphic sentences, and lexical choices that expose her narrator's callous insensitivity. This quality is sealed by the story's last line. Interestingly, it is absent from the *Harper's* edition of "Child's Play," published in February 2007, and its addition to the final version tells us something of the writer's boldness.[19] She is prepared to take risks in this collection, and several are illustrated in this disturbing narrative.

Almost every collection Munro publishes "contains more than you saw the last time."[20]

Afterword

In October 2013, the Swedish Academy in Stockholm announced that the Nobel Prize in Literature, given to a writer for a lifetime's body of work, had that year been awarded to Alice Munro. In the *New York Times* on October 11, Julie Bosman reported that news of this achievement was greeted with affectionate tributes and jubilation, in Canada and beyond, along with congratulatory messages rolling in from readers, politicians, publishers, editors and fellow writers.[1]

The award seemed particularly poignant as it was announced in a year when Munro had stated firmly she would write no more. In an article titled "Alice Munro Puts Down Her Pen to Let the World In," Charles McGrath, Munro's former editor at the *New Yorker*, explained that the writer had told him there would be no more books after *Dear Life*, published in 2012.[2] This resolve was apparently reiterated at the Nobel Award ceremony in Sweden in December 2013 when Munro's daughter Jenny accepted the prize for her mother. At a banquet afterward, she read a statement from the writer, in which she asserted, "I've been writing since I was about 10, and it's really time to have a different take on life."[3]

The writer's intention to write no more stories after *Dear Life* was perhaps hinted at by her decision to preface the "final four works" in the collection with the description, "the first and last—and the closest—things I have to say about my own life" (p. 255).[4] If indeed *Dear Life* is to be the writer's last book of new stories, then it is a finale with a flourish, for the book has garnered customarily laudatory reviews. Peter Kemp, for example, in the *Sunday Times*, called it "a triumph of imaginative vitality."[5]

Faithful readers of Munro's fiction will find much that is familiar in *Dear Life*. Most of the material was published before in locations as diverse as *Tin House*, *Narrative Magazine*, *Harper's*, *Granta*, and the *New Yorker*, which has a first-refusal contract with the writer. Seven of the fictional pieces came out in the same year as the book, giving the impression of preemptive haste on the part of agent and/or publisher. As ever, there are thought-provoking differences between the versions published in journals and magazines and those of the final collection, notably in the case of "Corrie," which I refer to later in this afterword. The stories

in *Dear Life* illustrate many distinguishing features, hallmarks of her narrative art; however, I believe that, as with every new collection Munro
publishes, there are some surprising innovations.

The sense of place—namely Ontario but with forays to Vancouver,
British Columbia—is strongly evoked in *Dear Life*. Indeed, references
to authentic locations, institutions, and events that are specifically
Canadian permeate the collection. In the stories not "autobiographical in feeling" (p. 255), Toronto is, remarkably, mentioned more than
thirty times, most often in "Train," where various well-known places,
such as Avenue Road, Eaton's store, Eglinton, Chinatown, and the
Royal Ontario Museum, are also named, substantiating the concrete-
ness of the setting. In other stories, characters travel to, pass near,
or think of Goderich, Kitchener, Windsor, Cobourg, Muskoka, Lake
Simcoe, and the Grey-Bruce border. That most Canadian of institutions, the United Church, appears nine times in the collection;
Tommy Douglas, the socialist premier of Saskatchewan from 1944 to
1961, is named, as is Pierre Trudeau, who served as Canada's premier
twice, from 1968 to 1979 and from 1980 to 1984.

But all this "Canadianness" is not merely for purposes of authenticity.
Munro uses aspects of the setting and landscape to suggest certain character indices, to accord importance to particular scenes or moments in the
narrative, modifying the reader's perception of them. Jackson, the protagonist of "Train," leaps off onto the rails before his journey would take
him toward a town near Lake Huron and a reunion with his intended
bride, Ileane. Instead, he settles for some years in a platonic relationship with Belle on a ramshackle farm that had been her wealthy parents'
summer cottage; in the story's final scene, twenty years later, having left
Belle and now on his own without any ties, he is back on a train heading for Kapuskasing, a lumbering town in north Ontario, where he will
find work and where he is "encouraged by the cooler air" (p. 216). The
train journey affords him escape from emotional commitment and from
burdening expectations; by identifying the geographical remoteness he
seeks, Munro conveys her character's elective solitariness. In "Amundsen," the narrator also makes a journey high into northern Ontario—to
a sanatorium where she will teach children suffering from tuberculosis.
The building is situated near a frozen, snow-covered lake that is "not level
but mounded along the shore, as if the waves had turned to ice in the act
of falling" (p. 32). In her new surroundings, the young narrator, Vivien,
sees "everything austere, northerly, black-and-white under the high dome
of clouds" (p. 32). The image emerges as an apt perception of the sanatorium's doctor, Alister Fox, an ascetic, self-absorbed, briskly practical man

who purposefully courts Vivien, then jilts her on the day of the marriage, leaving her "dazed and full of disbelief" (p. 66).

Details in the Canadian setting can sometimes appear as propitious or inauspicious omens. The sexually bold protagonist Greta in "To Reach Japan" makes a hopeful journey from her home in Vancouver to Toronto, where she is to look after a friend's house for a month. She has hopes of being reunited with a journalist she met at a poets' party in Vancouver and has sent him a whimsical message with details of her arrival, thinking it has little chance of reaching him. The final scene in the narrative is of her arriving "in the bright lofty light of Union Station," and this pleasing image of expansive clarity augurs well for Greta, preparing her for the "determined and celebratory" (p. 29) kiss with which she is greeted by the man who has taken her suitcase from her hand. The kiss, and Greta's reaction to it, described as "a tumbling in [her] insides" (p. 30), mark the beginning of another sexual adventure for her.

The story "To Reach Japan" is set in the early 1960s, as the reference to the 1959 film *The Four Hundred Blows* indicates. The narrator discloses that it was one of several "European movies such as were beginning to be shown in Vancouver at that time" (p. 9). Temporal disruptions are neither radical nor frequent in this story, the time scale of which is quite compact, as indeed it is in several other narratives—for example "Amundsen," "Pride," and "Corrie," where the action takes place in the 1940s or 1950s. "Haven" is set wholly in the 1970s, as the narrator declares in the opening sentence (p. 110), and there are few disarrangements in a retrospective account of the year she spent with her repressed aunt and her rigidly controlling uncle. The temporal levels in *Dear Life* are generally more settled than in previous collections: yes, there are customary analepses, and years can scroll out over decades, as they do markedly in "Train." But in most of the stories, narrative time remains for long periods constant and uninterrupted. It is often at a story's conclusion that the first person or third-person narrator brings retrospective action back to the contemporaneous level of narration.

It is in several of the conclusions that I determine a marked difference between *Dear Life* and, certainly, *Too Much Happiness* for this recent collection is generally more affirmative. I have already remarked on the almost joyous optimism in Greta's arrival at Toronto's Union Station, the "Japan" of her desire. In other endings, the narrator or protagonist has similarly reached a welcome destination, like Jackson has in Kapuskasing when he breathes in the cooler air and feels sure of finding work in the lumbering town. At the conclusion of "Leaving Maverley," Ray, bereft by the recent death of his partner Isabel, finds some consolation, "relief out of all proportion" (p. 90), when he meets up again with Leah, whom he had first known and grown fond of when she was a gauche young woman, isolated and impoverished by her upbringing. At that time, he was a policeman in Maverley and in that capacity had helped her and shown an interest in her welfare and her future; indeed, when she suddenly left the town, eloping with the United Church minister's son, Ray was surprised at how desolate and "offended" he had felt (p. 79).

The story "Pride" is also principally concerned with the life of a male character; he is not, however, the subject of the focalization but the unnamed first person narrator. Such a choice of narration is rare in Munro's body of published work: only two stories, "Thanks for the Ride" (*Dance of the Happy Shades*) and "Face" (*Too Much Happiness*) feature a male narrator. "Pride" is narrated by a terse, reticent bookkeeper who is fearful of any emotional display and commitment, mainly because he is too conscious of his disfigurement: a badly stitched harelip. The narrator documents the stages in his relationship with Oneida, the daughter of the town's disgraced banker, a woman who first seeks the narrator's financial advice and then his regular company. Their developing friendship leads her to imagine a future together in the house he occupies alone: she tells him that if she were to leave her rented flat and live with him, they could "look after each other like brother and sister and it would be the most natural thing in the world" (p. 148). But this proposal horrifies the narrator, who instantly discourages her, telling her he plans to sell his house. This he swiftly does, and he absurdly buys an apartment in the same block as Oneida, for there are few places available in town that suit him. The story could have ended on a miserable note—the lasting recollection being of two proud characters destined to live separate lives, occupying separate small apartments near one another. In the story's ultimate scene, Oneida visits the narrator in the midst of his packing, telling him of her vague intentions to travel. She looks out of the window and catches sight of flurries of movement in the backyard. Munro leaves the reader with a memorable description of what she and the narrator then observe: little black and white skunks, playfully dancing in the birdbath, "flashing and dancing and never getting in each other's way" before they leave the water and walk smartly across the yard. The narrator observes how Oneida is "dazzled" by the brilliance of the sighting, and he is too because he concludes, "We were as glad as we could be" (p. 153). This laconic assertion is hopeful, for it is an admission of a shared joy, something that may be repeated.

My favorite story in *Dear Life*, "Corrie," might not immediately appear affirmative, for it deals with a cynic's deceitful exploitation of a gullible young woman disabled by polio. The third-person narrator recounts her involvement with Howard Ritchie, an architect engaged by Corrie's rich father to restore the tower of the town's Anglican church. Corrie begins a relationship with this married man, and their affair—made easier by the fact that Ritchie's work often requires travel, and Corrie is now alone in her house since the death of her father—proceeds smoothly. Trouble emerges when Ritchie discloses that Lillian Wolfe, a young girl who had cleaned for Corrie and is now employed by another family, has written to him, threatening to tell his wife about his infidelity, which she has inferred from seeing Ritchie with two different women in amorous poses. The blackmailing demands of which Ritchie tells Corrie are very specific: cash in envelopes twice a year, which Corrie quickly agrees to pay, reassuring him that money is "nothing to [her]" and that in any case it would be difficult for him to make the sacrifice, "taking it away from [his] family" (p. 161). Years later, with the affair still flourishing, albeit at a gentler pace, Corrie finds out that Lillian Wolfe has died prematurely. She attends the funeral party, where she learns from mourners about how loved Lillian was and how grateful she had always been to Corrie, who had once given her money for typing lessons, "so that she could better herself" (p. 159).

A clamorous ellipsis immediately follows the scene in which Corrie makes this discovery about Lillian. In this hiatus, the reader might comprehend the full extent of Howard Ritchie's treachery if he or she is alert to pieces of information and significant character indices adroitly inserted before this scene, for this protagonist is presented in a poor light. As she does in "Lichen," discussed in Chapter 2 of this book, Munro begins with an external focalizer and then aligns the perspective with an internal one, the male character, who is, especially at the outset, the subject of the focalization. Via free indirect discourse, Munro exposes his reductive, captious reaction to Corrie, who sits opposite him at dinner in the story's opening scene. He decides she has a "conventional mind" and is "not a soft woman. Not much meat on the bone," thinking her both "unmannerly" and "spoilt" when she dares to light a cigarette (pp. 156–57). He dislikes her "forwardness, her self-satisfaction," which "would become tiresome" but then qualifies his objections with a salutary aside, one that in a second reading, announces itself as dramatic irony. As such, it conveys his cupidity: "Of course, there was money, and to some men that never became tiresome" (p. 157).

If the reader has not already formed suspicions about Ritchie's motivations and deviousness, then he or she would have wondered why the recipient of the blackmailing letter should have burned it and not shown it to the coaccused in his acts of infidelity. The reader might also wonder why someone so trusted and respected by Corrie should suddenly turn treacherous and why Corrie could so easily assume treachery. The practice of handing over the stipulated sums of money to Ritchie, for deposit in a postal box, becomes a ritual, one so regular and routine that eventually the pair did not even speak of it. The narrator makes several references, however, to the financial comfort Ritchie and his family enjoy over the years—holidays in Europe (pp. 164, 165), a move from Kitchener to Toronto, and the summer cottage in Muskoka (p. 171)—and these encourage the impression that Corrie's payments are supporting her lover's successful, solidly respectable family life.

The final scenes in the narrative concern Corrie's response to the revelation of Lillian Wolfe's death. The differences between the version published in New Yorker[6] and that in Dear Life are significant, and I would argue they further substantiate my claim that this collection of stories is more affirmative than Munro's previous publications. In both versions, Corrie realizes she has been deceived, waking up from sleep with "a cavity everywhere, most notably in her chest" (p. 173), thinking on how she will act with this new knowledge. In the New Yorker version, she does nothing, sure that Ritchie will never learn of the woman's death and accepting that if what she does demands payment, then "she is the one who can afford to pay."[7] In the book version of the ending, she sends Howard Ritchie a brief message with the information and turns off her phone. The narrator reports that she receives an equally laconic letter, stating, "All well now, be glad. Soon" (p. 147). Munro uses free indirect discourse in the last paragraph to express Corrie's resignation and maybe her relief: "So that's how they're going to leave it. Too late to do another thing. When there could have been worse, much worse" (p. 174).

Which ending is preferable? In one ending, the man's deceit may be acknowledged, but its rewards remain, and Corrie's cynical lover and his family are kept comfortably off; in the revised version, Corrie does at least put a stop to the payment of her sexual dues, and she may also have caused some consternation with her "special delivery" note to Ritchie's office. What bothers me is that in neither version does Corrie clear the innocent Lillian's (or Sadie's) name, and in neither version does Corrie come across as anything but needy, desperate, and hypocritical. But what I like about this story is the exposure of the male character's fastidious sexual prejudice and instrumental, carefully planned deceit. The ending of the story published in Dear Life at least shows the female protagonist with some degree of agency, a little more nous.

These, then, are some of the differences I discern between the stories of *Dear Life* and those of previous collections, notably *Too Much Happiness*. Of course, probably the most remarkable innovation in the book (and one noted by most reviewers) is the inclusion of four pieces prefaced by "FINALE" and described by the writer as "autobiographical in feeling" (p. 255). These I don't intend to comment on, since my book is a study, using the tools of narratology and literary linguistics, of the writer's *fiction*.

In the years ahead, there will assuredly be more monographs published on Alice Munro's work, as there will be many single essays published in academic journals and volumes of scholarly criticism. The Modern Language Association's list of cited works under her name grows longer each time I consult it. At the time of writing, there are planned symposiums in Ottawa and Paris, with prestigious academics and authors poised to contribute.[8] In 2012, the contents of *Narrative*, the journal of the International Society for the Study of Narrative,[9] consisted entirely of analyses of and dialogues on a single Munro story, "Passion," from *Hateship, Friendship, Courtship, Loveship, Marriage* (2001). Her fiction has in the last decade become particularly attractive to researchers from the disciplines of narrative studies, stylistics, and corpus linguistics, and this fact is a source of both pleasure and optimism for me. It is with the enriching and elucidating tools of these disciplines that I have come to appreciate and better understand Munro's fiction. And more recently, shortly after *Narrative Art* was published in 2011, I discovered yet another source of illumination for my subject.

In his research on lexical patterning, reader expectation, and emotionally immersive language in literary narrative, for example, British linguist Michael Toolan[10] has produced exciting, insightful work on the various ways Munro engages and sustains reader empathy, how she concentrates "a moment or passage of exceptional emotional resonance that draws the reader in and holds them moral captive."[11] To write fiction with this sort of power is a momentous achievement.

NOTES

INTRODUCTION

1. Helen Hoy, "'Rose and Janet': Alice Munro's Metafiction," *Canadian Literature* 121 (1989): 59–83.
2. Robert Thacker, *Alice Munro: Writing Her Lives* (Toronto: McClelland and Stewart, 2005), 414.
3. Alice Munro, quoted in Thacker, *Alice Munro,* 417, italics in original.
4. Jeanne McCulloch and Mona Simpson, "Alice Munro: The Art of Fiction CXXXVIII," *Paris Review* 131 (1994): 227–64.
5. Alice Munro, "What Is Real?" *Canadian Forum* (September 1982): 5, 32.
6. Catherine Sheldrick Ross, *Alice Munro: A Double Life* (Toronto: ECW Press, 1992), 88. The interview from which Ross quotes, entitled "Interview: Alice Munro," is with Kevin Connolly, Douglas Freake, and Jason Sherman, and is published in *What* (September–October 1986): 8–10.
7. Daphne Merkin, "Northern Exposure," *New York Times Magazine* (October 24, 2004): 20–23.
8. Aida Edemariam, "Riches of a Double Life," *Guardian Review* (September 24, 2003): 20–23.
9. Alice Munro continues to publish in the *New Yorker.* On October 11, 2010, the short story "Corrie" was published (pp. 94–101), and on January 31, 2011, "Axis" (pp. 62–69). She has also published recently in *Harper's*: the story "Pride" appeared in April 2011 (pp. 59–67).
10. Eleanor Wachtel, "An Interview with Alice Munro," *Brick* 40 (1991): 48–53.
11. Catherine Sheldrick Ross, "'Too Many Things': Reading Alice Munro's 'The Love of a Good Woman,'" *University of Toronto Quarterly* 71, no. 3 (Summer 2002): 786–808.
12. Dennis Duffy, "'A Dark Sort of Mirror': 'The Love of a Good Woman' as Pauline Poetic," *Essays in Canadian Writing* 66 (Winter 1998): 169–90.
13. Coral Ann Howells, "The Telling of Secrets/The Secrets of Telling," *Open Letter* Eleventh Series no. 9, Twelfth Series no. 1 (2003–4): 39–54.
14. Héliane Ventura, "Introduction," *Open Letter* (2003–4): 15–22.
15. Caterina Ricciardi, "The Secrets of Intertextuality: Alice Munro's 'Pictures of Ice,'" *Open Letter* (2003–4): 121–37.
16. Ajay Heble, *The Tumble of Reason: Alice Munro's Discourse of Absence* (Toronto: University of Toronto Press, 1994), 3.
17. Danielle Fuller and Susan Billingham, "CanLit(e): Fit for Export?" *Essays on Canadian Writing* 71 (Fall 2000): 114–28.

18. Alison Lurie, "The Lamp in the Mausoleum," *New York Review of Books* (December 21, 2006): 22–30.

19. Alice Munro, *Something I've Been Meaning to Tell You* (Toronto: McGraw-Hill Ryerson, 1974). The edition used in this book is published by Penguin (London 1985).

20. Stephen Reagan, "'The Presence of the Past': Modernism and Postmodernism in Canadian Short Fiction," in *Narrative Strategies in Canadian Literature*, ed. Coral Ann Howells and Lynn Hunter (Milton Keynes: Open University Press, 1992), 108–34.

21. Gerald Prince, "Narratology," in *The Johns Hopkins Guide to Literary Theory and Criticism*, ed. Michael Groden and Martin Kreiswirth (Baltimore: Johns Hopkins University Press, 1994), 524–28.

22. Karen McCauley, "Russian Formalism," in *The Johns Hopkins Guide to Literary Theory and Criticism*, 634–37.

23. David Darby, "Form and Context: An Essay in the History of Narratology," *Poetics Today* 22, no.4 (Winter 2001): 829–52.

24. David Herman, "Introduction," in *Narratologies*, ed. David Herman (Columbus: Ohio State University Press, 1999), 1–30.

25. Ibid., 3.

26. Shlomith Rimmon-Kenan, *Narrative Fiction* (London: Routledge, 2003), 135.

27. Ibid., 5.

28. Ibid., 137.

29. Ibid., 16–17.

30. Alice Munro, "Lichen," from *The Progress of Love* (1986). The edition used in this book was published by Fontana (London, 1988). Further references are included in the text.

31. Coral Ann Howells, *Contemporary Canadian Women's Writing* (London: Palgrave Macmillan, 2003), 56.

32. Alice Munro, *The Beggar Maid* (London: Penguin, 1980), 136. Further references to the collection are included in the text.

33. Rimmon-Kenan, *Narrative Fiction*, 52.

34. Gerald Prince, *A Dictionary of Narratology* (Lincoln: University of Nebraska Press, 2003), 25.

35. Mieke Bal, *Introduction to the Theory of Narrative* (Toronto: University of Toronto Press, 1985), 105.

36. Alice Munro, "Five Points," from *Friend of My Youth* (Toronto: McClelland and Stewart, 1990), 35. Further references to the collection are included in the text.

37. Rimmon-Kenan, *Narrative Fiction*, 61.

38. Ibid., 67.

39. Michael Toolan, *Narrative: A Critical Linguistic Introduction*, 2nd ed. (London: Routledge, 2001), 60.

40. Bal, *Introduction to the Theory of Narrative*, 105. Bal uses the spelling "focalizor," whereas "focalizer" is preferred by American and British narratologists.

41. Prince, *A Dictionary of Narratology*, 45.

42. Katie Wales, *A Dictionary of Stylistics* (Harlow: Pearson Education, 2001), 164.
43. Geoffrey Leech and Mick Short, *Style in Fiction* (Harlow: Pearson Education, 2007). See chapter 10.
44. Ibid., 260.
45. Alice Munro, *Runaway* (Toronto: McClelland and Stewart, 2004). Further references to the collection are included in the text.
46. Mikhail Bakhtin, *Problems of Dostoevsky's Poetics*, ed. and trans. Caryl Emerson (Manchester: Manchester University Press, 1984), 6.
47. Ildikó de Papp Carrington, *Controlling the Uncontrollable: The Fiction of Alice Munro* (DeKalb: Northern Illinois University Press, 1989), 52.
48. Coral Ann Howells, *Alice Munro* (Manchester: Manchester University Press, 1998), 142.
49. Rimmon-Kenan, *Narrative Fiction*, 89.
50. Herman, *Narratologies*, 2.
51. Louis K. MacKendrick, *Some Other Reality: Alice Munro's Something I've Been Meaning to Tell You* (Toronto: ECW Press, 1993), 65.
52. Héliane Ventura, "The Setting up of Unsettlement in Alice Munro's 'Tell Me Yes or No,'" in *Postmodern Fiction in Canada*, ed. Theo D'Haen and Hans Bertens (Amsterdam: Rodopi, 1992), 105–23.
53. Deborah Heller, "Getting Loose: Women and Narration in Alice Munro's *Friend of My Youth*," in *The Rest of the Story: Critical Essays on Alice Munro*, ed. Robert Thacker (Toronto: ECW Press, 1999), 60–81.
54. Alice Munro, *The Moons of Jupiter* (Toronto: Macmillan, 1982). The writer's introduction is found in the paperback edition published by Macmillan of Canada (Toronto, 1986), xiii–xvi.
55. Wendy Lesser, "The Munro Doctrine," in *New Republic* (October 1994): 51–53.
56. Andrew Hiscock, "'Longing for a Human Climate': Alice Munro's *Friend of My Youth* and the Culture of Loss," *Journal of Commonwealth Literature* 32, no. 2 (1997): 17–33.
57. Sheldrick Ross, "Too Many Things," 787.
58. Peter Kemp, "A Journey into her Heart of Darkness," *Sunday Times Review* (August 16, 2009), 40.
59. Ibid., 40.

CHAPTER 1

1. Robert Thacker, *Alice Munro: Writing Her Lives* (Toronto: McClelland and Stewart, 2005), 91.
2. Ibid., 132.
3. J. R. (Tim) Struthers, "'The Real Material': An Interview with Alice Munro," in *Probable Fictions: Alice Munro's Narrative Acts*, ed. Louis K. MacKendrick (Toronto: ECW Press, 1983), 5–36.
4. Sheila Munro, *Lives of Mothers & Daughters: Growing Up with Alice Munro* (Toronto: McClelland and Stewart, 2001), 138.

5. Robert Thacker, "'Clear Jelly': Alice Munro's Narrative Dialectics," in *Probable Fictions: Alice Munro's Narrative Acts*, ed. Louis K. MacKendrick (Toronto: ECW Press, 1983), 37–60.

6. Harper Lee, *To Kill a Mockingbird* (London: Penguin, 1963), 285.

7. Margaret Laurence, *A Bird in the House* (Toronto: McClelland and Stewart, 1970), 191.

8. Alice Munro, *Dance of the Happy Shades* (Toronto: Ryerson Press, 1968). The edition I use was published in London (Penguin, 1983). Further references to the collection are included in the text.

9. Randolph Quirk, Sidney Greenbaum, Geoffrey Leech, and Jan Svartnik, *A Comprehensive Grammar of the English Language* (London: Longman, 1985), 179.

10. Millicent Bell, "Narrative Gaps/Narrative Meaning," *Raritan: A Quarterly Review* 6, no.1 (1986): 84–102.

11. Geoffrey Leech, *A Glossary of Grammar* (Edinburgh: Edinburgh University Press, 2006), 64.

12. Helen Hoy, "'Dull, Simple, Amazing and Unfathomable': Paradox and Double Vision in Alice Munro's Fiction," *Studies in Canadian Literature* 5 (1980): 100–115.

13. Coral Ann Howells, *Alice Munro* (Manchester: Manchester University Press, 1998), 23.

14. J. R. (Tim) Struthers, "Interview with Alice Munro," in *Probable Fictions: Alice Munro's Narrative Acts*, ed. Louis K. MacKendrick (Toronto: ECW Press, 1983), 21.

15. Louis K. MacKendrick, *Some Other Reality: Alice Munro's Something I've Been Meaning to Tell You* (Toronto: ECW Press, 1993), 39.

16. Ibid., 45.

17. Alice Munro, *Something I've Been Meaning to Tell You* (London: Penguin, 1984). Further references are included in the text.

18. Ildikó de Papp Carrington, *Controlling the Uncontrollable: The Fiction of Alice Munro* (DeKalb: Northern Illinois University Press, 1989), 29.

19. MacKendrick, *Some Other Reality*, 40.

20. Patricia Waugh, *Metafiction: The Theory and Practice of Self-Conscious Fiction* (London: Routledge, 1984), 2.

21. Quirk et al., *Comprehensive Grammar*, 1469.

22. MacKendrick, *Some Other Reality*, 42.

23. Ibid., 41.

24. Ajay Heble, *The Tumble of Reason: Alice Munro's Discourse of Absence* (Toronto: University of Toronto Press, 1994), 85.

CHAPTER 2

1. Robert Thacker, "'Clear Jelly': Alice Munro's Narrative Dialectics," *Probable Fictions: Alice Munro's Narrative Acts, ed. Louis K.* MacKendrick (Toronto: ECW Press, 1983), 27.

2. Helen Hoy, "'Rose and Janet': Alice Munro's Metafiction." *Canadian Literature* 121 (1989): 80.

3. Robert Thacker, *Alice Munro: Writing Her Lives* (Toronto: McClelland and Stewart, 2005), 399.

4. Alice Munro, *The Moons of Jupiter* (Markham, Ontario: Penguin, 1986), 11.

5. Robert Thacker, *Writing Her Lives*, 408.

6. Virginia Pruitt, "Alice Munro's 'Fits': Secrets, Mystery and Marital Relations," *Psychoanalytic Review* 89, no. 2 (April 2002): 157–67.

7. Caitlin J. Charman, "'There's Got to Be Some Wrenching and Slashing': Horror and Retrospection in Alice Munro's 'Fits,'" *Canadian Literature* 191 (Winter 2006): 13–32.

8. Ildikó de Papp Carrington, *Controlling the Uncontrollable: The Fiction of Alice Munro* (DeKalb: Northern Illinois University Press, 1989), 52.

9. Alice Munro, *The Progress of Love* (London: Fontana, 1988), 10. All further references to the collection are included in the text.

10. Randolph Quirk, Sidney Greenbaum, Geoffrey Leech, and Jan Svartnik, *A Comprehensive Grammar of the English Language* (London: Longman, 1985), 354.

11. Charman, "'There's Got to Be Some Wrenching and Slashing,'" 17.

12. Pruitt, "Alice Munro's 'Fits': Secrets, Mystery and Marital Relations," 159.

13. Ajay Heble, *The Tumble of Reason: Alice Munro's Discourse of Absence* (Toronto: University of Toronto Press, 1994), 152.

14. Héliane Ventura, "'Fits': A Baroque Tale," *Recherches Anglaises et Nord Americaines* 22 (1989): 89–97.

15. Carrington, *Controlling the Uncontrollable*, 55.

16. Pruitt, "Alice Munro's 'Fits': Secrets, Mystery and Marital Relations," 164.

17. Ibid., 158.

18. Munro, *The Moons of Jupiter*, 35.

19. Mieke Bal, *Narratology: Introduction to the Theory of Narrative* (Toronto: University of Toronto Press, 1985), 105.

20. Michael Toolan, *Narrative: A Critical Linguistic Introduction* (London: Routledge, 2001), 62.

21. Magdalene Redekop, *Mothers and Other Clowns: The Stories of Alice Munro* (New York: Routledge, 1992), 183.

22. Geoff Hancock, *Canadian Writers at Work: Interviews with Geoff Hancock* (Toronto: Oxford University Press, 1987), 224.

23. Carrington, *Controlling the Uncontrollable*, 162.

24. Marianne Micros, "Et in Ontario Ego: The Pastoral Ideal and the Blazon Tradition in Alice Munro's 'Lichen,'" *The Rest of the Story: Critical Essays on Alice Munro*, ed. Robert Thacker (Toronto: ECW Press, 1999), 44–60.

25. Ibid., 52.

26. Redekop, *Mothers and Other Clowns*, 191.

27. Terence Hawkes, *Metaphor* (London: Methuen, 1972), 3.

28. Carrington, *Controlling the Uncontrollable*, 165.

29. Héliane Ventura, "Le Trace de L'écart ou L'origine du Monde Reinventée dans 'Lichen' d'Alice Munro," *Texte/Image: Nouveaux Problèmes*, dir. Lilianne Louvel et Henri Scepi (Rennes: Universitaires de Rennes, 2005), 269–81.

CHAPTER 3

1. Deborah Heller, "Getting Loose: Women and Narration in Alice Munro's *Friend of My Youth*," in *The Rest of the Story: Critical Essays on Alice Munro*, ed. Robert Thacker (Toronto: ECW Press, 1999), 60.
2. Coral Ann Howells, *Alice Munro* (Manchester: Manchester University Press, 1998), 101.
3. Gérard Genette, *Narrative Discourse: An Essay in Method*, trans. Jane E. Lewin (Ithaca, NY: Cornell University Press, 1980), 232.
4. Andrew Hiscock, "'Longing for a Human Climate': Alice Munro's *Friend of My Youth* and the Culture of Loss," *Journal of Commonwealth Literature* 32 (1997): 28.
5. Mark Nunes, "Postmodern 'Piecing': Alice Munro's Contingent Ontologies," *Studies in Short Fiction* 34, no. 1 (1997): 11–26.
6. Heller, "Getting Loose," 66.
7. Gerald Prince, *A Dictionary of Narratology*, rev. ed. (Lincoln: University of Nebraska Press, 2003), 50.
8. Heller, "Getting Loose," 66.
9. Gayle Elliott, "'A Different Tack': Feminist Metanarrative in Alice Munro's *Friend of My Youth*," *Journal of Modern Literature*, XX (Summer 1996): 75–84.
10. Ibid., 80
11. Ibid., 84.
12. Susan S. Lanser, "Toward a Feminist Narratology," in *Feminisms: An Anthology of Literary Theory and Criticism*, ed. Robyn Warhol and Diane Price Herndl (Basingstoke: Macmillan, 1997), 674–94.
13. Ibid., 680.
14. Ibid., 684.
15. Ibid., 680.
16. Alice Munro, *Open Secrets* (London: Chatto and Windus, 1984). Further references to the collection are included in the text.
17. Ildikó de Papp Carrington, "Double-Talking Devils: Alice Munro's 'A Wilderness Station,'" *Essays on Canadian Writing* 58 (1996): 71–92.
18. Christopher Gittings, "The Scottish Ancestor: A Conversation with Alice Munro," *Scotlands* 1994: 83–96.
19. Christopher Gittings, "Constructing a Scots-Canadian Ground: Family History and Cultural Translation in Alice Munro," *Studies in Short Fiction* 34, no. 1 (1997): 27–37.
20. Carrington, "Double-Talking Devils," 88.
21. Patrocinio Schweickart, "Reading Ourselves: Toward a Feminist Theory of Reading," in *Feminisms*, ed. Robyn R Warhol and Diane Price Herndl (Basingstoke: Macmillan, 1997), 609–35.

22. Carrington, "Double-Talking Devils," 88–89.
23. Ildikó de Papp Carrington, *Controlling the Uncontrollable: The Fiction of Alice Munro* (DeKalb: Northern Illinois University Press, 1989), 182.
24. Ibid., 143, italics in original.
25. Beverly Rasporich, *Dance of the Sexes: Art and Gender in the Fiction of Alice Munro* (Edmonton: University of Alberta Press, 1990).
26. Howells, *Alice Munro*, 128.
27. Gittings, "Constructing a Scots-Canadian Ground," 32.
28. Michael Toolan, *Narrative: A Critical Linguistic Introduction* (London: Routledge, 2001), 135.
29. Carrington, "Double-Talking Devils," 81.
30. Ibid., 83.
31. Ibid., 84, italics in original.
32. Ibid., 83–84.
33. Ibid., 84.
34. Lanser, "Toward a Feminist Narratology," 685–88.
35. Howells, *Alice Munro*, 128.
36. Lanser, "Toward a Feminist Narratology," 688.
37. George Woodcock, "The Secrets of Her Success," *Quill & Quire* (August 1994): 25.
38. Val Ross, "A Writer Called Alice," *Globe and Mail* (October 1, 1994): C1, C21.
39. Eleanor Wachtel, "An Interview with Alice Munro," *Brick* 40 (1991): 49–53.
40. Alice Munro, "Introduction," *The Moons of Jupiter* (Markham, Ontario: Penguin Canada, 1986), xv. Further references are included in the text.

CHAPTER 4

1. Wendy Lesser, "The Munro Doctrine," *New Republic* (October 1994): 51–53.
2. Pleuke Boyce and Ron Smith, "A National Treasure: Interview with Alice Munro," *Meanjin* 54 (1995): 222–32.
3. Andrew Hiscock, "'Longing for a Human Climate': Alice Munro's *Friend of My Youth* and the Culture of Loss," *Journal of Commonwealth Literature* 32 (1997): 30.
4. Judith Maclean Miller, "Deconstructing Silence: The Mystery of Alice Munro," *Antigonish Review* 129 (Spring 2002): 43–52.
5. Donna Bennett, "Open Secret. Telling Time in Munro's Fiction" and Russell Morton Brown, "Open Secrets? Alice Munro and the Mystery Story," *Open Letter*, Eleventh Series no. 9 and Twelfth Series no. 1 (2003–4): 185–209.
6. Ildikó de Papp Carrington, "Talking Dirty: Alice Munro's 'Open Secrets' and John Steinbeck's *Of Mice and Men*," *Studies in Short Fiction* 31 (1994): 595–606.
7. Robert Thacker, *Alice Munro: Writing Her Lives* (Toronto: McClelland and Stewart, 2005), 453.
8. Val Ross, "A Writer Called Alice," *Globe and Mail* (October 1, 1994): C1.

9. Alice Munro, *The Love of a Good Woman* (Toronto: McClelland and Stewart, 1998). Further references to the collection are included in the text.
10. Alice Munro, "Contributors' Notes," in *The Best American Short Stories 1999*, ed. Amy Tan with Katrina Kenison (Boston: Houghton Mifflin, 1999), 387–88.
11. Alice Munro, "Save the Reaper," in *The Best American Stories 1999*, 280. The story runs from page 273 to page 294.
12. Randolph Quirk, Sidney Greenbaum, Geoffrey Leech, and Jan Svartnik. *A Comprehensive Grammar of the English Language* (London: Longman, 1985), 202.
13. Ildikó de Papp Carrington, "Where Are You, Mother? Alice Munro's 'Save the Reaper,'" *Canadian Literature* 173 (Summer 2002): 34–51.
14. Miller, "Deconstructing Silence," 50.
15. Georges Roque, "Graphic Presentation as Expressive Device," in *Routledge Encyclopedia of Narrative Theory*, ed. David Herman, Manfred Jahn, and Marie-Laure Ryan (London: Routledge, 2005), 209–10.
16. Gillian Brown and George Yule, *Discourse Analysis* (Cambridge: Cambridge University Press, 1983), 95–97.

CHAPTER 5

1. John Gerlach, "To Close or Not to Close: Alice Munro's 'The Love of a Good Woman,'" *Journal of Narrative Theory* 37, no. 1 (Winter 2007): 146–58.
2. Catherine Sheldrick Ross, "'Too Many Things': Reading Alice Munro's 'Love of a Good Woman,'" *University of Toronto Quarterly* 71 (Summer 2002): 808.
3. Dennis Duffy, "'A Dark Sort of Mirror': 'The Love of a Good Woman' as Pauline Poetic," *Essays on Canadian Writing* 66 (Winter 1998): 179.
4. Heta Pyrhönen, "Retardatory Devices," in *Routledge Encyclopedia of Narrative Theory*, ed. David Herman, Manfred Jahn, and Marie-Laure Ryan (London: Routledge, 2005), 499–500.
5. Ross, "'Too Many Things,'" 804.
6. Ibid., 796.
7. Ibid., 803.
8. Coral Ann Howells, *Alice Munro* (Manchester: Manchester University Press, 1998), 151.
9. Judith McCombs, "Searching Bluebeard's Chambers: Grimm, Gothic, and Bible Mysteries in Alice Munro's 'The Love of a Good Woman,'" *American Review of Canadian Studies* 30, no. 3 (2000): 327–45.
10. Ibid., 11
11. Duffy, "'A Dark Sort of Mirror,'" 184.
12. Ross, "'Too Many Things,'" 794.
13. Randolph Quirk, Sidney Greenbaum, Geoffrey Leech, and Jan Svartnik, *A Comprehensive Grammar of the English Language* (London: Longman, 1985), 1088.
14. Gerlach, "To Close or Not to Close," 154.
15. Duffy, "'A Dark Sort of Mirror,'" 184.
16. Ross, "'Too Many Things,'" 808.

CHAPTER 6

1. Alice Munro, *Hateship, Friendship, Courtship, Loveship, Marriage* (Toronto: McClelland and Stewart, 2001), 109, 135. The title is abbreviated to *Hateship*, and references to the collection are included in the text.

2. Alice Munro, *Runaway* (Toronto: McClelland and Stewart, 2004), 161. Further references are included in the text.

3. Michael Ravitch, "Fiction in Review," *Yale Review* 90, no. 4 (2002): 160–70.

4. Monika Fludernik, "Chronology, time, tense and experientiality in narrative," *Language and Literature* 12, no. 2 (2003): 117–34.

5. Ibid., 119.

6. Stephen Regan, "'The Presence of the Past': Modernism and Postmodernism in Canadian Short Fiction." In *Narrative Strategies in Canadian Literature*, ed. Coral Ann Howells and Lynette Hunter. (Buckinghamshire, UK: Open University Press, 1991), 127.

7. Fludernik, "Chronology," 121.

8. Robin Lakoff, "Remarks on This and That," *Proceedings of the Tenth Regional Meeting of the Chicago Linguistic Society*, ed. Michael W. La Galy, Robert A. Fox, and Anthony Bruck (Chicago: Chicago Linguistic Society, 1974), 345–56.

9. Stephen E. Levinson, *Pragmatics* (Cambridge: Cambridge University Press, 1983), 64.

10. Fludernik, "Chronology," 122.

11. Ravitch, "Fiction in Review," 165.

12. Peter Gzowski, "You're the Same Person at 19 That You Are at 60: Interview with Alice Munro," *Globe and Mail* (September 29, 2001): F4–F5.

13. Ken Ireland, "Temporal Ordering," *Routledge Encyclopedia of Narrative Theory*, ed. David Herman, Manfred Jahn, and Marie-Laure Ryan (London: Routledge, 2005), 591–92.

14. Geoff Hancock, *Canadian Writers at Work: Interviews with Geoff Hancock* (Toronto: Oxford University Press, 1987), 200.

15. Shlomith Rimmon-Kenan, *Narrative Fiction* (London: Routledge, 2003), 57.

16. Gzowski, "Interview with Alice Munro," F4.

17. Dorrit Cohn, *The Distinction of Fiction* (Baltimore: Johns Hopkins University Press, 1999), 127.

18. Lester E. Barber, "Alice Munro: The Stories of Runaway," *ELOPE: English Language Overseas Perspectives and Enquiries* 3, no. 1/2 (2006): 143–56.

CHAPTER 7

1. Alice Munro, "Introduction," *Selected Stories* (New York: Vintage International, 1997), xiii–xxi.

2. Helen Hoy, "'Rose and Janet': Alice Munro's Metafiction," *Canadian Literature* 121 (1989): 67.

3. Catherine Sheldrick Ross, *Alice Munro: A Double Life* (Toronto: ECW Press, 1992), 71.

4. Chris Gittings, "The Scottish Ancestor: A Conversation with Alice Munro," *Scotlands* 1994: 91.

5. Alice Munro, "Working for a Living," first published in *Grand Street* 1, no. 1 (1981): 9–37. References to this version are included in the text under *Grand Street*; references to the version published in *The View from Castle Rock* are included in the text under *Castle Rock*. "Home" was first published in *New Canadian Stories*, ed. David Helwig and Joan Harcourt (Ottawa: Oberon Press, 1974), 133–53. References to this version are included in the text. A version of "Home" was published in *New Statesman* (December 17, 2001–January 7, 2002): 84–93. Where reference is made to this version, it is included in the text under *New Statesman*. References to "Home" from *The View from Castle Rock* are included in the text. The story "Hired Girl" was first published in the *New Yorker* (April 11, 1994): 82–89. References to it are included in the text (*New Yorker*). References to the version published in 2006 are included in the text (*Castle Rock*).

6. Charles Foran, "Alice in Borderland," *The Walrus* (September 2009): 41–46.

7. Val Ross, "Lunch at Alice's Restaurant," *Globe and Mail Weekend Review* (October 8, 2006): R1, R8.

8. Gittings, "The Scottish Ancestor," 87.

9. Aida Edemariam, "Riches of a Double Life," *Guardian Review* (October 4, 2003): 23.

10. Jeanne McCulloch and Mona Simpson, "Alice Munro: The Art of Fiction CXXXVIII," *Paris Review* 131 (1994): 260.

11. Dorrit Cohn, *The Distinction of Fiction* (Baltimore: Johns Hopkins University Press, 1999), 27.

12. Ross, "Lunch at Alice's Restaurant," R8.

13. Readers will likely know that Alice Munro's mother died in 1959, having suffered for many years from Parkinson's disease.

14. Robert Thacker, *Alice Munro: Writing Her Lives* (Toronto: McClelland and Stewart, 2005), 316.

15. Ibid., 5.

16. Ildikó de Papp Carrington, *Controlling the Uncontrollable: The Fiction of Alice Munro* (DeKalb: Northern Illinois University Press, 1989), 194.

17. Hoy, "Rose and Janet," 79.

18. Geoff Hancock, *Canadian Writers at Work: Interviews with Geoff Hancock* (Toronto: Oxford University Press, 1987), 205.

19. Ibid., 206.

20. Thacker, *Writing Her Lives*, 82.

21. Ross, *A Double Life*, 46.

22. Eleanor Wachtel, "An Interview with Alice Munro," *Brick* 40 (1991): 49.

23. Roxanne Rimstead, *Remnants of a Nation: On Poverty Narratives by Women* (Toronto: University of Toronto Press, 2001), 105.

24. Ibid., 216.

25. Ibid., 105.

26. References to the story are included in the text.

27. George Woodcock, "The Plots of Life: The Realism of Alice Munro," *Queen's Quarterly* 93, no. 2 (Summer 1986): 235–50.

28. Carrington, *Controlling the Uncontrollable*, 105.

29. *The Oxford English Dictionary Online*, http://dictionary.oed.com/cgi/entry (accessed April 11, 2007).

30. Stephen E. Levinson, *Pragmatics* (Cambridge: Cambridge University Press, 1983), 101–18.

31. Ibid., 101.

32. Ibid., 105.

33. John Lyons, *Semantics*, vol. 2 (Cambridge: Cambridge University Press, 1977), 638.

34. Katie Wales, *Personal Pronouns in Present-Day English* (Cambridge: Cambridge University Press, 1996), 54.

35. Ibid., 44.

36. Rimstead, *Remnants of a Nation*, 105.

37. Ibid., 215.

38. Geoffrey Leech, "The Distribution and Function of Vocatives in American and British English," in *Out of Corpora: Studies in Honour of Stig Johansson*, ed. Hilde Hasselgård and Signe Oksefjell (Amsterdam: Rodopi, 1999), 108–21.

39. Ibid., 116.

40. Sara Mills, *Feminist Stylistics* (London: Routledge, 1995), 110.

41. Rimstead, *Remnants of a Nation*, 105.

42. Ibid., 215.

43. Geoff Pevere, "Munro Explores the Darker Side," *Toronto Star* (August 30, 2009): IN7.

44. Philip Marchand, "Her Dark Materials," *National Post* (Saturday 29, 2009): WP10.

CHAPTER 8

1. Alice Munro, *Too Much Happiness* (Toronto: McClelland and Stewart, 2009). References to the collection are included in the text.

2. The title of this chapter is taken from the story "Deep-Holes" (p. 115). Several of the characters in *Too Much Happiness* are extreme outsiders, distanced by choice or circumstance from close family and friends, like Kent in "Deep-Holes," Mr. Crozier in "Some Women," Roy in "Wood," and Lloyd in "Dimensions."

3. Joyce Carol Oates, "Who Do You Think You Are?" *New York Review of Books*, vol. 19 (December 3, 2009): 42–44.

4. Peter Kemp, "A Journey into Her Heart of Darkness," *Sunday Times Review* (August 16, 2009), 40.

5. Gerald Prince, *A Dictionary of Narratology*, rev. ed. (Lincoln: University of Nebraska Press, 2003), 25.

6. Gérard Genette, *Narrative Discourse*, trans. Jane E. Lewin (Oxford: Blackwell, 1980), 52.

7. Michael Gorra, "Mortal Fear," *Times Literary Supplement* (August 28, 2009): 3–4.
8. Ibid., 3.
9. Randolph Quirk, Sidney Greenbaum, Geoffrey Leech, and Jan Svartnik, *A Comprehensive Grammar of the English Language* (London: Longman, 1985), 1629.
10. Brian Richardson, *Unnatural Voices: Extreme Narration in Modern and Contemporary Fiction* (Columbus: Ohio State University Press, 2006), 36.
11. Eleanor Wachtel, "An Interview with Alice Munro," *Brick* 40 (1991): 53.
12. Pleuke Boyce and Ron Smith, "A National Treasure: Interview with Alice Munro," *Meanjin* 54 (1995): 228.
13. Coral Ann Howells, "Alice Munro," in *Encyclopedia of Literature in Canada*, ed. W. H. New (Toronto: University of Toronto Press, 2002), 769–72.
14. Catherine Sheldrick Ross, "'Too Many Things': Reading Alice Munro's 'Love of a Good Woman,'" *University of Toronto Quarterly* 71 (Summer 2002): 786.
15. Alice Munro, "Introduction," *Selected Stories* (New York: Vintage International, 1997), xx.
16. Ibid., xvii.
17. Judith Maclean Miller, "Deconstructing Silence: The Mystery of Alice Munro," *Antigonish Review* 129 (Spring 2002): 51.
18. Michael Ravitch, "Fiction in Review," *Yale Review* 90 (2002): 170.
19. Alice Munro, "Child's Play," *Harper's* (February 2007): 73–85.
20. Munro, "Introduction," xx.

AFTERWORD

1. Julie Bosman, "Alice Munro, Storyteller, Wins Nobel in Literature," *New York Times* (October 11, 2013). Online.
2. Charles McGrath, "Alice Munro Puts Down her Pen to Let the World in," *New York Times Review* (July 1, 2013). Online.
3. Sandra Martin, "A Storied Prize: The Ordinary Scenes of an Extraordinary Day," *Globe and Mail* (December 11, 2013): A1.
4. Alice Munro, *Dear Life* (Toronto: McClelland and Stewart, 2012).
5. Peter Kemp, "Review of Dear Life," *Sunday Times Review* (November 11, 2012). Online.
6. "Corrie" was first published in the *New Yorker* (October 11, 2010): 94–101. In this earlier version, Munro uses the forename "Sadie," not "Lillian."
7. Ibid., 101.
8. The Alice Munro Symposium, Department of English, University of Ottawa, May 9–11, 2014. Another Munro symposium, titled "Rehabilitating the Fugitive," was held in April 2014 at Université Paris-Ouest Nanterre.
9. *Narrative* 20, no. 2 (May 2012).
10. Michael Toolan, *Narrative Progression in the Short Story: A Corpus Stylistic Approach* (Amsterdam: John Benjamins, 2009).
11. Ibid., 224.

BIBLIOGRAPHY

Bakhtin, Mikhail. *Problems of Dostoevsky's Poetics.* Translated by Caryl Emerson. Manchester: Manchester University Press, 1984.

Bal, Mieke. *Narratology: Introduction to the Theory of Narrative.* Toronto: University of Toronto Press, 1985.

Barber, Lester E. "Alice Munro: The Stories of Runaway." *ELOPE: English Language Overseas Perspectives and Enquiries* 3 (2006): 143–56.

Barthes, Roland. "Introduction to the Structural Analysis of Narrative." *Image Music Text.* Translated by Stephen Heath. New York: Hill and Wang, 1977.

Bell, Millicent. "Narrative Gaps/Narrative Meaning." *Raritan: A Quarterly Review* 6, no. 1 (1986): 84–102.

Bennett, Donna. "Open Secret. Telling Time in Munro's Fiction." *Open Letter* Eleventh Series no. 9 and Twelfth Series no. 1 (2003–4): 185–209.

Beran, Carol L. "The Luxury of Excellence: Alice Munro in the *New Yorker*." In *The Rest of the Story: Critical Essays on Alice Munro*, edited by Robert Thacker, 204–301. Toronto: ECW Press, 1999.

Bosman, Julie. "Alice Munro, Storyteller, Wins Nobel in Literature." *New York Times* (October 11, 2013): Online.

Boyce, Pleuke, and Ron Smith. "A National Treasure: Interview with Alice Munro." *Meanjin* 54 (1995): 222–32.

Brown, Gillian, and George Yule. *Discourse Analysis.* Cambridge: Cambridge University Press, 1983.

Brown, Russell Morton. "Open Secrets? Alice Munro and the Mystery Story." *Open Letter* Eleventh Series no. 9 and Twelfth Series no. 1 (2003–4): 185–209.

Carrington, Ildikó de Papp. *Controlling the Uncontrollable: The Fiction of Alice Munro.* DeKalb: Northern Illinois University Press, 1989.

———. "'Don't Tell on Daddy': Narrative Complexity in Alice Munro's 'The Love of a Good Woman.'" *Studies in Short Fiction* 34, no. 2 (1997): 159–70.

———. "Double-Talking Devils: Alice Munro's 'A Wilderness Station.'" *Essays on Canadian Writing* 58 (1996): 71–92.

———. "Talking Dirty: Alice Munro's 'Open Secrets' and John Steinbeck's *Of Mice and Men*." *Studies in Short Fiction* 31 (1994): 595–606.

———. "Where Are You, Mother? Alice Munro's 'Save the Reaper.'" *Canadian Literature* 173 (Summer 2002): 34–51.

Charman, Caitlin J. "'There's Got to Be Some Wrenching and Slashing': Horror and Retrospection in Alice Munro's 'Fits.'" *Canadian Literature* 191 (Winter 2006): 13–32.

Cohn, Dorrit. *The Distinction of Fiction.* Baltimore: Johns Hopkins University Press, 1999.

Cox, Ailsa. *Alice Munro.* Tavistock: Northcote House, 2004.

Darby, David. "Form and Context: An Essay in the History of Narratology." *Poetics Today* 22, no. 4 (Winter 2001): 829–52.

D'Haen, Theo, and Hans Bertens, eds. *Postmodern Fiction in Canada.* Amsterdam: Rodopi, 1992.

Duffy, Dennis. "'A Dark Sort of Mirror': 'The Love of a Good Woman' as Pauline Poetic." *Essays on Canadian Writing* 66 (Winter 1998): 169–90.

Edemariam, Aida. "Riches of a Double Life." *Guardian Review* (October 4, 2003): 20–23.

Elliott, Gayle. "'A Different Tack': Feminist Meta-Narrative in Alice Munro's 'Friend of My Youth.'" *Journal of Modern Literature* 20, no. 1 (Summer 1996): 75–84.

Fludernik, Monika. "Chronology, Time, Tense and Experientiality in Narrative." *Language and Literature* 12, no. 2 (2003): 117–34.

Foran, Charles. "Alice in Borderland." *The Walrus* (September 2009): 41–46.

Fuller, Danielle, and Susan Billingham. "CanLit(e): Fit for Export?" *Essays on Canadian Writing* 71 (Fall 2000): 114–28.

Genette, Gérard. *Narrative Discourse.* Translated by Jane E. Lewin. Oxford: Blackwell, 1980.

Gerlach, John. "To Close or Not to Close: Alice Munro's 'The Love of a Good Woman.'" *Journal of Narrative Theory* 37, no. 1 (Winter 2007): 146–58.

Gittings, Chris. "The Scottish Ancestor: A Conversation with Alice Munro." *Scotlands* 1994: 83–96.

Gittings, Christopher E. "Constructing a Scots-Canadian Ground: Family History and Cultural Translation in Alice Munro." *Studies in Short Fiction* 34, no. 1 (1997): 27–37.

Gorra, Michael. "Mortal Fear." *Times Literary Supplement* (August 28, 2009): 3–4.

Groden, Martin, and Michael Kreiswirth. *The Johns Hopkins Guide to Literary Theory & Criticism.* Baltimore: Johns Hopkins University Press, 1994.

Hancock, Geoff. *Canadian Writers at Work: Interviews with Geoff Hancock.* Toronto: Oxford University Press, 1987.

Hasselgård, Hilde, and Signe Oksefjell. *Out of Corpora: Studies in Honour of Stig Johansson.* Amsterdam: Rodopi, 1999.

Hawkes, Terence. *Metaphor.* London: Methuen, 1972.

Heble, Ajay. *The Tumble of Reason: Alice Munro's Discourse of Absence.* Toronto: University of Toronto Press, 1994.

Heller, Deborah. "Getting Loose: Women and Narration in Alice Munro's *Friend of My Youth.*" In *The Rest of the Story: Critical Essays on Alice Munro*, edited by Robert Thacker, 60–81. Toronto: ECW Press, 1999.

Herman, David, Manfred Jahn, and Marie-Laure Ryan, eds. *Routledge Encyclopedia of Narrative Theory.* London: Routledge, 2005.

Hiscock, Andrew. "'Longing for a Human Climate': Alice Munro's *Friend of My Youth* and the Culture of Loss." *Journal of Commonwealth Literature* 32, no. 2 (1997): 17–33.

Howells, Coral Ann. *Alice Munro.* Manchester: Manchester University Press, 1998.

———. *Contemporary Canadian Women's Fiction.* Basingstoke, Hampshire: Palgrave Macmillan, 2003.

———. "The Telling of Secrets/The Secrets of Telling." *Open Letter* Eleventh Series no. 9 and Twelfth Series no. 1 (2003–4): 39–54.

Howells, Coral Ann, and Lynette Hunter, eds. *Narrative Strategies in Canadian Literature*. Milton Keynes, Buckinghamshire: Open University Press, 1991.

Hoy, Helen. "'Dull, Simple, Amazing and Unfathomable': Paradox and Double Vision in Alice Munro's Fiction." *Studies in Canadian Literature* 5, no. 5 (1980): 100–115.

———. "'Rose and Janet': Alice Munro's Metafiction." *Canadian Literature* 121 (1989): 59–83.

Ireland, Ken. "Temporal Ordering." In *Routledge Encylopedia of Narrative Theory*, edited by David Herman, Manfred Jahn, and Marie-Laure Ryan, 591–92. London: Routledge, 2005.

Kemp, Peter. "A Journey into Her Heart of Darkness." *Sunday Times Review* (August 16, 2009): 40.

———. "Review of *Dear Life*." *Sunday Times Review* (November 11, 2012): Online.

Lakoff, Robin. "Remarks on This and That." In *Proceedings of the Tenth Regional Meeting of the Chicago Linguistic Society*, edited by Michael W. La Galy, Robert A. Fox, and Anthony Bruck, 345–56. Chicago: Chicago Linguistic Society, 1974.

Lanser, Susan S. "Toward a Feminist Narratology." In *Feminisms,* edited by Robyn R. Warhol and Diane Price Herndl, 674–94. Basingstoke, Hampshire: Macmillan, 1997.

Laurence, Margaret. *A Bird in the House.* Toronto: McClelland and Stewart, 1970.

———. *The Diviners.* London: Macmillan, 1974.

Lee, Harper. *To Kill a Mockingbird.* London: Heinemann, 1960.

Leech, Geoffrey. "The Distribution and Function of Vocatives in American and British English." In *Out of Corpora: Studies in Honour of Stig Johansson*, edited by Hilde Hasselgård and Signe Oksefjell, 108–21. Amsterdam: Rodopi, 1999.

———. *A Glossary of English Grammar.* Edinburgh: Edinburgh University Press, 2006.

Leech, Geoffrey, and Mick Short. *Style in Fiction.* Harlow, Essex: Pearson Education, 2007.

Lesser, Wendy. "The Munro Doctrine." *New Republic* (October 1994): 51–53.

Levinson, Stephen C. *Pragmatics.* Cambridge: Cambridge University Press, 1983.

Lurie, Alison. "The Lamp in the Mausoleum." *New York Times Review of Books* (December 21, 2006): 22–30.

Lyons, John. *Semantics*, vol. 2. Cambridge: Cambridge University Press, 1977.

Marchand, Philip. "Her Dark Materials." *National Post* (September 29, 2009): WP10.

Martin, Sandra. "A Storied Prize: The Ordinary Scenes of an Extraordinary Day." *Globe and Mail* (December 11, 2013): A1.

MacKendrick, Louis K., ed. *Probable Fictions: Alice Munro's Narrative Acts.* Toronto: ECW Press, 1983.

———. *Some Other Reality: Alice Munro's Something I've Been Meaning to Tell You.* Toronto: ECW Press, 1993.

McCauley, Karen A. "Russian Formalism." *In The Johns Hopkins Guide to Literary Theory and Criticism*, edited by Michael Groden and Martin Kreiswirth, 634–37. Baltimore: Johns Hopkins University Press, 1994.

McCombs, Judith. "Searching Bluebeard's Chambers: Grimm, Gothic, and Bible Mysteries in Alice Munro's 'The Love of a Good Woman.'" *American Review of Canadian Studies* 30, no. 3 (2000): 327–45.

McCulloch, Jeanne, and Mona Simpson. "Alice Munro: The Art of Fiction CXXXVIII." *Paris Review* 131 (1994): 227–64.

McGrath, Charles. "Alice Munro Puts Down her Pen to Let the World in." *New York Times Review* (July 1, 2013): Online.

Merkin, Daphne. "Northern Exposure." *New York Times Magazine* (October 24, 2004): 58–62.

Micros, Marianne. "Et in Ontario Ego: The Pastoral Ideal and the Blazon Tradition in Alice Munro's 'Lichen.'" In *The Rest of the Story: Critical Essays on Alice Munro*, edited by Robert Thacker, 44–60. Toronto: ECW Press, 1999.

Miller, Judith Maclean. "Deconstructing Silence: The Mystery of Alice Munro." *Antigonish Review* 129 (Spring 2002): 43–52.

Mills, Sara. *Feminist Stylistics.* London: Routledge, 1995.

Munro, Alice. "Axis." *New Yorker* (January 31, 2011): 62–69.

———. *The Beggar Maid.* London: Penguin, 1980.

———. "Child's Play." *Harper's* (February 2007): 73–85.

———. "Corrie." *New Yorker* (October 11, 2010): 94–101.

———. *Dance of the Happy Shades.* Toronto: Penguin, 1983.

———. *Dear Life.* Toronto: McClelland and Stewart, 2012.

———. "Everything Here is Touchable and Mysterious." *Globe and Mail Weekend Supplement* (May 11, 1974): 33.

———. *Friend of My Youth.* London: Chatto and Windus, 1990.

———. *Hateship, Friendship, Courtship, Loveship, Marriage.* Toronto: McClelland and Stewart, 2001.

———. "Hired Girl." *New Yorker* (April 11, 1994): 82–88.

———. "Home." In *New Canadian Stories*, edited by David Helwig and Joan Harcourt, 133–153. Ottawa: Oberon, 1974.

———. *Lives of Girls and Women.* Toronto: McGraw-Hill, 1971.

———. *The Love of a Good Woman.* Toronto: McClelland Stewart, 1998.

———. *The Moons of Jupiter.* Markham, Ontario: Penguin, 1986.

———. *Open Secrets.* London: Chatto and Windus, 1994.

———. *The Progress of Love.* London: Fontana, 1988.

———. *Runaway.* Toronto: McClelland and Stewart, 2004.

———. *Something I've Been Meaning to Tell You.* London: Penguin, 1984.

———. "Sunday Afternoon." *Canadian Forum* (September 1957): 127–30.

———. *Too Much Happiness.* Toronto: McClelland and Stewart, 2009.

———. *The View from Castle Rock.* Toronto: McClelland and Stewart, 2006.

———. "What Is Real?" *Canadian Forum* (September 1982): 5, 36.

———. "Working for a Living." *Grand Street* 1, no. 1 (1981): 9–37.

Munro, Sheila. *Lives of Mothers and Daughters: Growing up with Alice Munro.* Toronto: McClelland and Stewart, 2001.

———. *Narrative* 20, no. 2 (May 2012).

New, W. H., ed. *Encyclopedia of Literature in Canada.* Toronto: University of Toronto Press, 2002.

Nunes, Mark. "Postmodern 'Piecing': Alice Munro's Contingent Ontologies." *Studies in Short Fiction* 34, no. 1 (1997): 11–26.

Oates, Joyce Carol. "Who Do You Think You Are?" *New York Review of Books* 56, no. 19 (December 2009): 42–44.

The Oxford English Dictionary Online. http://dictionary.oed.com/cgi/entry (accessed April 11, 2007).

Pevere, Geoff. "Munro Explores the Darker Side." *Toronto Star* (August 30, 2009): IN7.

Phelan, James, and Peter J Rabinowitz, eds. *A Companion to Narrative Theory.* Oxford: Blackwell, 2005.

Prince, Gerald. *A Dictionary of Narratology,* rev. ed. Lincoln: University of Nebraska Press, 2003.

———. "Narratology." In *The Johns Hopkins Guide to Literary Theory and Criticism,* edited by Michael Groden and Martin Kreiswirth, 524–27. Baltimore: Johns Hopkins University Press, 1994.

Propp, Vladimir. *Morphology of the Folk-tale.* Translated by Laurence Scott. Revised by Louis A. Wagner. Austin: University of Texas Press, 1968.

Pruitt, Virginia. "Alice Munro's 'Fits': Secrets, Mystery and Marital Relations." *Psychoanalytic Review* 89, no. 2 (April 2002): 157–167.

Pyrhönen, Heta. "Retardatory Devices." In *Routledge Encyclopedia of Narrative Theory,* edited by David Herman, Manfred Jahn, and Marie-Laure Ryan, 499–500. London: Routledge, 2005.

Quirk, Randolph, Sidney Greenbaum, Geoffrey Leech, and Jan Svartnik. *A Comprehensive Grammar of the English Language.* London: Longman, 1985.

Rasporich, Beverly J. *Dance of the Sexes: Art and Gender in the Fiction of Alice Munro.* Edmonton: University of Alberta Press, 1990.

Ravitch, Michael. "Fiction in Review." *Yale Review* 90, no. 4 (2002): 160–70.

Regan, Stephen. "'The Presence of the Past': Modernism and Postmodernism in Canadian Short Fiction." In *Narrative Strategies in Canadian Literature,* edited by Coral Ann Howells and Lynette Hunter, 108–34. Milton Keynes, Buckinghamshire: Open University Press, 1991.

Ricciardi, Caterina. "The Secrets of Intertextuality: Alice Munro's 'Pictures of Ice.'" *Open Letter* Eleventh Series no. 9 and Twelfth Series no. 1 (2003–4): 15–22.

Richardson, Brian. *Unnatural Voices: Extreme Narration in Modern and Contemporary Fiction.* Columbus: Ohio State University Press, 2006.

Rimmon-Kenan, Shlomith. *Narrative Fiction.* London: Routledge, 2003.

Rimstead, Roxanne. *Remnants of Nation: On Poverty Narratives by Women.* Toronto: University of Toronto Press, 2001.

Roque, Georges. "Graphic Presentation as Expressive Device." In *The Routledge Encyclopedia of Narrative Theory,* edited by David Herman, Manfred Jahn, and Marie-Laure Ryan, 209–10. London: Routledge, 2005.

Ross, Catherine Sheldrick. *Alice Munro: A Double Life.* Toronto: ECW Press, 1992.

———. "'Too Many Things': Reading Alice Munro's 'Love of a Good Woman.'" *University of Toronto Quarterly* 71, no. 3 (Summer 2002): 786–808.

Ross, Val. "A Writer Called Alice." *Globe and Mail* (October 1, 1994): C1, C21.

———. "Lunch at Alice's Restaurant." *Globe and Mail Weekend Review* (October 28, 2006): R1, R8.

Schweickart, Patrocinio P. "Reading Ourselves: Toward a Feminist Theory of Reading." In *Feminisms*, edited by Robyn R. Warhol and Diane Price Herndl, 609–35. Basingstoke, Hampshire: Macmillan, 1997.

Struthers, J. R. (Tim). "The Real Material: An Interview with Alice Munro." In *Probable Fictions: Alice Munro's Narrative Acts*, edited by Louis K. MacKendrick, 5–36. Toronto: ECW Press, 1983.

Tan, Amy, with Katrina Kenison, ed. *The Best American Short Stories 1999*. Boston: Houghton Mifflin, 1999.

Tennyson, Alfred Lord. *Poems and Plays*. London: Oxford University Press, 1965.

Thacker, Robert. *Alice Munro: Writing Her Lives*. Toronto: McClelland and Stewart, 2005.

———. "'Clear Jelly': Alice Munro's Narrative Dialectics." In *Probable Fictions: Alice Munro's Narrative Acts*, edited by Louis K. MacKendrick, 37–61. Toronto: ECW Press, 1983.

———, ed. *The Rest of the Story: Critical Essays on Alice Munro*. Toronto: ECW Press, 1999.

Todorov, Tzvetan. *Grammaire du Décameron*. The Hague: Mouton, 1969.

Toolan, Michael. *Narrative: A Critical Linguistic Introduction*. London: Routledge, 2001.

———. *Narrative Progression in the Short Story: A Corpus Stylistic Approach*. Amsterdam: John Benjamins, 2009.

Ventura, Héliane. "'Fits': A Baroque Tale." *Recherches Anglaises et Nord Americaines* 22 (1989): 89–97.

———. "Introduction." *Open Letter* Eleventh Series no. 9 and Twelfth Series no. 1 (2003–4): 15–22.

———. "The Setting Up of Unsettlement in Alice Munro's 'Tell me Yes or No.'" In *Postmodern Fiction in Canada*, edited by Theo D'Haen and Hans Bertens, 105–23. Amsterdam: Rodopi, 1992.

———. "Le tracé de l'écart ou l'origine du monde reinventée dans 'Lichen' d'Alice Munro." In *Texte/Image: Nouveaux Problèmes*, dir. Lilianne Louvel et Henri Scepi, 269–81. Rennes: Universitaires de Rennes, 2005.

Wachtel, Eleanor. "Alice Munro: A Life in Writing." *Queens Quarterly* 112, no. 2 (2005): 267–80.

———. "An Interview with Alice Munro." *Brick* 40 (1991): 48–53.

Wales, Katie. *A Dictionary of Stylistics*. Harlow, Essex: Pearson Education, 2001.

———. *Personal Pronouns in Present-day English*. Cambridge: Cambridge University Press, 1996.

Warhol, Robyn R., and Diane Price Herndl, eds. *Feminisms: An Anthology of Literary Theory and Criticism*, rev. ed. Basingstoke, Hampshire: Macmillan, 1997.

Waugh, Patricia. *Metafiction*. London: Routledge, 1984.

Woodcock, George. "The Plots of Life: The Realism of Alice Munro." *Queen's Quarterly* 93, no. 2 (Summer 1986): 235–50.

———. "The Secrets of Her Success." *Quill & Quire* (August 1994): 25.

INDEX

CPSIA information can be obtained at www.ICGtesting.com
Printed in the USA
LVOW10s2304150416

483839LV00013B/300/P